The American Novel series provides students of American literature with introductory critical guides to the great works of American fiction. Each volume begins with a substantial introduction by a distinguished authority on the text, giving details of the novel's composition, publication history, and contemporary reception, as well as a survey of the major critical trends and readings from first publication to the present. This overview is followed by a group of new essays, each specially commissioned from a leading scholar in the field, which together constitute a forum of interpretative methods and prominent contemporary ideas on the text. There are also helpful guides to further reading. Specifically designed for undergraduates, the series will be a powerful resource for anyone engaged in the critical analysis of major American novels.

Henry Roth's *Call It Sleep*, praised when it first appeared in the 1930s, neglected for decades, and reissued to wide acclaim in the 1960s, has been finally hailed as the finest Jewish-American novel of the first half of the century and one of the richest modernist novels to appear in America. The introduction by Hana Wirth-Nesher locates the novel in its cultural context and in terms of contemporary debates about ethnic literature, minority writing, and the problem of representativeness. Leslie Fiedler, who played an instrumental role in the book's reissuance, offers a new reading in light of the work's canonization. Mario Materassi traces the controversial history of its reception, and Ruth Wisse connects the immigration theme with the existential hero. Each of the following three essays addresses the question of modernism from a different perspective: Brian McHale focuses on Roth's modernist rather than postmodernist poetic, Karen Lawrence on the maternal and paternal powers that forge the inner life so basic to the modernist novel, and Werner Sollors on the "ethnic modernism" of second-generation immigration literature. Thus the volume sets out to consider Roth's hybrid status – as an American writer, a Jewish writer, and a European modernist.

NEW ESSAYS ON CALL IT SLEEP

GENERAL EDITOR

Emory Elliott
University of California, Riverside

Other works in the series:

The Scarlet Letter   *Sister Carrie*
The Great Gatsby   *The Rise of Silas Lapham*
Adventures of Huckleberry Finn   *The Catcher in the Rye*
Moby-Dick   *White Noise*
Uncle Tom's Cabin   *The Crying of Lot 49*
The Last of the Mohicans   *Walden*
The Red Badge of Courage   *Poe's Major Tales*
The Sun Also Rises   *Rabbit, Run*
A Farewell to Arms   *Daisy Miller and The Turn of the Screw*
The American   *Hawthorne's Major Tales*
The Portrait of a Lady   *The Sound and the Fury*
Light in August   *The Country of the Pointed Firs*
The Awakening   *Song of Solomon*
Invisible Man   *Wise Blood*
Native Son   *Go Tell it on the Mountain*
Their Eyes Were Watching God   *The Education of Henry Adams*
The Grapes of Wrath   *Go Down, Moses*
Winesburg, Ohio

New Essays on
Call It Sleep

Edited by
Hana Wirth-Nesher

CAMBRIDGE
UNIVERSITY PRESS

CAMBRIDGE UNIVERSITY PRESS
Cambridge, New York, Melbourne, Madrid, Cape Town, Singapore,
São Paulo, Delhi, Dubai, Tokyo

Cambridge University Press
The Edinburgh Building, Cambridge CB2 8RU, UK

Published in the United States of America by Cambridge University Press, New York

www.cambridge.org
Information on this title: www.cambridge.org/9780521456562

First published 1996

A catalogue record for this publication is available from the British Library

Library of Congress Cataloguing in Publication data
New essays on Call it sleep / edited by Hana Wirth-Nesher.
p.   cm. – (The American novel)
Includes bibliographical references.
ISBN 0-521-45032-2 (hardcover). – ISBN 0-521-45656-8 (pbk.)
1. Roth, Henry. Call it sleep.   2. Modernism (Literature) – United
States.   3. Jews in literature.   I. Wirth-Nesher, Hana, 1948–
II. Series.
PS3535.0787C3436   1996
813´.52 – dc20   95-4655

ISBN 978-0-521-45032-4 Hardback
ISBN 978-0-521-45656-2 Paperback

Transferred to digital printing 2009

Contents

Contents

Series Editor's Preface

In literary criticism the last twenty-five years have been particularly fruitful. Since the rise of the New Criticism in the 1950s, which focused attention of critics and readers upon the text itself – apart from history, biography, and society – there has emerged a wide variety of critical methods which have brought to literary works a rich diversity of perspectives: social, historical, political, psychological, economic, ideological, and philosophical. While attention to the text itself, as taught by the New Critics, remains at the core of contemporary interpretation, the widely shared assumption that works of art generate many different kinds of interpretations has opened up possibilities for new readings and new meanings.

Before this critical revolution, many works of American literature had come to be taken for granted by earlier generations of readers as having an established set of recognized interpretations. There was a sense among many students that the canon was established and that the larger thematic and interpretative issues had been decided. The task of the new reader was to examine the ways in which elements such as structure, style, and imagery contributed to each novel's acknowledged purpose. But recent criticism has brought these old assumptions into question and has thereby generated a wide variety of original, and often quite surprising, interpretations of the classics, as well as of rediscovered works such as Kate Chopin's *The Awakening*, which has only recently entered the canon of works that scholars and critics study and that teachers assign their students.

The aim of The American Novel Series is to provide students of American literature and culture with introductory critical guides to American novels and other important texts now widely read and studied. Usually devoted to a single work, each volume begins with an introduction by the volume editor, a distinguished authority on the text. The introduction presents details of the work's composition, publication history, and contemporary reception, as well as a survey of the major critical trends and readings from first publication to the present. This overview is followed by four or five original essays, specifically commissioned from senior scholars of established reputation and from outstanding younger critics. Each essay presents a distinct point of view, and together they constitute a forum of interpretative methods and of the best contemporary ideas on each text.

It is our hope that these volumes will convey the vitality of current critical work in American literature, generate new insights and excitement for students of American literature, and inspire new respect for and new perspectives upon these major literary texts.

Emory Elliott
University of California, Riverside

Henry Roth died shortly before this volume went to press.
It is warmly dedicated to his memory.

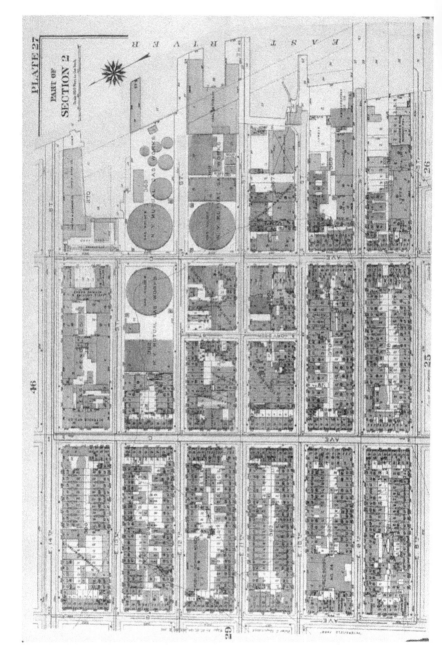

1

Introduction

HANA WIRTH-NESHER

IN 1966 Henry Roth published a story in *The New Yorker* entitled "The Surveyor." An American tourist is apprehended by the police in Seville for conducting surveying operations at a public thoroughfare without a permit and for suspiciously laying a wreath at the site later that day. "What is this surveying about?" asks the policeman before bringing him to the local precinct. "Well," answers the tourist, "I tried to locate a place of some sentimental value to myself."[1] A state attorney dismisses the charges when he suspects that the wreath marked the site where heretics found guilty by the Inquisition were burned to death, among them "relapsed *conversos,* those Catholics who secretly clung to their Judaic faith."[2] Startled to find that the state attorney shares this knowledge, the tourist turns interrogator, "Why is everyone ignorant of it but you?" "There may have been personal reasons," the Spaniard replies, and reveals that his family had the strange habit of lighting a candle on Friday night. Each insists on the personal, private nature of his knowledge; yet each shares a collective memory that sets him apart from the mainstream community. Where exactly is this place, this site of sentimental value not easily recognized by others? This is the question raised by both this story and Roth's monumental novel, *Call It Sleep.*

In February of 1992, at the age of 86, Henry Roth completed the manuscript of a second book, more than sixty years after the completion of *Call It Sleep.* Towering over his desk in his living room in Albuquerque, New Mexico, is a many times enlarged photograph of New York's Lower East Side at the turn of the century, and on his desk is a copy of the daily newspaper delivered to his door, *The Jerusalem Post*. The small wooden bookcase across from the desk holds dozens of copies of *Call It Sleep*, in a great many languages. The space of Roth's private world contains artifacts that point to worlds elsewhere: to a Yiddish world of New York's Jewish immigrant neighborhoods, now relegated to history – "Who would have believed," says Roth, "that I would have seen Yiddish disappear in one lifetime?"[3], to a Hebrew world in Israel that has a hold on Roth's memory and imagination but is inaccessible to him as a means of communication; to a literary world where he is read internationally in translation as a representative Jewish, American, and modernist writer. Places and languages to which he has no access haunt and captivate him, just as they define the space inhabited by his character David Schearl in *Call It Sleep*.

The publication history of this remarkable novel is itself a dramatic story that uncannily plays out the motif of inaccessibility so evident in his fiction. Published in 1934, at the height of the Depression, the book was acclaimed as a great contribution to American literature. John Chamberlain in *The New York Times* wrote, "Mr. Roth has done for the East Side what James T. Farrell is doing for the Chicago Irish. . . . The final chapters in the book have been compared to the Nighttown episodes of Joyce's *Ulysses;* the comparison is apt."[4] Edwin Seaver of the *New York Sun* called him "a brilliant disciple of James Joyce,"[5] and Alfred Hayes observed "There has appeared in America no novel to rival the veracity of this childhood. It is as honest as Dreiser's *Dawn*, but far more sensitive. . . . It is as brilliant as Joyce's *Portrait of the Artist*, but with a wider scope, a richer emotion, a deeper realism."[6] Kenneth Burke found in *Call It Sleep* the same pattern of magic traced by Frazer in *The Golden Bough:* "The great virtue of Roth's book, to my way of thinking, was in the fluent and civilized way in which he found, on our city streets, the new equivalents of the ancient jungle."[7] In the Sunday *New York Herald-Tribune Book Review*, Fred T. Marsh claimed that *Call It Sleep* was "the most compelling and moving, the most accurate and profound study of an American slum childhood that has yet appeared in this day. . . . Henry Roth has achieved the detach-

ment and universality of the artist."[8] And then, as Harold Ribalow noted, "*Call It Sleep* vanished, and so did its author."[9]

For almost twenty-five years the novel was out of print,
passed from hand to hand among a cult of devoted readers
who searched for battered copies of it in secondhand bookshops.
Inaccessible, marginal, nearly forgotten. Its revival is by now a
legend in American literary history. For the twenty-fifth anni-
versary of the Phi Beta Kappa journal, *The American Scholar*, the
editors ran a special feature entitled "The Most Neglected Books
of the Past 25 Years." The only title to be mentioned more than
once was *Call It Sleep*, cited by both Alfred Kazin and Leslie
Fiedler. In Kazin's words, "if you imagine the patient sensibility
of Wordsworth and the unselfconscious honesty of Dreiser
brought to the shock of his [Roth's] environment upon the
senses, you may have some inkling of the slowness, the patience
and the strange inner serenity of this book – as of something
won, very far deep within, against the conventional cruelties of
modern city life."[10] Fiedler was as lavish with his praise, "For
sheer virtuosity, *Call It Sleep* is hard to best; no one has ever
distilled such poetry and wit from the counterpoint between the
maimed English and the subtle Yiddish of the immigrant. No one
has reproduced so sensitively the terror of family life in the
imagination of a child caught between two cultures. To let another year go without reprinting it would be unforgiveable."[11]

It made a miraculous comeback. Harold Ribalow negotiated a
reissuance of the novel in 1960, with a critical introduction by
Maxwell Geismar. Four years later Peter Mayer, who had been
introduced to the out-of-print book by a New York cabbie, used
his tiny budget at Avon where he had just landed a publishing
job to purchase the rights and reissue it in paperback. It sold a
million copies. *Call It Sleep* became the first paperback edition of
a work ever to be reviewed on the front page of *The New York
Times Book Review*, where Irving Howe called it "one of the few
genuinely distinguished novels written by a 20th-century American."[12] A book that had become inaccessible except to a coterie
of admirers was transformed overnight into more than a best-
seller – "*Call It Sleep* has become a classic," observed the novelist
William Styron, "it's embedded, a landmark in our literature."[13]

Its first accolades linked it either with high experimental modernism in the context of Joyce, Eliot, and Frazer or with the American naturalism of Dreiser and Farrell, as a powerful exposé of slum life. The generation that attended its rebirth underscored these earlier judgments but also added another dimension to its reception – its Jewishness. Themselves the children of immigrants, Irving Howe, Leslie Fiedler, and Alfred Kazin were all moved by the novel as a document of cultural passage, the one that they had made from Eastern European Yiddish-speaking homes to the American university and the last stronghold of Protestant culture, the Department of English. Fiedler designated *Call It Sleep* a *"specifically* Jewish book, the best single book by a Jew about Jewishness written by an American certainly through the thirties and perhaps ever."[14] For Kazin it is "the most profound novel of Jewish life that I have ever read by an American."[15] Irving Howe acknowledged that although "structured according to the narrative strategies of modernism . . . Henry Roth's *Call It Sleep* draws its substance, the whole unfolding of socioethnic detail, from the Jewish immigrant experience."[16] A whole new generation of readers seized upon the book as quintessentially representative of Jewish-American literature.

The ever-increasing interest in *Call It Sleep* throughout the 1960s and 1970s coincided with a rise in ethnicity studies, with the ideological shift from the melting pot to what we have come to call multiculturalism. Along with the book's impeccable credentials as a modernist masterpiece it now acquired the added dimension of ethnic chronicle. As a new wave of university students two generations removed from immigration participated in a nationwide search for national roots beyond the Atlantic, *Call It Sleep* became a staple of Jewish literature and Jewish studies curricula.[17]

The life of the author of *Call It Sleep* is no less dramatic than the story of its reception. Roth was two when his parents immigrated to the United States from the Austro-Hungarian province of Galitzia to join masses of Eastern European Jewish immigrants on New York's Lower East Side. In 1914 the family moved to Harlem, away from what he remembered as a homogeneous, protected Jewish environment, and he was suddenly "plunged into an Irish Catholic neighborhood."[18] By 1925 he was a student at City College reading English (and Irish) modernist literature while still living in his Yiddish-speaking Harlem home. Two years later he met Eda Lou Walton, a New York University literature instructor and poet who transformed his life by encouraging him to write. In her Greenwich Village apartment he composed *Call It Sleep* on university examination booklets, completing a whole booklet in pencil every day. She also introduced him to *Ulysses*, which she had smuggled into the country from France; reading Joyce taught Roth "that I could talk about urban squalor and develop it into a work of art."[19] But despite the security that saw him through the writing of a successful first novel, Roth was uneasy about his relationship with Walton and the Bohemian Village life she represented. The comforts he had been enjoying as a young writer at a time when other artists and Americans generally were enduring the hunger and despair of the Depression years brought with them a guilty conscience. His growing commitment to Communism, moreover, made him acutely sensitive to rebukes such as that of the anonymous *New Masses* reviewer who bemoaned the fact that "so many young writers drawn from the proletariat can make no better use of their working class experience than as material for introspective, febrile novels."[20]

In a futile attempt to integrate his moral and political commitments with his artistic ambitions, he embarked on a novel commissioned by Maxwell Perkins of Scribner's about a midwestern factory worker which he abandoned despite Perkins' encouragement. What followed was Roth's legendary writer's block, a sixty-year spell of silence broken only in 1994 with the publication of *A Star Shines Over Mt. Morris Park* and *A Diving Rock on the Hudson*, the first two volumes of a multivolume autobiographical fiction entitled *Mercy of a Rude Stream*.[21] In those sixty years he worked as a precision tool grinder, an attendant at a psychiatric hospital, a Latin tutor, and a waterfowl breeder on a farm which he and his wife, Muriel Parker, purchased in Maine. During the McCarthy years, he burned his journals and other literary papers that might have contained incriminating information about himself and his friends. When *Call It Sleep* was reissued in paperback by Avon in 1964, reporters flocked to his Maine farm seeking out the reclusive writer. They published photographs that fed the legend of a curmudgeon in the snow, a nonentity thrust into a literary limelight that he eyed with a mixture of humility and cynicism. Book sales enabled the Roths to sell their farm and retire to a mobile home park in Albuquerque where he began to work on *Mercy of a Rude Stream,* originally intended for posthumous publication.

From the Yiddish world of his parents' home and the Lower East Side, Roth became Americanized first through the slang of street urchins who taunted him for being Jewish and then through the cadences of English literature. The raw material for his first novel is the world from which he felt he had escaped; the treatment of that material is a dazzling display of modernist techniques, gleaned from Joyce and Eliot among others. Roth admitted that he had begun the book as an autobiography but that it sprouted fictional possibilities that he first resisted and to which he eventually succumbed. Despite the indictment of the book by the reviewer in *New Masses,* it is partly naturalistic, reproducing with excruciating detail the grit of the slum streets, the charred metal of the Statue of Liberty, the dialect of the immigrant poor, the foods, smells, and noises of the Lower East Side. Almost every reader has commented on the work's cacophony, or as Stephen Adams has aptly put it, "The Noisiest Novel Ever Written."[22] But like the naturalism of Joyce, the sounds and objects in Roth's universe all have symbolic resonances. The coarse dialogues of bar talk, for example, take on symbolic dimensions, such as these remarks over poker: "Dare's a star fer yeh! Watch it! T'ree kings I god. Dey come on huzzbeck! Yee! Hee! Hee! Mary! Nawthin' to do but wait fer day light and go home. To a red cock crowin'."[23] Not only do sexual and Christian religious connotations merge in this discourse, but the speech also refers to Emma Lazarus' poem "The Crowing of the Red Cock," a survey of the persecution of Jews throughout Western civilization. These few words, then, drift away from their naturalistic environment to a textual play that signals both Christian and Jewish culture simultaneously, and that draws attention to itself as art.

The child protagonist David Schearl has been identified by readers as the young artist, Henry Roth, attempting to wend his way between the Scylla of his father's wrath and the Charybdis of the slum streets. Narrated almost exclusively from his perspective, it is an account of a child's gradual and dim awareness of his parents' ordeal as immigrants and of the dark history which dogs their attempts to begin a new life in the Goldineh Medina, the Golden Land of America. The reader knows that both parents have been guilty of sins which have made them pariahs in the old country: the father for having been complicitous in patricide and the mother for having consummated her love for a gentile who abandoned her. By transgressing the authority of the father and of the community, they have been thrust into their marriage as a form of penance.

The shadow cast over this story is the father's suspicion that the child is not his, which motivates his callousness and the child's uncanny defense against an accusation of which he is ignorant: He fabricates an alternative past for himself, one in which his father is the Christian organist who signifies a romantic gentile world both seductive and treacherous. Brutalized by his father and nurtured to the point of suffocation by his mother, David seeks a power greater than that of his parents for protection and solace. Inspired by the text of Isaiah read to him in his *cheder* class and stunned by the sparks between the trolley car tracks, he thrusts his father's milk ladle into the cracks between the rails, nearly electrocuting himself. He survives, buoyed up by the crowds of immigrants who witness his near death, to see his Thorlike father chastened and resigned to his paternity precisely when the child appears to have freed himself from its stranglehold. His biological paternity palls beside the suggestion that the young man has been reborn as an American who can assume an English voice and a gentile past. This is the covenant of America. Or so it seems.

The internal struggle for self-definition is enacted in the novel as a *kulturkampf*, a battleground of languages. Although the book is written in English, it is experienced by the reader as if it were a translation, for David's main actions and thoughts are experienced in Yiddish. Yet this "original" source language is almost entirely absent, occasionally reproduced in transliteration or alluded to as the language of dialogue. Throughout the work David is in the process of constructing a self out of the languages that make up his world. First and foremost there is Yiddish, the language of home and the mother tongue, associated with his own nurturing mother and the Yiddish neighborhood of the Lower East Side. The formidable rival to that language is English, represented in the novel by the street lingo of immigrant dialects but also by the self-consciously literary passages that testify to the presence of a mind schooled in Anglo-American civilization. Also looming as a powerful linguistic force in the book is Hebrew, counterpoint to the mother tongue as it represents the Law of the Father in the words of the Biblical prophets and the liturgy of Jewish ceremony. Hebrew and its partner in ritual, Aramaic, function in the novel as the repository of the Divine, associated with paternal power. The role of Polish is strangely a silent mirror image of English, for it is an inaccessible language for David, the vehicle for conveying secrets between adults that contain within them the key to his parents' past and to the circumstances of his own origins. He can overhear his mother and aunt conversing in Polish about their girlhood and the Old Country, but he can only guess at the meaning and those guesses are born of his own desires. Polish is as inaccessible to David and to the reader as English is inaccessible to his mother. In each case, it is a language of assimilation into a majority non-Jewish culture, away from Yiddish, which was central to Eastern European Jewish life and marginal in both Poland and America.[24]

David's consciousness is divided among these languages, and the competing claims for his allegiance emerge from Henry Roth's location at the nexus of competing cultures. At first the polarities seem self-evident: Hebrew, Aramaic, and Yiddish function as Jewish languages and English and Polish as gentile ones. The ability to understand a language is not always commensurate with the power it wields over its listeners. Hebrew, despite its being a "foreign" language for David, is the unchallenged "home" language as the holy tongue uniting Jews historically and geographically. Furthermore, Hebrew and Aramaic are

linked to texts, namely the Book of Isaiah and the Passover
Haggadah recounting the story of the Exodus from Egypt, the
liberation from slavery, that signify Jewish civilization, whereas
intertextual references in English are drawn from nursery
rhymes, folklore, and secular literature. It might seem that this
novel charts the course of assimilation from a clearly defined
ethnic parent culture to a clearly recognizable Anglo-American
identity, from the mother tongue Yiddish and the father tongue
Hebrew to the adopted tongue English. But it is not that simple.

Yiddish is associated with his mother, but it is the language of
the father as well. And although Hebrew signifies the language
of Judaism and thus serves to reinforce his ties to his family, it is
represented in the King James translation, evoking Christian
Western culture as much as it does Jewish civilization. In fact,
the passage from Isaiah Roth cites is read in Christian hermeneu-
tics as a prophecy of the coming of Christ, just as the Chad Godya
song, with its link to the sacrificial lamb and the Passover seder,
signifies both Jewish and Christian traditions. Furthermore, the
lyrical and symbolic resonances of the Biblical text, with its
metaphorical angel coal in contrast to the literal coal of his cellar,
captivate David's imagination and mark a turning point in his
movement away from his parents and toward his development
as an artist. The Book of Isaiah functions, therefore, as both a
movement toward and away from his Jewish heritage. Aramaic
serves as yet another instance of how tidy oppositions of Jewish
and gentile worlds are challenged by this novel. In one sense,
the Aramaic stanzas from the Chad Godya, by virtue of their
being embedded in a Jewish ritual, have become Judaized
through context. But Aramaic was an official language in the
Persian Empire and served to some extent as a lingua franca
among peoples, much as English has in this century. Aramaic is
also an important influence as a second language in the Bible.
What may serve in this novel as an authentic Jewish medium is
thus also a classic example of the bilingualism and biculturalism
that has characterized Jewish civilization over the ages.[25]

As an immigrant writer who made the dramatic journey from
a Yiddish tenement home to a Greenwich Village literary world,

Roth himself is situated between languages. Bound to Yiddish emotionally, he is also estranged from it intellectually, having never achieved genuine literacy in that language and having never read Yiddish literature. Yet despite mastery of and inventiveness in his nearly native English, he is estranged from it emotionally, for it has remained in his mind the repository of the Christian world. Evident in Roth's novel is not only the importance of language in the construction of David's self, but also the unstable referent of the different languages that make up his world. The non-English and therefore "ethnic" components of his identity spring not from inherent characteristics, but arise interactively, in the context of the other culture. To discuss *Call It Sleep* as an ethnic novel can be constructive, then, if we discard the notion that ethnicity provides an essential and stable identity in confrontation with a monolithic mainstream culture. Instead, ethnicity itself may be a type of invention, as Werner Sollors has argued so persuasively in his studies on ethnicity in American culture.[26] In Homi Bhabha's terms, "The representation of difference must not be hastily read as the reflection of *pre-given* ethnic or cultural traits set in the fixed tablet of tradition. The social articulation of difference, from the minority perspective, is a complex, on-going negotiation that seeks to authorize cultural hybridities that emerge in moments of historical transformation."[27]

David Schearl's Jewish identity may be comprised of pre-given texts, languages, and rituals, but it is activated by its dialogue with aspects of American culture in a given time and place. His hybrid Jewish-American identity, therefore, is forged in the clash of languages and dialects coursing through his consciousness in the book's climactic chapters. It is located in an in-between zone, interstices that are both Henry Roth's individual artistic space and the communal space of a particular generation in Jewish-American culture. "He might as well call it sleep." The evocative opening sentence of the book's last paragraph, thus moves into another indeterminate space, between waking and sleeping, that signifies the indeterminate cultural spaces David inhabits so uneasily. The long series of synecdoches that follows intensifies the problem of representativeness that is the novel's signature.

... the perpetual blur of shod and running feet, the broken shoes, new shoes, stubby, pointed, caked, polished, buniony, pavement-beveled, lumpish, under skirts, under trousers, shoes, over one and through one, and feel them all and feel, not pain, not terror, but strangest triumph, strangest acquiescence. One might as well call it sleep. He shut his eyes.[28]

Each shoe is a tangible particular in his world. Yet each shoe is also a part representing the whole person, and a part representing categories of people, the wearers of caked or polished shoes. David's reverie emphasizes types, groups, collective identities, but at the same time it is the urban child's equivalent of counting sheep before nodding, a silent display of the masses that comprise his world. By shifting into "*one* [my emphasis] might as well call it sleep" in the last sentence, Roth foregrounds the issue of representativeness, since "one" is both a general term uniting author, readers, and characters, and a reference to David's individual consciousness in a form of free indirect discourse. Who speaks for whom in "One might as well call it sleep"? Who is doing the calling? David acquiesces to the existing world that has been named before him, and David also triumphs; he names his state by calling it sleep. Roth has located David in a trancelike state where he both invents his identity through naming and bows to the categories that precede him.

Like Stephen Dedalus, whose name is derived from conflicting cultures, David Schearl's name is oxymoronic. In Hebrew David means beloved; in Yiddish schearl means scissors. What the power of love restores for the child is rent again and again by the power of mind. And what the inheritance of generations provides, the act of immigration severs. Yiddish surnames historically have had the domesticating function of designating vocation or locale. Schearl may mean little more than livelihood from tailoring, humble origins. David, on the other hand, is a name that cannot contract into its etymological link to love alone, for it too has a historical dimension, the most beloved King of Israel, ancestor of the Messiah. To call him David Schearl is to make him representative in the most complex of ways. It is to draw attention to the very act of calling.

This new collection of essays takes a fresh look at the question of representativeness. By recognizing the book's power back in 1956, Leslie Fiedler played a major role in its comeback and canonization. At that time he called it a *"specifically* Jewish book" and, as cited earlier, "the best single book by a Jew about Jewishness written by an American." In his essay for this volume, Fiedler recalls the poem that he wrote but never published as his initial response to *Call It Sleep,* a poem that locates the book in the eternal swing of Yin and Yang and in the rickety moment of the child's entry into that play. His essay returns to his moment of discovery upon his first reading, reconstructed with the hindsight of the transformation of *Call It Sleep* into a classic of Jewish-American literature. It also oscillates between the particularity of one ethnic and religious tradition and the general archetypal structures in the work that can be reached only through the particular. This is evident in Fiedler's rhetoric as well as his theme, for like Henry Roth, he draws on a repertoire of Hebrew and Yiddish expressions some of which have entered general American colloquial usage and some of which have not. By aiming for more than one readership in this essay, Fiedler has challenged the notion of a homogeneous American audience.

Mario Materassi offers a history of the reception of *Call It Sleep,* charting the novel as representative high modernist work, as proletariat novel, as Freudian case study. Moreover, by reading Roth's New York against maps and social accounts of the period, Materassi demonstrates how the author represented his Lower East Side world as a homogeneous Jewish community despite historical evidence to the contrary. The numbing and paralyzing effect of being stripped of a sustaining community and a multi-generational culture, according to Ruth Wisse in her reading of the book, turns David Schearl into an existential hero. Although Roth tried to make deprivation work for him, writes Wisse, his novel is a searing record of the price of disinheritance paid by immigrants, as childhood in this work is representative of immigration.

The following three essays by Brian McHale, Karen Lawrence, and Werner Sollors all place the novel within recent debates about and revisions of the concept of modernism with emphases on form, gender, and ethnicity respectively. Using Joyce as a model for drawing the boundary between modernism and post-modernism, Brian McHale offers a descriptive poetics of Roth's prose by tracing his experimental narrative strategies within the context of other American experimental fiction. Karen Lawrence uses Roth to question one of the basic tenets of modernism, the inner life. What is the forging of a consciousness when the interior world is not sealed off from the grit of the world but rather comprised of it? Conceding that the oedipal paradigm underlies the novel, Lawrence, by drawing on Deleuze and Guattari, demonstrates how maternal and paternal powers are represented within larger systems of desire having to do with the city and with migration. Her question, "How can one be a Jewish writer, an American writer, a European modernist?" is also addressed by Werner Sollors in his concept of "ethnic modernism," whereby Roth's novel is representative of second-generation immigrant literature. In such texts, Jewish immigrant childhood (or any ethnic immigrant upbringing) merges with American modernism to form "a haunting bilateral descent myth." Sollors challenges simple notions of origins, as Lawrence challenges simple notions of the inner life. And in tracing the numerous implications of the novel's multilingualism, Sollors draws our attention to the problem of split audience posed by any ethnic literature.

Each of these readings is an attempt to define the cultural space implied by the tourist in Roth's story "The Surveyor" when he silently tried "to locate a place of some sentimental value to myself." David the individual shares in the collective memory of more than one language, more than one people, more than one culture. And because each of these memories is itself dynamic, David can be representative of more than one group. David the Jewish-American child protagonist inhabits a book that has been hailed as the great representative work of Jewish-American literature. Yet *Call It Sleep* is a novel that challenges the very notion of typicality. This could be identified as the book's central theme. To "call it sleep" is not to lay to rest the problem of ethnic and minority identity in America; it is to draw our attention to the act of calling, as both recognition and invention, even in the moment of utmost weariness.

NOTES

1 Henry Roth, "The Surveyor," *The New Yorker,* August 6, 1966. Reprinted in *Jewish-American Stories,* ed. Irving Howe (New York: New American Library, 1977), 57.

2 Ibid., 64.

3 Unpublished interview with Hana Wirth-Nesher, February 1992. I am grateful to Henry Roth for hospitality and kindness and to H. M. Daleski for being both mentor and catalyst.

4 Harold Ribalow, "The History of Henry Roth and *Call It Sleep,*" introduction to *Call It Sleep* (Paterson, N.J.: Pageant Books, 1960), xiii.

5 Ibid.

6 Ibid., xiv.

7 Kenneth Burke, "More About Roth's *Call It Sleep,*" *New Masses,* 14, February 26, 1935, 21.

8 Fred T. Marsh, "A Great Novel about Manhattan Boyhood," *New York Herald-Tribune Books,* February 17, 1935, 6.

9 Ribalow, xiv.

10 Alfred Kazin, "The Most Neglected Books of the Past 25 Years," *The American Scholar* 25 (Autumn 1956), 478.

11 Leslie Fiedler, "Neglected Books," 486.

12 Irving Howe, "Life Never Let Up," *The New York Times Book Review,* 25, October 1964, 1, 60–61.

13 Jonathan Rosen, "The 60-Year Itch," *Vanity Fair,* February 1994, 22.

14 Leslie Fiedler, "The Jew in the American Novel," *To The Gentiles* (New York: Stein and Day, 1972), 96.

15 Alfred Kazin, "Introduction" to *Call It Sleep* (New York: Farrar, Straus & Giroux, 1991), ix.

16 Irving Howe, *World of Our Fathers* (New York: Harcourt Brace Jovanovich, 1976), 588.

17 In an attempt to explain the radiant urgency of writers such as Roth, Saul Bellow, Delmore Schwartz, and Bernard Malamud, Irving Howe noted that "a subculture finds its voice and its passion exactly at the moment that it approaches disintegration." Ibid., 586.

18 Hana Wirth-Nesher, interview with Henry Roth, February 1992.

19 Ibid.

20 Review of *Call It Sleep, New Masses,* February 12, 1935, 27.

21 Henry Roth, *Mercy of a Rude Stream.* Vol. I, *A Star Shines Over Mt. Morris Park* (New York: St. Martin's Press, 1994); *Mercy of a Rude*

Stream. Vol. 2, *A Diving Rock on the Hudson* (New York: St. Martin's Press, 1995). In these books Roth raises the theme of the transgression of boundaries – ethnic, religious, linguistic, and sexual – to an even higher pitch, as Ira Stigman, the adolescent and guilt-ridden David Schearl, submits to self-denigrating Americanization.

22 Stephen J. Adams, "The Noisiest Novel Ever Written: The Soundscape of Henry Roth's *Call It Sleep,*" *Twentieth Century Literature* (Spring 1989): 43–64.

23 Henry Roth, *Call It Sleep* (New York: Farrar, Straus & Giroux), 418–419.

24 For a more detailed discussion of the function of multilingualism in the novel, see Hana Wirth-Nesher, "Between Mother Tongue and Native Language in *Call It Sleep,*" "Afterword" to the 1991 edition of *Call It Sleep,* 443–462.

25 For a discussion of bilingualism in Jewish culture see Baal-Makhshoves, "One Literature in Two Languages," in *What Is Jewish Literature?* ed. Hana Wirth-Nesher (Philadelphia: The Jewish Publication Society, 1994), 69–78.

26 See Werner Sollors, *Beyond Ethnicity: Consent and Descent in American Culture* (New York: Oxford University Press, 1986) and Werner Sollors, ed. *The Invention of Ethnicity* (New York: Oxford University Press, 1989).

   The imagining and inventing of national identity that has been the subject of historians such as Hobsbawm and Anderson is clearly applicable to the forging of ethnic identities within America. See Benedict Anderson, *Imagined Communities* (London: Verson, 1983) and Eric Hobsbawm, *The Invention of Tradition* (Cambridge: Cambridge University Press, 1992).

27 Homi Bhabha, *The Location of Culture* (London: Routledge, 1994), 2.

28 *Call It Sleep,* 441.

2

The Many Myths of Henry Roth

LESLIE FIEDLER

SIX decades have passed since Henry Roth's first and only
novel appeared, but he has been far from silent during that
time, talking and writing compulsively about his long block and
his abortive attempts to break through it. Recently, Mario
Materassi, an Italian critic, has gathered together under the title
of *Shifting Landscape* all that Roth has to say on this subject –
along with the fragmentary stories and essays he published during his presumably terminal silence, thus revealed as more
mythic than real. In this, which amounts to a second book
(ghostedited to be sure, if not quite ghostwritten), we learn that
Roth has attempted three other long fictions since *Call It Sleep.*
    The first, begun while he was still young, is written from the
point of view of and in the language of a kind of super *goy*, a
labor organizer. The second, started when he was already
middle-aged, deals with the simultaneous expulsion of the Jews
from Spain and the genocidal invasion of America by the Con-
quistadores. The third, not undertaken until he was old, is an
odd mixture of reminiscence and invention, based on the un-
spectacular events of Roth's later life. The first two have long
since been abandoned; but the last, rather disconcertingly, has
developed into a multivolumed long fiction, *Mercy of a Rude
Stream*, the first two volumes of which, *A Star Shines Over Mt.
Morris Park* and *A Diving Rock on the Hudson*, were published
during the last two years as Roth approaches his ninetieth
birthday.
    He has, that is to say, lived long enough to give the lie to his
own myth of himself as the writer who would never, *never* write
again, a persuasive myth through which, I confess, I, like many

17

other critics, have long seen Roth – along with certain other failed authors of the 1930s with whom he associates himself. All of them, and especially himself, he considers victims not of their own weaknesses but of the contradictory demands of the age. Sometimes, to be sure, he suggests more personal reasons for his own plight, referring, for instance, to a lifelong depression, first triggered (it seems evident to me) by the breakup of his affair with Eda Lou Walton, to whom he dedicated his book.

This older gentile woman, already a professor at New York University when he first met her, was to him not merely a mistress, but a surrogate mother and a cultural cicerone. During the bleakest years of the Great Depression, she fed, clothed, and sheltered him, meanwhile inducting him into the mysteries of Modernist High Art (in particular T. S. Eliot's *The Waste Land*) and – despite her own initial reservations – Stalinist politics. Both of these, paradoxically enough, served for him a single purpose: providing him with a way out from the impoverished parochial culture of the ghetto into an ecumenical one, whose aspirations and ideals made ethnic and class distinctions irrelevant. Both, that is to say, enabled him to begin ceasing to be a Jew.

Later in life, when the 1967 war between Israel and the Arabs had shaken his faith in the Communist "line," and time had eroded his allegiance to Modernist High Art, he began to suspect that his double apostasy, the deliberate cutting of his roots, was what had crippled him as an artist. As late as 1963, however, he was still able to insist in print that "to the great boons Jews have already conferred on humanity, Jews in America might add the last and greatest one: of orienting themselves toward ceasing to be Jews." This assimilationist "final solution" Roth not merely advocated but for a long time sought to live. To begin with, all the great loves of his life were *goyim*. These include not just Eda Lou Walton and the *shikse* whom he married and lived with happily for the rest of his life, but also Bill Coy, the *shegetz* organizer whom he passionately admired and used as a model for the protagonist of his aborted second novel.

Moreover, once Roth left New York, he always chose to live in nearly *judenrein* enclaves of America, like rural Maine and suburban New Mexico, places in which his stubbornly unassimilated mother refused to join him. After 1967, Roth did a complete about-face on that score. Not only did he disavow Stalinism in favor of Zionism; he actually considered for a while moving permanently to Israel. Though his proposed *aliyah* finally did not work out, his Jewish identification has remained firm. His return to his roots did not immediately and magically release him from his block, however, and he therefore continued to search for its causes elsewhere.

In any case, he had all along been aware that his plight was not unique. It was shared by many other writers of his generation, including not just other assimilated Jews like Nathanael West, Daniel Fuchs, and Edward Dahlberg, but also birthright American *goyim* like John Steinbeck, James T. Farrell, Hart Crane, and Leonie Adams. "One author after another," he once observed, "whether he was Gentile or Jew, stopped writing, became repetitive, ran out of anything new to say, or just plain died artistically." The problem, he decided, was that they were all caught between what he calls "personal expression" and "social obligation," between, that is to say, a desire to make canonical art as defined by bourgeois society and a conviction that the values of that society must be radically changed. It is a theory too simplistic and reductive to fit all the facts, more myth than objective analysis; but like all true myths, it creates a grid of perception through which those facts can be newly perceived. It is, at any rate, through that archetypal grid that I have (not so much believing as suspending disbelief) continued to perceive not just Roth's single novel and his subsequent long silence, but the work and fate of his contemporaries as well.

He has, in short, not merely mythicized himself, like, say, Poe and Whitman and Byron, but, unlike them, an entire generation too. Reflecting on this, I have come to realize that the greatest of his many artistic gifts is his mythopoeic power, and have therefore felt obliged to reread *Call It Sleep* in a new way. That it is not just incidentally but essentially a mythic book I have always been dimly aware. And how could I not, since I have always known that the two works which most influenced Roth at the moment he wrote it were James Joyce's *Ulysses* and T. S. Eliot's *The Waste Land?*

For reasons I do not quite understand, Roth has in later life attempted to conceal this fact. He declared, for instance, in a speech he gave in Italy in 1987, which Materassi reprints in his collection, "I drew my inspiration from many, many sources, living and dead. From Mark Twain, from Victor Hugo, from Dante and Shakespeare." Several earlier comments, however, also reproduced by Materassi, make it abundantly clear that he was really reading at the moment he conceived *Call It Sleep* not those long-established and therefore unproblematical masters but the two pioneers of Modernism, who had not yet been fully accepted either by the bourgeois critical establishment or the Marxist advocates of "proletarian literature." The latter, indeed, were especially hostile, and when Roth's novel was first published, scolded him for having used as his model such "decadent" elitists.

It is possible, moreover, that Roth may also have read and been influenced by T. S. Eliot's essay on Joyce called "Ulysses, Order and Myth," first published in *The Dial* of 1925. In it, Eliot begins by meditating on how Joyce was one of the first writers to have realized that the conventional novel was "dead," incapable "of controlling, of ordering, of giving significance to the immense panorama of futility and anarchy which is contemporary history." From which it follows, Eliot concludes, that "Instead of the narrative method, we may now use the mythic method . . . as a step toward making the modern world possible for art." Whether or not he had actually read Eliot's manifesto, it is evident in retrospect that Roth identified himself with that Modernist "we."

Call It Sleep contains at its heart an old-fashioned Aristotelian plot, complete with a reversal and recognition; but it strains against the limits of linear narrative more and more as it moves toward its chaotic close. Though it ends in a kind of exhausted tranquillity, its penultimate climactic scene (reminiscent of the Nighttown episode in *Ulysses*, and the second canto of *The Waste Land*) dissolves into a cacophony of disembodied voices, clearly symbolizing the "futility and anarchy" of modern life which only myth can order and control. The myths which Roth uses in his quest for order, however, unlike Joyce's and Eliot's, are drawn not from the lore of Christian Humanism but from the Judaic tradition. That is to say, instead of evoking the legend of the Holy Grail or ironically retelling the story of Odysseus' long voyage home, Roth turns in his quest for archetypal subtexts to the Torah and the *Haggadah* for *Pesach*.

The first of these he finds in the eleventh chapter of *Genesis*, that cryptic account of the fall of the Tower of Babel and the ensuing confusion of tongues, so mysteriously intruded into the genealogy of Shem, the firstborn son of Noah, who is the mythic progenitor of the Jews. Roth never quotes directly from those verses, and, indeed, even the word "babel" appears in his novel only once – uncapitalized, as if it were a common noun.

It is impossible, however, to read *Call It Sleep* without being reminded of the divine curse imposed on the first presumptuous stormers of heaven: "Let us go down, and there confound their language, that they may not understand one another's speech./ So the Lord scattered them abroad from thence upon the face of all the earth." But is this not the very paradigm of the mass migration to America, the setting of Roth's tale, and of the consequent failure of communication among the polyglot immigrants, one of his major themes?

Many critics have commented on the multiple languages spoken in Roth's novel, but none that I know of seems to have noticed that what especially obsesses him are the negative aspects of that heteroglossia. He makes clear, to begin with, how the various dialects of fractured English used by refugees from different lands are mutually incomprehensible, so that even the name of the street on which David lives – as he and his mother pronounce it – cannot be understood by the non-Jews to whom they are obliged to turn for directions or rescue. But he points out, too, that even within single ethnic groups, the generations are more separated than joined by their imperfectly shared languages, old and new.

David, for instance, cannot make sense of the Polish in which his mother and his aunt exchange secrets about their lives and loves in the Old World. No more can the teacher in his *cheder*

21

comprehend the whispered comments of the young hooligans in his charge, since they are couched in a language learned on the streets and in public school which he rejects as unredeemably *goyish*. They in turn cannot understand the holy texts in Hebrew and Aramaic which he forces them to learn by rote. Nowhere does Roth explicitly deal with the question of why this second confusion of tongues has befallen Jew and gentile alike in the New World. It is, however, everywhere suggested that it has been incurred because of a second attempt to reach heaven without leaving the earth, which is to say, by subscribing to the dream of creating a secular Eden in what latter-day immigrants to America called "the Golden Land" and its founding fathers "a City on a Hill."

* * * * *

In any case, the cacophony of confused tongues mounts incrementally through *Call It Sleep*, climaxing in the parodic chorus of obscenities, barroom banalities, and political slogans, in the midst of which – despairing of ever understanding his parents or being understood by them – David almost electrocutes himself. He is seeking between the electrified rails a cleansing and an illumination that will release in him a voice his elders will not merely listen to but actually hear. If he believes that only supernal fire will do so, this is because there has long been echoing in his head the *Haftorah* for *Yitro*, a passage from the sixth chapter of *Isaiah*, which he first overheard in *cheder*.

This passage Roth quotes in full in a transliteration of the Hebrew text. In English he gives us only a translation of the Rabbi's Yiddish paraphrase. Thus what clearly constitutes a second key archetypal text of *Call It Sleep* appears only at a double remove from the original. Ever since my first reading, therefore, I have kept returning to the King James version of that mythic account of the calling of a reluctant prophet. "I am a man of unclean lips," Isaiah protests in that version, struck dumb by his vision of God in all his glory, "and I dwell in the midst of a people of unclean lips." When, however, those sullied lips are touched by a burning coal in the hands of a Seraph, he is able to answer as a proper prophet should, "Here am I. Send me."

Here is another obvious paradigm, since David, too, feels himself called but unworthy. After all, he also is the foul-mouthed child of a foul-mouthed world, in which the preferred metaphor for the act of love is putting the *petzel* in the *knish*. Consequently, he seeks to purify himself in a supernal conflagration, though – ironically enough – this time from below rather than from above. At first – even more ironically – he seems to find not illumination but darkness and total silence, which is to say, death. He does not quite die, of course, but is somehow reborn short of total extinction; and as he struggles back to full consciousness, a new voice speaking in a new tongue, elegantly phrased and cadenced, begins to cut through the inchoate uproar of the new Babel.

Italicized and enclosed in noncommittal parentheses, the provenance of that voice seems uncertain, but clearly it is the voice of the adult who will someday be able to write a prophetic book much like the one we are reading. Disconcertingly, however, that new holy language by which the confusion of tongues will be at long last resolved, turns out to be much like the transatlantic *goyish* English of the elite High Modernists. This does not appear to have disturbed Roth as it does me. At any rate, he uses it once more for the book's last word: the final paragraph in which a redeemed David lies in a state of suspended animation for which neither he nor his author can find a better word than "sleep."

* * * * *

From the very start, however, two other archetypally resonant texts have been counterpointing the passage from *Isaiah* which triggers David's nearly fatal quest. At the moment he first hears it, *Pesach* (the only festival of the Jewish year which seems to interest Roth) is approaching, and therefore he and his fellow students in the *cheder* are being schooled in the *Haggadah* for Passover. This is appropriate enough, since the reading from the Law which that *Haftorah* follows begins with the thirteenth chapter of *Exodus*, in which Moses tells to his gentile father-in-law, Jethro, the tale of Israel's deliverance from Egypt. This is the same mythic narrative which the *Haggadah* fixes in ritual form, so that, recited annually, its memory may never die.

To prepare them for their role in this ceremonial rehearsal, David and his classmates have been set to memorizing in Hebrew and Yiddish "The Four Questions" traditionally posed by the youngest male present at the Seder, thereby cueing the recitation by the rest of those assembled of that often-told story. There is irony in this, in light of the fact that many of the boys learning them – especially David as Roth's surrogate – are terminal Jews, destined to break the chain forever. There is, however, no irony implicit in Roth's evocation of the second set piece we overhear the *cheder* boys reciting: the Aramaic folk song, *Chagadya*, chanted at the Seder's end.

Beginning with the line "one kid, one kid, my father bought for two pennies," it evokes images of filial sacrifice, reminding some critics of Abraham's binding of Isaac and others of the story of the death on the Cross of the one who claimed to be the earth-born Son of the Heavenly Father. But as the song continues, the father disappears completely, except in the choral repetitions of the first line. It is a cat who kills and consumes the kid, then is in turn bitten by a dog, who is beaten by a stick, which is burned by a fire, etc., etc., etc. It seems at first as if this tale of universal destruction, so disarmingly reduced to the cadences of a nursery rhyme, can end only in total annihilation. At the very last minute, however, the Divine Father of us all intervenes, slaying the Angel of Death, who has slain the slaughterer, who has slaughtered the ox, which has drunk the water, which had put out the fire. . . . And we are unexpectedly and triumphantly through with all etceteras, since death itself has died.

Reflecting on this, we are reminded that on the first *Pesach*, the dread hand of the *malaach-ha-mavit* was also stayed by divine intervention. His threat to our frail flesh was not ended forever, but he was induced to pass over the dwellings of the Israelites without slaying their eldest sons. It is this which the archetypal subtext of *Exodus* symbolizes for Roth, who tends to downplay the sense in which it also signifies the passage from bondage to freedom, the reentry into the Holy Land, and the defeat of all who seek to destroy the Chosen People.

David, after all, is another in that line of firstborn males barely snatched from the jaws of death, which includes Moses himself as well as the generation which survived the Tenth Plague. But David is threatened not by a heathen oppressor or the wrath of God that oppressor has provoked. The enemy who hounds him to the very verge of death is his own father, made half mad and nearly impotent by indurated paranoia and guilt. He is haunted, on the one hand, by a suspicion that David is not his son but a bastard spawned by his wife's adulterous affair with a *goy*, and on the other, by a sense of guilt for his hated father's death. That father was fatally gored by an ox, but the surviving son cannot forget that he had been in a position to prevent it.

His subsequent "hardening of the heart" is attributed by Roth not, like that of the Pharaoh, to the inscrutable will of God, but to his own troubled psyche. Consequently, it is no traditional Judaic source which provides the archetypal subtext for a chief plot line of *Call It Sleep:* the patriarchal-filial conflict foreshadowed in the novel's introduction and not finally resolved until its very end. It is rather to the myth of Oedipus we must turn, not as originally imagined by Sophocles but as re-imagined by Sigmund Freud, which is to say, by another prophet, who, however secular, is undeniably Jewish. Freud delivered his first important lectures to the B'nai Brith, and almost all his patients as well as his most faithful disciples were Jews.

Roth never mentions the name of the founder of psychoanalysis – or for that matter that of the mythic killer of his father and lover of his mother so central to the "Jewish science." Nonetheless, David seems finally a textbook case of the "Oedipus Complex." Not only does he love his mother passionately; he is obsessed by erotic images of her naked flesh, which he compulsively fantasizes being stared at by strangers and ravished in his father's planned absence by a boarder who pretends to be his friend. This time, however, whatever the oedipal son may have dreamed, his father does not die. He himself is the only one who even comes close to death, nearly slain by his own hand. In this ironic version of the myth he has introjected the father by performing for him what amounts to a preemptive counterattack.

He has also usurped the paternal role by the way in which he attempts to destroy himself, thrusting a milk ladle into a dark gap in the earth. Surely, this parody of phallic penetration and the nearly fatal orgasm which ensues represent both his infringement of the ultimate erotic taboo and his self-punishment for it. But this is not all; even earlier his introjection of the father had already begun, when in an excess of blind rage he strikes down another boy in the street. Nor does his internalization of the Oedipal conflict stop with his father; when he does not die but is reborn, he takes on the mother's role as well, delivering his new self in a travail like that of birthing.

But he has already emulated her in other respects, whoring like her after the gods of strangers and lusting for the strangers' flesh. Though she had not, as David's father suspects, betrayed him in an extramarital affair with a *shegetz,* she had, before her marriage, betrayed her own Jewish father by coupling with a church organist. But David – having half-understood her confession of the affair to her sister – half-believes himself to be the bastard begotten of that miscegenational union, and publicly announces that fact in a moment of panic. He had already recapitulated her imagined infidelity by carrying on what amounts to a long-term flirtation with a *goyish* hooligan called Leo, a flirtation vicariously consummated when he helps Leo seduce the sluttish stepdaughter of his (David's) Aunt Bertha.

To complicate matters even further, that gross and vulgar aunt is clearly the alter ego of David's mother, the dark side of Roth's own mother (he has confessed in print), split off for fictional purposes. In yet another turn of the mythic screw, as a reward for serving as a pimp David is given a rosary. To David this seems only a kind of secular amulet, no different than the torn-off leaves of the calendar he has earlier hoarded. But when it falls from his pocket at the novel's crisis point, his horrified Jewish elders recognize it as a symbol of the adoration of Mary, the

Great Goddess of Mediterranean paganism, reborn as the Mother of the Messiah rejected by the Jews.

* * * * *

Reflecting on this, we begin to realize how Roth has been sub-verting the narrow Freudian interpretation of the Oedipus myth. Not only does he interiorize it, as we have already noticed; he generalizes it as well – in a way that seems more Jungian than Freudian. Rather than interpreting the generational conflict at its heart as symbolizing the subconscious tensions present in even the most loving of nuclear families, he takes it to signify the bipolar oppositions which define the very nature of existence. These oppositions are most conspicuously represented by the two secular icons which hang on the walls of David's childhood home: the picture of a field of golden wheat, the symbol of her forbidden dalliance, so dear to the heart of his mother, and ox horns mounted on a plaque, the symbol of parricide, cherished by his father.

Though thus identified as "female" and "male," in the rest of Roth's text these primal antinomies assume a myriad of shapes and forms. Sometimes they appear as mere abstractions, like hot and cold, light and dark, in and out, up and down, lost and found – or more grandly, love and hate, life and death. But sometimes more specifically they are represented by what seem at first inert aspects of the novel's plot, setting, background, or decor: the roof and the cellar, the house and the street, the Old World and the New, gentile and Jew, *kosher* and *treif*, the Eve of Passover and "all other nights."

Yin and Yang are the traditional Chinese terms which sub-sume them all and though Roth never uses them he seems as aware as any Taoist sage of the mystery they signify. A major theme of his book is the necessity for each of us to restore to these cosmic principles, sundered in the here and now, their original timeless unity. So, at any rate, David does, thus falling into a tranquil sleep from which he will awake with a new vision, rather than blinding or killing himself like the tragic protagonists of the Oedipus myth.

Though this seems to me obvious now, it has taken me nearly fifty years of rereading Roth's novel to perceive it. Yet I must have dimly surmised it from the start, since after my initial reading I wrote the following little poem, which I have never forgotten, though I publish it here for the first time:

Call It Sleep

One must kill,
One betray.
Yang's anger,
The yielding of Yin.
Under the random evasion of play,
How does the child begin?

3

Shifting Urbanscape:
Roth's "Private" New York

MARIO MATERASSI

SINCE the end of the fifties a minor legend has grown around
the figure of Henry Roth, long known to the literary world
as a one-novel author. There are many chapters in this legend:
the early success of *Call It Sleep*, the writer's block that paralyzed
Roth soon afterward, his disappearance from the literary scene
at the beginning of the forties, his burning of the manuscript of
a second novel for which Scribner's had advanced one thousand
dollars, his rediscovery as a waterfowl farmer in Maine, the
revival of *Call It Sleep* in the early sixties and its subsequent
recognition as one of the masterpieces of twentieth-century literature. Recently, another chapter was added with the publication
of *A Star Shines over Mt. Morris Park*, the initial section of a
multivolume opus with the general title of *Mercy of a Rude Stream*.
The appearance of the new work has disclosed a fact of which
only few had been aware: In 1979, at the age of seventy-three,
Henry Roth had resumed writing in a regular and highly disci-
plined way, and this belated, miraculous outburst of creativity
has resulted in a "novel in memoir form," as he calls it, which is
well over 4,000 pages long.[1]

So the Roth legend continues to grow. It is a legend that over
the course of half a century has accrued by the slow accumula-
tion of disconnected fragments of a unique, decidedly odd existence in and out of the literary world and of the public eye. Each
chapter of the legend is isolated by long periods of silence; each
contradicts the previous one and in turn is contradicted by the
one that follows. Phoenixlike, Henry Roth appears, disappears,
reappears out of the ashes of his prior avatars. Ghostlike in his

rare, sudden returns to the scene, he seems to mock the common, expected model of development, ripening, and decline.

The pattern of discontinuity and fragmentation manifest in the legend took possession of Roth's life at an early stage. When still an infant he was "imported" from the Old into the New World, a disruption whose possibly far-reaching consequences are hinted at in the prologue of *Call It Sleep*.[2] A second, decidedly traumatic break occurred when he was eight years old: In 1914, just prior to the outbreak of World War I, the Roth family moved from the Lower East Side to Harlem. Roth has always blamed this move for most of the unhappiness that ensued, repeatedly asserting that it destroyed the safe, harmonious, self-contained world which he knew and left him stranded in alien territory, deprived of his familiar emotional and cultural moorings.

Henry Roth never recovered the congruity and the harmony he had experienced as a child on the Lower East Side. It could be argued that he has spent his adult life trying to recapture that sense of belonging, first by affiliating himself with Edna Lou Walton's circle of intellectuals in the Village, then by joining the Communist Party, later by withdrawing into his secluded family life in rural Maine, and still later through his newborn interest in and partisanship for the state of Israel. As a writer, Roth has delved over and over again into his lifelong obsession with the paradigmatic sequence of belonging, estrangement, and subsequent loss of identity. This theme consistently runs through *Call It Sleep*, through most of the short pieces in *Shifting Landscape*, and through *Mercy of a Rude Stream*. Whether in an overt fashion or under a thin disguise, Roth's writing obsessively recounts the life story of a peculiarly erratic individual: a Jew who rejected Judaism and broke away from his heritage, a Marxist who repudiated the party line to embrace the cause of Israel, a promising writer who gave up his literary career, became a farmer and a hermit, then cast off that life of self-deceit to try once again the way of writing.[3] A fundamentally autobiographical writer, Henry Roth has never been interested in any story other than the anguished one of a man who, throughout his life, has contradicted each of his previously held positions and beliefs.

Arguably, *Call It Sleep* can be read as a vehicle through which, soon after breaking away from his family and his tradition, young Roth used some of the fragments of his childhood to shore up the ruins of what he already felt was a disconnected self. Forty-five years later, Roth embarked on another attempt to bring some retrospective order to his life's confusion: *Mercy of a Rude Stream*, which he has long called a "continuum," can be read as a final, monumental effort on the part of the elderly author to come to terms with the pattern of rupture and discontinuity that has marked his life.

I have suggested elsewhere that this pattern is the constant which gives Roth's existence its peculiarly paradoxical quality.[4] One of the major constants in his writing, and his primary metaphor for fragmentation, is New York City. Like most metropolitan settings in twentieth-century literature, Henry Roth's New York is a place of division and isolation where the individual's aspiration toward self-fulfillment is thwarted into a haphazard struggle to conquer or retain a minimum of integration both within the self and within the social context. Never, in Roth's fiction, is the reader allowed to forget that temporal discontinuity marks the existence of millions who have left behind them centuries of cultural and emotional continuity; never can one lose sight of the fact that spatial discontinuity is stamped on every facet of urban life, which is conditioned at all levels by the overwhelming reality of ethnically and economically defined neighborhoods. Rifts within the self, the family, and the community, and the desire to somehow heal this rupture, predominate in Henry Roth's almost totally urban fiction.

* * * * *

New York has always loomed large in Roth's imagination, both as a specific physical environment and as a social laboratory where diverse experiments in collective relationships are effected. In an embryonic fashion it is present in the very first piece of writing Roth ever produced, "Impressions of a Plumber," a paper he wrote as an assignment in one of his English courses at CCNY in 1925. In this paper, which his teacher deemed worthy of publication in the college magazine, young Roth described one typical workday of the previous summer when he had held a temporary job as a plumber's helper. Emerging from the subway, an emblem of the alienating city for many American writers, the sprightly youth reaches his destination, "the skeleton houses stand[ing] out crudely against the sky."[5]

This passage marks the birth of the setting in which Henry Roth was later to place his characters, from *Call It Sleep* to *Mercy of a Rude Stream* through many of the short stories and occasional pieces collected in *Shifting Landscape*.[6] The humorous self-portrait of the artist as a plumber's helper in the Bronx shows a lively high school student fully immersed in his temporary job. His acute observations on the other laborers, his frank delight in the quirky personality of the older plumber, and his minute, almost loving description of every phase of his work give life to the protagonist of this sketch as an individual keenly focused on his surroundings. Like the Lower East Side buildings in and out of which little David Schearl will later conduct his moving search for a sense of self, these still gaping buildings are more than simply a backdrop: They are the catalyst of the young man's experience, as limited as it is in this early piece.

One should not make too much of "Impressions of a Plumber" as an antecedent of *Call It Sleep* although, by virtue of its being the *only* extant antecedent of that novel, the temptation is quite strong.[7] "Impressions of a Plumber" is an occasional piece of writing composed for a nonliterary purpose. Still, one must note the curious coincidence that a few years after this sketch on plumbers and plumbing, the first chapter of *Call It Sleep* opens with a paragraph focused on plumbing. In this paragraph, the center of interest is the sink in the Schearls' kitchen, its drain, and the unreachable brass faucets which to little, thirsty David are stark reminders that "this world had been created without thought of him."[8] The first questions that David asks himself in this novel of quest concern the mysterious world of plumbing:

Where did the water come from that lurked so secretly in the curve of the brass? Where did it go, gurgling in the drain? What a strange world must be hidden behind the walls of a house. (15)

The young plumber's helper knows all the answers to David's questions. Past the age of wonder and initiated into the prosaic realities of the everyday world, he knows that "keeping pipe out of sight is the modern philosophy of plumbing" (*Shifting Landscape* 7).

Undoubtedly, the fact that Book I of *Call It Sleep* begins with a passage echoing the main thematic concern of the early sketch is but a coincidence, and any self-referential intent on the part of the more mature writer should be excluded. This coincidence, however, helps us perceive that as early as 1925 Henry Roth already knew how to structure referential reality by concentrating on one element in the everyday life of the character and describing it with great precision so as to establish a cogent relationship between the character and his environment. Of the two texts focused on plumbing – the early sketch and the initial paragraph of the novel's first chapter – the first is particularly meticulous in the description: "Visualize a tree, a poplar, whose trunk extends straight upward but whose branches make an acute angle with the trunk. There you have the six-by-two 'Y,' the trunk six inches and the branches two inches. To these branches the drain pipes of the wash basins, bathtubs, and flush bowls are connected" (*Shifting Landscape* 6). The passage in *Call It Sleep* conveys with immediacy the child's impression of the kitchen sink: "the brass faucets . . . gleamed so far away, each with a bead of water at its nose, slowly swelling, falling" (15).

In both texts, the probing spotlight on the mundane plumbing components serves to highlight the protagonists' character, their position vis-à-vis their surroundings and, ultimately, their role in the respective stories. In the sketch, the youth leaves work noticeably less grimy than the plumber because the dirt accumulated on his skin from handling tools and pipes the whole day has yet to become ingrained as it has with the plumber. In the novel, the boy experiences the first of his many frustrations when his attempt to reach the refreshing water is thwarted by "the iron hips of the sink [which] rested on legs tall almost as his own body" (15).

Whether he wrote of installing a pipe or straining for a faucet

33

out of reach, unloading a truck stuck under the Elevated ("Broker") or roasting chestnuts on the sidewalk on a wintry evening (*A Star Shines* 47), Roth consistently singled out with laserlike precision one physical element and transformed it into an eloquent emblem of the character's rapport with his environment.

* * * * *

Since its publication in 1934, Roth's treatment of the urban environment in *Call It Sleep* has been hailed by critics as particularly successful.

He knows the smell of alleys, the noise of hawkers as they wheel their pushcarts on the refuse coated pavements in the neighbourhoods of Hester Street,

wrote one of the earliest reviewers, who went on to say:

The whine of beggars, the hum of city traffic and the drone of old men as they repeat the sacred words from the Holy Books are noises he has heard, understood and helped to make.[9]

Another critic observed that *Call It Sleep* reveals "more of the actual conditions of living in New York's East Side than any other book I have ever read."[10]
Writing at a time when the canons of proletarian literature were prevailing, some of the first reviewers stressed the "accuracy" of Roth's descriptions of the East Side slums: "the sidewalk humor and the better-than-Milt-Gross dialect is accurate; the cruelty and obscenity of these tenement children are genuine," commented one critic.[11] "The most accurate ... study of an American slum childhood that has yet appeared," confirmed another reviewer in the Books section of the same paper.[12]
The accuracy of Roth's representation of his environment was, however, not universally acknowledged. One reviewer wrote: "There are times when [Mr. Roth's] desire to paint a picture makes him resort to colors too vivid to be accurate."[13] A similar view, couched in terms of extreme negativity, was voiced by the anonymous reviewer of *New Masses:*

The child's reactions to the hectic squalor of the streets ... are done with vigor, understanding and a sensitivity which, however, often degenerates into impressionism on a rampage.

The review ended with these often quoted words:

It is a pity that so many young writers drawn from the proletariat can make no better use of their working class experience than as material for introspective, febrile novels.[14]

The first reviewers of *Call It Sleep*, then, can be grouped into three broad categories: those who liked the book because it went beyond the tenets of social realism, those who liked it *although* it did, and those who did not like it precisely for that reason.

Accuracy in the depiction of slum life – that is, the possible documentary value of the novel – was a key issue in the critical discussion at the time. All reviewers tacitly agreed on the desirability of accuracy. They only disagreed on the extent to which *Call It Sleep* was accurate. Those who questioned the faithfulness of Roth's depiction of his slums found fault with his impressionistic poetics or with his desire to "paint a picture" – where the recurring, implicitly damning reference to the visual arts belies their impatience as Marxists with the use that the middle class makes of this "superstructure."

By the time Roth's long-forgotten novel was reissued in 1960, social realism was no longer the dominant criterion by which contemporary literature was judged.[15] The prevailing view of *Call It Sleep* from the early sixties on is best expressed by Leslie Fiedler in his pioneering essay on the novel:

Roth's turning to childhood enables him to render his story as dream and nightmare, fantasy and myth – to escape the limits of that realism which makes of other accounts of ghetto childhood documents rather than poetry.[16]

Marie Syrkin put it in similar words:

Call It Sleep cannot be pigeon-holed as a social document or a slice of life in the slums of Brownsville and the East Side. ... In Roth fidelity to the depiction of the environment is always complemented by the imaginative capacity to weld the drab details of the outer world into the transport of the child's vision.

And again:

If East Side life were glimpsed only through David's febrile awareness, the novel would still be powerful but limited in range. Roth, however, always lets you feel the "real" outer texture of the objective experience which the child suffers subjectively.[17]

Subjectivity, almost a forbidden word in much of the criticism of the thirties, became the new critical banner. Long past were the days when David could be branded as "an absurdly sensitive child"[18] and readers could be counted on to share in the reviewer's dismissal of such a character. The general critical stress on the boy's inner world began to push upstage the outer world within which David's search for a grasp on reality takes place. The environment, both physical and social, became "subordinate to [the boy's] inward fears and private obsessions,"[19] a backdrop to be studied as a function of David's vision rather than in relation to the referential world it depicts. "[T]he *paysage intérieur* of David Schearl," to borrow Naomi Diamant's words, became "the central element of the novel as a whole."[20]

An excursus through some of the most representative or influential interpretations of *Call It Sleep* in the past three decades may be instructive in highlighting the variety of views offered by critics. Some of these views echo each other, their differences being mostly a question of emphasis when not of nuance. Others prove to be totally unreconcilable, though they may be equally convincing. Considering that the wide range of critical instruments used in the analysis of the novel has been fairly consistent throughout the thirty years under scrutiny, one must draw the conclusion that the text of *Call It Sleep* provides substantial support to each of the expressed views. As I hope to make clear in this essay, the nature of Roth's novel calls for an integration of all the critical instruments hitherto employed in its analysis, whether they be Freudian theory, Marxist theory, Biblical exegesis or more strictly literary approaches such as the study of symbols or of myth. More broadly, it calls for an integration of all the ideologies, be they political, religious, cultural, or critical, from which these instruments are derived.

As is the case with all methodologically defined critical discourses, interpretations of *Call It Sleep* based on Freudian theory vary in their dependence on the chosen model. Certain critics explicitly rely on Freudian concepts and terminology. "If we may understand the cellar as representing not only sexual fear and contamination but the dark oedipal forces of the id," wrote Ethan Place, "then David, by embracing these forces and touching the rail, is metaphorically consummating the repressed desire for his mother while simultaneously investing himself with the light of purity from God the Father."[21] Others, taking for granted that "the chief influence of the book [is] Freudianism," do not feel the necessity of supporting their assertion with more than a sporadic exemplification.[22] Still others do not specifically refer to Freud, although they make use of his terminology in their study of the novel's symbolism.[23]

These variances notwithstanding, readings of *Call It Sleep* based on Freudian theory often reach conclusions that do not significantly differ except on matters of emphasis or in the treatment of particulars. There is a general consensus as regards the oedipal triangle, the symbolic equation of the cellar with the unconscious, the phallic connotations of the milk dipper, the sexual implications of David's words to his *melamed* about the "big light in the middle, between the crack" of the trolley tracks (346), as well as other passages that admit Freudian interpretations. This consensus is shared by certain critics who do not necessarily adopt a Freudian perspective but draw on Freudian readings of the novel and subsume these findings in a new interpretation. Such is the case of Bonnie Lyons.[24] Lyons, the scholar who has devoted perhaps the greatest attention to the symbolic level of *Call It Sleep*, referred only in passing to Freud but her general discussion of the boy's psyche is clearly indebted to Freudian concepts and terminology.

In her exhaustive analysis of the "organic symbolic structure" that gives *Call It Sleep* its tightly woven unity, Bonnie Lyons expanded William Freedman's convincing discussion of the all-pervading light/darkness dichotomy in the novel and its symbolic connotations.[25] Lyons also elaborated on Freedman's view of the final scene at the rail as "a transcending experience" in which David finds "[r]edemption from guilt through the pain of electric jolt" (Freedman 1967, 114). Freedman's interpretation, which was based on the myths of redemption and rebirth, initiated a line of thinking as regards the conclusion of *Call It Sleep* which Tom Samet in his essay referred to as "a remarkable sort of critical orthodoxy" (Samet 569). Disregarding certain early warnings that "[i]n the interplay of ironies and evasions the final meaning of the failed sacrifice, the private apocalypse . . . is never made quite clear"[26] and that "[t]he search for an apocalypse is ironic and doomed" (Syrkin 91), many commentators found in David's near self-electrocution a highly positive significance based on those universal myths.[27]

The ample consensus on this interpretation cut across cultural lines, as it was shared by those who felt, with Sam B. Girgus, that "David's awakening marks his resurrection as a Jew from a living death,"[28] as well as by those who, like Gordon Poole, saw David as a Christ figure.[29] Lyons understood David's experience at the rail in terms of both the Jewish and the Christian mystical tradition, although of the two, the former was given much greater emphasis. Mary Edrich Redding identified "an extensive system of pagan and folk myths" that "does not require a denial of the presence of Hebraic sacred themes" (Redding 180), whereas Ita Sheres found the four sections of the novel suggestive of Lurianic mysticism and of "biblical prophetic motifs related to exile and redemption."[30]

At the end of the essay, however, Sheres conceded that "[t]he concluding 'sleep' episode is the most disturbing to the notion of redemption" and asked a highly relevant question: "how can one equate redemption with sleep?" Sheres's question reflected the lack of unanimity among critics concerning the positivity of the short circuit scene. Forcefully downplaying the symbolic reverberation of this scene, Tom Samet called David's "moments of illumination . . . essentially bogus – images of betrayal rather than salvation," as the "electric current, the bogus vision, cannot alter the permanent facts of David's intractable world" (570, 571). In a sobering, no-nonsense approach to the question, Gary Epstein reinforced Samet's argument: "Even logic would reveal to anyone who spends a moment of serious thought on the subject that touching the third rail of a trolley track is, in fact, nothing at all like a mystical experience."³¹ Epstein found Reb Pankower's pronouncement, "God's light is not between car-tracks" (346), to be "peculiarly relevant to David's fate" as in the short circuit the boy "finds nothing but electricity, symbolic of nothing but brute, dumb force."³² Predictably, the conflicting interpretations of the final explosion at the rail had far-reaching consequences on the conclusions critics drew as to the meaning of the novel.

Fiercely clashing conclusions were also reached in assessing the significance of David's relationship to his social environment. As noted earlier, even critics who shared the conviction that David's experience is ultimately a redemptive one could take wholly unassimilable positions in their identification of the over-all ideologic implications of the boy's story, which could be seen either as totally within the Jewish tradition or as definitely point-ing to a repudiation of Judaism in favor of Christianity. Analo-gous disparities can be observed in the positions of critics particu-larly attentive to the social environment. In Bernard Sherman's opinion, "[un]questionably, the materials of the novel are those of the [Jewish] education novel: the sentient six-year-old and the teeming ghetto replete with Jewish gangs to corrupt and gentile ones to ambuscade"; for the critic, "Christianity . . . is one more source of guilt to the chronically terrified David," whereas it is "Judaism which supplies [him] with sublimity."³³ No such role is granted Judaism by Helge Norman Nilssen, who saw *Call It Sleep* as a *Bildungsroman* which, through a "substantial render-ing of the life of the streets and the characteristic lower class urban speech of the inhabitants," describes a "subtle reorienta-tion from isolation to community, in sociological terms," to the point that David is seen "developing attitudes that are American and Emersonian."³⁴ Gordon Poole went one step further, claim-ing that the novel's progressive abandonment of Judaism reaches an almost anti-Semitic overtone (134, n2).

Sam B. Girgus took an intermediate position between Sher-man's and Poole's opposite views. For Girgus, *Call It Sleep* "func-tions as a paradigmatic, Jewish novel of initiation" and its young protagonist "emerges as a new American consciousness, a pro-phetic Jewish 'kup' dramatizing in modern setting the cultural democracy and pluralism of the American idea."[35] On the other hand, Diane Levenberg struck an explicit Marxian posture when she wrote that "Roth offers to David and to his readers all the raw power inherent in the proletariat. It is the workers, with their dreams, their visions, their hope of a restful night, who save David and bring him home."[36] In her essay on this "semiotic *Bildungsroman,*" Naomi Diamant concentrated on a different sort of rawness, "the raw material of actuality" which "the experiencing self dominates . . . transmuting it arbitrarily – from smoke stack to paling, from paling to teeth, and so on – and creating a parallel world of the imagination as compelling, or perhaps even more compelling, than the real" (344).[37]

Two observations are in order at the end of this excursus through some of the studies devoted to *Call It Sleep* in the last three decades. The first concerns the excellent quality of many of these hermeneutic efforts, the depth of insights displayed, and the wealth of individual discoveries unearthed from within the text. The second observation concerns the variety of conflicting views, all of which are at least partially supported by textual evidence. Such interpretative divergences arise when greater emphasis – at times, *exclusive* emphasis – is placed on some of the textual components at the expense of others, as when the dialectic tension between opposing world views (for instance, Marxism versus Freudianism or Judaism versus Christianity) is ignored and one of the two poles is privileged over the other. A consequence of the circumscribed perspective is that the dynamic interaction of the many levels present in the text – be they the historical or the sociological, the political or the religious, the psychological, the symbolic, or the mythical – is downplayed if not totally overlooked. This is not always the case. A number of critics have made the focus of their inquiry into *Call It Sleep* inclusive rather than exclusive, therefore succeeding in accounting for more than just one of the textual levels. Ultimately, these are the readings of Roth's novel that prove the most rewarding, as the methodologic flexibility of the interpreter matches the complexity and variety of the author's interests.

With the possible exception of Levenberg, today's critics of *Call It Sleep* proceed from theoretical premises that are quite distant from those once supporting the concept as well as the expectation of accuracy of representation: that is, the firm belief in the solidity of reality and the equally firm belief in a direct relation between literature and referential reality. Unlike most critics in the thirties, we now differentiate between reality and the writer's *idea* of reality, and concentrate on the latter fully convinced that the fictional environment is, as Hana Wirth-Nesher puts it, "inseparable from the frame of mind of the characters and the vision of life held by the author."[38] We are, therefore, well aware that the New York City we study in *Call It Sleep* is Roth's idea of the city and, as such, does not have to stand up for verification and certification against the "real" New York – except insofar as an understanding of the peculiarity of the writer's possible alteration of his model sheds light on the function his treatment of the environment has within the whole.

Roth has often declared that it was Joyce who revealed to him the feasibility of using the elements of his everyday reality as material for a work of art (Friedman 31). This included both his private life and the world outside his home – the crowded tenements, the throngs in the streets, the poverty, the filth. The extent to which Roth utilized his own past in writing the story of little David Schearl, as well as the profound distortions and basic omissions to which he subjected his private life in recreating it for literary purposes, are questions that will be best addressed once the whole of *Mercy of a Rude Stream* is made public. For the time being, all that need be said is that David's story follows quite closely Henry Roth's life up to the time of the family's move to Alphabet City in the Lower East Side, to the point that the real-life and the fictional youngsters lived on the same fourth floor of the same five-story corner building between Avenue D and 9th Street to which both the real-life and the fictional families moved in 1910.[39]

If there have been distortions and omissions in the use to which Roth put his old neighborhood in *Call It Sleep*, these have largely escaped critical notice. To my knowledge, since those first reviewers who argued that the writer had somewhat distorted his environment, no critic has questioned the accuracy of the Lower East Side neighborhood as portrayed in the novel. This

41

appears to be at odds with some of Roth's statements indicating that he had intentionally altered the environment to suit his dramatic ends.

"I decided to leave the realm of strict fact," Roth told an interviewer in 1987, and then proceeded to explain how he began treating people and events in his past as "objects that were just [his] to use."[40] Many a time, in his conversations, he has insisted that he compounded the East Side with Harlem, creating an American microcosm and placing it in the middle of what he has repeatedly referred to in his interviews and in *Mercy* as a kind of "Jewish ministate." More than once Roth has declared that while he lived on 9th Street no contact with Catholics was conceivable and that not until he left the Lower East Side did he encounter a non-Jewish way of life.[41] Even more forcefully, on page 507 of the typescript of *Mercy of a Rude Stream* (a passage yet to be made public) the writer has aging Ira wail:

Ah, Stigman, Stigman: Fourteen years you resided there. Couldn't you have simply chronicled the street? Fourteen years spent in polyglot Harlem, as against a few years on the homogeneous East Side, *which you warped out of shape anyway.*[42]

The available historical evidence neither supports nor flatly disproves Roth's claim as to the homogeneity of his old neighborhood. In 1900 – that is, four years before the peak period of Jewish immigration into the United States (1904–1909) – Jews already constituted seventy-nine percent of the Lower East Side population.[43] The area focused on in *Call It Sleep* is the upper portion of the formerly German neighborhood once known as *Kleindeutschland,* between 10th Street and Houston and between Avenue B and the river.[44] By 1910, when the Roths moved in, almost all of the German community had moved out as a consequence of the tragic death toll suffered in 1904 when the pleasure boat *General Slocum* sank and over 1,000 people – mostly German workers from the neighborhood – drowned in the East River. The neighborhood then became predominantly Jewish of Hungarian origin with a scattering of gentile families, either German or Slav.[45]

It is to be presumed that the children of these families attended the local public school. Undoubtedly, the overwhelming majority of the students were Jewish since in 1905, a few years before young Henry Roth went to school there, Jewish students already constituted almost ninety-five percent of the elementary school population on the Lower East Side. Still, Roth probably did come in contact with some gentile children; for certain, most, if not all, of his teachers were gentiles.[46] Other encounters with non-Jews could have occurred, and in all probability did occur, as a result of forays into adjoining "alien" neighborhoods. Tompkins Square, for example, referred to in the novel as simply "the open stretch of the park" (349) and which in the words of a Jewish immigrant from Rumania, a contemporary of Roth, rested in the middle of "the untracked wilds . . . which to me was the vast dark continent of the 'real Americans,' " lay only two long blocks away from the Roths' apartment.[47] An even closer stage for possible intercultural and interethnic encounters was 10th Street, just one short block north of where young Roth lived. This street marked the boundary between two neighborhoods, one predominantly Jewish and the other predominantly Irish. As a sort of no man's land, it provided a meeting point for people of different backgrounds – and, appropriately, in the penultimate chapter of *Call It Sleep*, 10th Street swarms with a motley crowd of Irish, Anglos, Italians, Blacks, Armenians, and, of course, Jews who in their differently maimed or broken English converge around David's limp body.

In any American city, and in New York in particular, the specific character of a neighborhood often changes drastically from one block to the next. This was true at the time of Roth's childhood as it is today. Therefore, it may very well be that from 1910 to 1914, East 9th Street between Avenues C and D was totally Jewish in composition. However, without a precise breakdown of the ethnic composition of that street and of the streets nearby for those years, it seems safe to assume that the passing of time may have caused Roth to forget or to minimize his encounters with individuals of different religious or ethnic backgrounds who could have been part of his neighborhood and whose presence could have rested within his circle of vision during his childhood on the Lower East Side.

Yet Roth's contention that not until he left the East Side did he encounter a non-Jewish way of life should be considered accurate if understood to convey the *sense* he had of his neighborhood as a child and, perhaps more important, of his own relation to it. His insistence on the homogeneity of the Lower East Side he knew is to be seen less as a sociological statement than as a reflection of the type of life he led there, the types of friends he had, and the types of influences he was subjected to in that neighborhood. It should not be taken literally but, rather, appreciated in its fundamental truthfulness once understood to mean that his probably frequent encounters with street urchins from different backgrounds, with gentile classmates who may have kept a low profile in school, with his teachers and the sundry passersby on the crowded streets, did not catch his attention long enough or deeply enough to offer him a cultural model capable of posing an alternative to his own way of life. Roth's East Side neighborhood was homogeneous because in his brief but intense five years of permanence there he filtered out everything that did not conform to his world.

The "warping" of his old neighborhood to which Ira Stigman refers in *Mercy* seems to allude, then, to something specifically literary – his author's compounding of two time frames: one prior and the other following the move to Harlem. In Leo Dugovka, the Polish boy through whose agency David is dramatically exposed to certain aspects of Catholic culture, the writer concentrated all the alien pressures young Henry Roth was to experience after his family's move uptown. By compounding the traumatic impact of these pressures within the time frame of the Lower East Side period, Roth lacerated its wholeness and opened it to the fragmented nature of the ensuing period. In other words, he submitted the first of his alleged literary alter egos to cultural influences that he did, indeed, experience but only later, and elsewhere.

* * * * *

In "Nature's First Green," a four-page piece published in 1979 that has since proved to be the seed of *Mercy of a Rude Stream,*

Roth declared: "Probably there are lots of reasons I won't write my memoir."[48] The fact that he then spent the following thirteen years writing a "novel in memoir form" would seem to suggest a contradiction of his original intention. Yet, although decidedly autobiographical, *Mercy of a Rude Stream* is not an autobiography. It certainly is not intended to set straight the record of Roth's childhood, youth, and manhood. As he had done with *Call It Sleep*, the author once again utilized elements from his life to write a *novel*. This novel concerns a boy named Ira Stigman who is quite different from David Schearl and perhaps more closely modeled after young Roth, but who is *not* Henry Roth. We also have another New York. Ira's neighborhood is East 119th Street between Park and Madison, just a few steps from the Elevated, and the surrounding areas: Mount Morris Park, Central Park, and the Cloisters further uptown. This is the East Harlem neighborhood where the Roths lived from mid-1914 on. We are given the exact address, as we were in *Call It Sleep*. Again, as in that novel, we are given lively portraits and colorful vignettes of neighbors, shopkeepers, and Ira's street chums.

The two works differ in that New York is an overwhelming presence throughout *Call It Sleep*, whereas in *Mercy of a Rude Stream* the impact of the city on the story tends to gradually diminish. Apart from the question of the genre labels (fiction in one case and fictionalized memoir in the other), *Call It Sleep* and *Mercy* tell an analogous story: the story of a Jewish youth who grows up in New York in the early part of the century and struggles to come to grips with his difficult environment. Moreover, the function of the urbanscape is the same in both works: the city must "reveal its essential 'mark'" on the two young protagonists.[49]

A Star Shines over Mt. Morris Park focuses on the destruction of the harmonious childhood experienced by Ira on the Lower East Side. The move to predominantly Catholic, hostile Harlem turns young Ira from a happily integrated individual into one who is alienated from both his new environment and his own background. Ira undergoes a traumatic shrinking of his inner as well as his outer world: thrown back upon himself for lack of any safe, constructive relationships with his peers, he sadly discovers that he has lost the innermost resources once sustained by his old surroundings. Nearly every page of the initial volume of *Mercy of a Rude Stream* points to the basic thematic concerns of rupture, loss of cultural identity, and splintered selfhood – the very themes that dominate in the final section of *Call It Sleep* when David's safe world is shattered by the corrosive influence of alien cultural pressures. In *A Star Shines* the situation is reversed because it is the young protagonist who invades, albeit unwillingly, the alien territory and must perforce face the young Irish thugs on their own turf. When they gleefully pounce on the new Jewish kid on the block, Ira tries to ingratiate himself with them by joining in their ridiculing of Jews, an act of cowardice and betrayal that launches him on a guilt-ridden, irreversible process of estrangement from his heritage.

Thematic as well as factual correspondences between *Call It Sleep* and *A Star Shines* abound, so much so that at times the two stories seem to merge and become one. An example of this overlapping is the poignant episode in the latter work when Ira and his mother go back to their old neighborhood for an afternoon visit. To Ira's hungering eyes, everything is once again familiar. In his impatience, he cannot reach the old street corner fast enough. Izzy, one of David's own playmates, charges in, screaming in delight at the unexpected reunion.

The effect of this scene is staggering: For an instant we are thrown back into *Call It Sleep*. The overlap of the time frames invites us to cast a backward glance to *Call It Sleep* in a nostalgic pilgrimage homologous to Ira's sentimental journey of revisitation to his lost childhood world of harmony. We immediately realize, however, that in this multilayered exercise in intertextuality the use of *Call It Sleep* is strictly functional to the development of the new story, leaving little room for our sudden impulse to conjure the enchantment of that novel. As for Ira, who just a couple of months before was one of the gang, he realizes with chilling grief that his departure from the East Side has made him "a guest now among his own kind."[50] Even as a guest, he is there under false colors. Having betrayed his Jewishness, he has betrayed himself. He no longer is who he was. In his own eyes, he is "excluded from belonging" (27), even to the physical world which he had long considered his.

The process whereby referential reality is incorporated into the text has been defined by Marcello Pagnini as "introjection": The referent, whatever its nature, is decontextualized from the world of reference and introjected (i.e., recontextualized) into its pertinent level of textual reality.[51] Here its function undergoes subtle modifications to the point that, quite often, its recognizability can prove to be a deceptive clue that misleads rather than sustains the reader in his or her attempt to chart the textual territory. This occurs when we merely *recognize* the introjected referents and automatically relate them to cultural contexts external to the text. In so doing, we bring into our reading experience certain personal as well as collective convictions that come to bear heavily on our understanding of the work, for they induce us to project our cultural presuppositions into the text.[52]

A reading based primarily on recognition, therefore, risks being inadequately receptive to the complexities of *Call It Sleep,* in which elements that are familiar within a specific cultural context may acquire unexpected connotations as the story unfolds and new, unfamiliar systems of cognition develop in the course of the narrative, forcing the reader to suspend his or her automatic responses. A case in point is the recognizable Ashcan School type of background. The familiar sights of the East River shoreline, the bustling lower Manhattan avenues, the everyday landmarks of stoops, fire escapes, water tanks, roof tops, and flapping clotheslines initially tempt the reader to place David's story within a correspondingly familiar framework loosely related to the Marxist world system. With its strong ideologic connotations, this framework appears sufficiently comprehensive to put into perspective a story rooted in the proletarian milieu while also profoundly Jewish. The Marxist frame of reference, however, gradually comes to clash against a recurrent, covert Christian dimension that subtly challenges its hold on the story long before David becomes fascinated with the Polish boy's intriguing Catholic icons, the rosary, the Sacred Heart, and the Christological fish.

The Christian dimension is introduced as early as the prologue, which Roth wrote after he finished Book IV. From the ferry that brings little David and his mother into the New York harbor, the Statue of Liberty is seen raising "a black cross against flawless light" (10). Later (Chapter XII, Book I), the telegraph poles endlessly climbing up and down the still undeveloped Brooklyn hills are transformed into crosses (118). At the end of Chapter VII, Book III, the man in the tugboat who saves David from falling into the river is presented in the position of the Savior, arms outstretched and "dark-blond head" lowered and turned aside (334). In the following chapter the city dump – a *locus classicus* of deterministic and, subsequently, proletarian literature – turns into a Christian icon as David, tin sword in hand, is forced by the three young Catholic ruffians to climb his malodorous backyard Golgotha.

The Marxist world system is not the only frame of reference to be divested of its professed hegemony over the organization of reality by this subterranean buildup of Christian icons and symbols culminating in their overt irruption in Book IV. The Jewish frame of reference is also undermined by the silent infiltration of alien values which these elements introduce. On the diegetic level this becomes apparent only in Book IV, when David comes in contact with certain objects of the Catholic cult. Their supposed talismanic power lures him into a mysterious new world, away from the safe universe whose familiar rituals had until then nurtured and protected him. Ultimately, they induce him to question, if only momentarily, the worth and validity of his traditions. On the exegetic level, the undermining of the Jewish frame of reference can be seen to begin with the image of the cross in the prologue, to continue throughout the course of the narrative until made explicit in David's encounter with the Polish boy. By Book IV, it is clear that the Jewish frame of reference is no longer adequate to provide unity and direction to a story in which the individual is first perfectly integrated in his Jewish environment, and then crosses the boundaries of his cultural milieu and associates himself, albeit tentatively, with a historically antagonistic ideology.

The inadequacy of any single frame of reference to originate and validate a comprehensive interpretation of *Call It Sleep* extends to the strictly literary level. Every model that may be perceived as constituting the structural foundation of the novel reveals itself, in time, to be only partially responsible for the organization of textual reality. The education novel, the proletarian novel, the novel of immigrant life, the novel of quest, all lay perfectly legitimate claim to centrality in *Call It Sleep*. None, however, can achieve predominance. Nor is there a fixed mode of discourse in the novel.[53] The realistic, the lyrical, the impressionistic, the comic, each in turn dictates the tone of the narrative, each relinquishing its hold as it is superseded by another.

The strategy of alternation is consistent in the treatment of the urbanscape, which is entrusted chiefly to the realistic and the impressionistic modes. The resulting shifts, corresponding to the shifts in the young protagonist's mood, create a kaleidoscope of images that present New York, from its widest vistas to its meanest detail, in the fluctuating light of these two perspectives. Whether rendered in close-ups or by means of long shots, the city is made the object of either precise, attentive descriptions in the naturalistic vein ("the shore sank beneath the mossy piles of the dock (these driven through blackened rocks, past oil-barrels, stove-in, moss-green and rusty, past scummy wreckage)," 330) or of delicate, metaphor-laden impressionistic sketches (*"and beyond, beyond the elevateds, . . . as in the pit of the west, the last . . . smudge of rose, staining the stem of . . . the trembling, jagged . . . chalice of the night-taut stone with . . . the lees of day,"* 568–569).

Roth does not offer, as Gelfant states is typical of the "city novelist," "a coherent, organized, and total vision of the city" consistent with a specific framework (Gelfant 6). Instead, he offers several visions of New York, each issuing from a different cultural framework and, therefore, each conveying a differing, exclusive sense of the city. This multiplication of visions leads to an effect of superimposition. Urban icons become compounded symbols incorporating disparate ideologies: The Statue of Liberty, for example, easily the most representative feature of the New York urbanscape and a universally recognized allegory of the American ethos, is presented, in succession, as an icon of the Industrial Age,[54] a Christian image, an emblem of American nationalism, and as the vehicle of a phallic pun.[55] The noisy streets, with their milling crowds seeking work or pleasure, security or oblivion, evoke with equal force and pertinence the world of Abraham Cahan or that of John Dos Passos. But the urbanscape can also be seen through modernist lenses that break up the whole and rearrange it into an aggregate of fragments – a recurrent procedure all the more effective when the scene is as vast as David's first overall view of the city from his sunny rooftop.[56]

The superimposition of these visions, some mutually exclusive, all potentially conflicting, prevents each one from achieving predominance. This situation of stalemate makes it problematic to univocally define the function of the environment on the basis of any of the phases through which the constantly shifting urbanscape evolves. "Everything shifted. Everything changed" (130), bemoans a panicky David stranded in an unfamiliar neighborhood where "the streets through his tear-blurred eyes began stealthily to wheel" (123). Deprived of his habitual coordinates, the boy is lost in a maze of directional alternatives: "About him vision tumbled into chaos."[57] As readers, we find ourselves in an homologous position for we, too, have entered a maze – the maze of semantic possibilities proffered by the text. But this labyrinth leads to understanding, not chaos. As we progress through it, we realize that if none of the conflicting models operating in the novel can overcome the others, if none can assert itself as the dominant framework that gives order to the text and dictates its sense, it is because they have all been drained of their totalizing energy. Having been introjected into the text as part of the cultural environment, as the Statue of Liberty, the *cheder*, or the wharf have been introjected as elements of the physical environment, and as the Jews, the Poles, or the Irish have been introjected as components of the social environment, these models have become actants.[58] As actants, they must perforce lose part of their extratextual nature, notably their tendency to seek hegemony. Consequently, pitched as they are one against the other within the controlled confines of the text, the various models bring about an ideologic deadlock, an apparently unresolvable intellectual impasse.

An impasse of like nature had devastating consequences for the author of *Call It Sleep*. In an interview with film producer Margie Goldsmith in 1983, Roth discussed the beginnings of the formidable writer's block that shortly after the publication of his novel stalled him in writing his second novel and eventually locked him into long years of silence. He spoke of "that horrendous indecision" which immobilized him, of "everything turning to jelly, everything turning fluid," of "so many alternatives, choices according to the way you looked at things" (*Shifting Landscape* 257). As he put it, "you could get into the most confused state of mind, where you absolutely evaporate everything you believed in, all your values and allegiances" (*Shifting Landscape* 44).

Although in the course of the years Roth has offered other explanations for his writer's block, ranging from a generational malaise to the deleterious influence of the Communist party's aesthetics of social realism, in the Goldsmith interview he was more outspoken than ever before in his public statements concerning what he considers a direct relationship of cause and effect between his ideologic impasse and his creative paralysis.[59] Clearly, this relationship does not extend to the novel itself, where the ideologic impasse does not constitute an insurmountable obstacle to the interpretation of the text. Whereas in the world of reference the multiplicity of perspectives became for Henry Roth a quagmire of equivalent possibilities and a nightmare of undifferentiated alternatives, in the world of literary reality the introjection of these seemingly incompatible perspectives into the text alters their exclusive nature and binds them into a singularly productive solidarity of intents that amplifies the significance of the novel. Textual reality can only be enriched by the complexity resulting from the interlarding of layers and layers of different, even contradictory, meanings. It thrives on the conflicts arising from alternatives, be they moral, cultural, or ideologic.

Roth's system of juxtaposing antagonistic world views and melding them into a composite whole is best illustrated in his treatment of the city and its icons. No slice of New York touched on in the novel, no single component of that myriad background maintains throughout the text the connotations with which it was charged when initially introduced. As if placed under the converging beams of various spotlights switched on now singly, now in pairs and now all together, each stoop, each cellar or sidewalk, each jagged profile of tenement or spire or bridge spanning the East River is bathed in a distinctive light that for a while sets the tone, and then suddenly is flooded with lights of different color which evoke new associations and produce further layers of meaning.

Meaning, in *Call It Sleep*, issues from accruement rather than selection. As exemplified in miniature by the Statue of Liberty construct, New York City steadily expands into a choral compound of all its textual manifestations, the epitome of "that Golden Land" where "no questions" (3) should ever be asked of those who come to her shores, and where the whole is always larger than the sum of its parts.

NOTES

1 I am referring here to the whole work which, upon completion in 1992, the author gave me in its entirety. Until late that year, Roth had intended for *Mercy of a Rude Stream* to be published only after his death. Previously, he had allowed the first one hundred pages to be translated and published in Italy (*Alla mercé di una brutale corrente*. Ed. and trans. Mario Materassi. Milano: Garzanti, 1990). He had also consented to the publication of two excerpts in English: "Trolley Car Runs," *RSA Journal* 1 (1990): 107–120, and "The Vanished Bus Line," *Blue Mesa Review* 5 (Spring 1993): 1–16. In large part, *Mercy of a Rude Stream* takes place in New York. Here I will consider the published portion of *Mercy*, limiting to a minimum all references to the rest of the work.

2 "The date of my importation into the US is a little vague," from a letter to this writer dated Jan. 26, 1964.

3 "I think I always knew that this was not what I ought to be doing, that this was not my life," Roth told me when I visited him on his farm in the winter of 1964.

4 Mario Materassi, introduction, *Shifting Landscape: A Composite, 1925–1987*, by Henry Roth (Philadelphia: Jewish Publication Society, 1987).

5   "Impressions of a Plumber," *Shifting Landscape* 5.

6   The exceptions to an urban setting are "Equipment for Pennies," "The Prisoners," "At Times in Flight: A Parable," "The Dun Dakotas," "Final Dwarf," and "Assassins and Soldiers." *The Maine Sampler*, as yet unpublished, is also set in a rural environment.

7   Roth recalls doing "one other thing" for a course in descriptive writing. This paper has not survived (*Shifting Landscape* 4).

8   Henry Roth, *Call It Sleep* (Paterson: Pageant, 1960) 15. Unless otherwise indicated, all quotations for *Call It Sleep* refer to this edition. "From this opening statement, it is apparent that Roth will use the child as representative of immigrant status in the New World"; cf. Hana Wirth-Nesher, "The Modern Jewish Novel and the City: Franz Kafka, Henry Roth, and Amos Oz," *Modern Fiction Studies* 24 (Spring 1978): 91–109.

9   S.A.L., "In the Ghetto of New York. Three Years of Jewish Boy Life," *Boston Evening Transcript* 9 Feb. 1935: E3.

10 Horace Gregory, "East Side World," *Nation* 27 Feb. 1935: 255. A quarter of a century later, analogous notes were sounded: "You see and smell the dingy streets and tenements," wrote Marie Syrkin in "Revival of a Classic," *Midstream* 7 (Winter 1961): 89–93. "We are spared nothing of the crudeness of cosmopolitan slum life and living," wrote Walter Allen: "the squalor and filth, the hopelessness and helplessness of slum-life are remorselessly presented and the cacophony never ceases – this must be the noisiest novel ever written"; cf. afterword, *Call It Sleep*, by Henry Roth (New York: Avon Books, 1964), 442–447.

11 Lewis Gannett, review of *Call It Sleep*, *New York Herald-Tribune*, 15 Feb. 1935: 9. "The book for the most part is documented with acute and sensitive details of tenement life," wrote Joseph Wolf; cf. "Portrait of the Artist as a Child," *Partisan Review*, April–May 1935: 95–96.

12 Fred T. Marsh, "A Great Novel about Manhattan Boyhood," *New York Herald-Tribune Books*, 17 Feb. 1935: 6. In the same vein and from an analogous perspective, Meyer Levin wrote that "from a sociological point of view [this novel] provides a recreation of the life from which the whole present generation of children-of-immigrants has come, typical not only for Jews, but for Irish, Germans, Poles, and for slum-city dwellers of every origin"; cf. "A Personal Appreciation," *Call It Sleep*, by Henry Roth (Paterson: Pageant, 1960), xlvi–li.

13 S.A.L., "In the Ghetto of New York."

14 Review of *Call It Sleep*, *New Masses* 12 Feb. 1935: 27. Another reviewer wrote that the novel's "sociological vision is securely, almost sternly, rooted in a psychological understanding complete enough to put out its own conclusions and indictments casually and powerfully as a tree declares its leaves. . . . But, while his intensity of personal feelings lights upon some very dark spots in the political and human moments, Roth does not persevere with his vision. He pleads diffuse poetry to the social light, puts his hands over his eyes, and pinkly through the flesh sees the angry sunset"; cf. Paul Wren, "Boy in the Ghetto," *New Republic* 27 Feb. 1935: 82.

15 This is not to say that *Call It Sleep* ceased to be read as an example of the proletarian novel. See Kenneth Ledbetter, "Henry Roth's *Call It Sleep:* The Revival of a Proletarian Novel," *Twentieth Century Literature* 12 (Oct. 1966): 123–130. See also Walter Rideout, *The Radical Novel in the United States: 1990–1954* (Cambridge: Harvard University Press, 1956); for Rideout, *Call It Sleep* was "the most distinguished single proletarian novel" (185). Roth flatly rejects this label: "[*Call It Sleep*] is not a proletarian novel"; cf. John S. Friedman, "On Being Blocked and Other Literary Matters: An Interview," *Commentary* Aug. 1977: 27–38.

16 Leslie A. Fiedler, "Henry Roth's Neglected Masterpiece," *Commentary* Aug. 1960: 102–107.

17 Syrkin 90, 92.

18 Wren 82.

19 Tom Samet, "Henry Roth's Bull Story: Guilt and Betrayal in *Call It Sleep*," *Studies in the Novel* 7 (1975): 569–583.

20 Naomi Diamant, "Linguistic Universes in Henry Roth's *Call It Sleep*," *Comparative Literature* 3 (1986): 336–355.

21 Ethan Place, "Henry Roth's Freudian Messiah," *Modernist Studies* 2.3 (1977): 37–43.

22 Bernard Sherman, *The Invention of the Jew: Jewish-American Education Novels (1916–1964)* (New York: Yoseloff, 1969), 82–92. According to the critic, "It is the series of phallic images at the end of the novel which makes the Freudian theme particularly apparent" (89). Allen Guttman, who termed *Call It Sleep* "the most Freudian of the great American novels," noted a widespread use of Freudian symbolism and an "allusion to club-footed King Oedipus" in David's scorched foot; cf. Allen Guttman, *The Jewish Writer in America: Assimilation and the Crisis of Identity* (New York: Oxford University Press, 1971), 48–57. Asked by an interviewer if he was "writing, in

effect, with Freud open on the table," Roth answered: "Of course I knew about Freud, but I had only a smattering of it. I knew only what almost everyone knew of Freud, and that wasn't a great deal. . . . I guess I must have occasionally thought about the relationships in Freudian terms, but I wouldn't say I was following Freud. Of course that's what an artist does. If he's good, and if he's working right, he doesn't need to be told"; cf. William Freedman, "A Conversation with Henry Roth," *Literary Review* 18.2 (1975): 149–157.

23 Tom Samet's interpretation is grounded on a persuasive analysis of the Schearls' oedipal triangle. Among the first, if not the very first, to mention the oedipal triangle in reference to the Schearl family were Leslie Fiedler (Fiedler 105) and Maxwell Geismar, "A Critical Introduction," *Call It Sleep*, by Henry Roth (Paterson: Pageant, 1960), xxxvi–xlv.

24 Cf. Bonnie Lyons, *Henry Roth: The Man and His Work* (New York: Cooper Square, 1976).

25 Lyons iii. Cf. William Freedman, "Henry Roth and the Redemptive Imagination," *The Thirties: Fiction, Poetry, Drama,* ed. Warren French (Deland: Everett/Edwards, 1967), 107–114. Also, William Freedman, "Mystical Initiation and Experience in *Call It Sleep*," *Henry Roth's Call It Sleep: 1934–1979,* ed. Bonnie Lyons, special issue of *Studies in American Jewish Literature* 5.1 (1979): 27–37.

26 Fiedler 107. Cf. also Kenneth M. Nelson, "A Religious Metaphor," *Reconstructionist* 26 Nov. 1965: 7–16 ("David Schearl who seeks the cleansing light promised by Isaiah and fails to find it, returns to his bed exhausted and burned to discover that it is only in the dreamy moments before sleep . . . that one finds the redemptive and uncorrupted light").

27 Guttman 54–55. For Mary Edrich Redding, David's directing "the dipper handle into the crack beneath the rail [is] a symbolic sexual gesture initiating rebirth. At this precise point, the concepts of revolution and redemption proclaimed by the street-people merge in the apocalyptic atmosphere of David's existential encounter with death," "Call It Myth: Henry Roth and *The Golden Bough*," *Centennial Review* 18 (Spring 1974): 180–195.

28 Sam B. Girgus, "A Portrait of the Artist as a Young Luther: Henry Roth," *The New Covenant: Jewish Writers and the American Idea* (Chapel Hill: University of North Carolina Press, 1984), 95–107.

29 Gordon Poole, "David in America: dalla etnicità ebraica all'americanismo cristiano," *Rothiana: Henry Roth nella critica italiana,* ed. Mario Materassi (Firenze: Giuntina, 1985), 105–117.

30 Ita Sheres, "Exile and Redemption in Henry Roth's *Call It Sleep*," *Markham Review* 6 (Summer 1977): 72–77.

31 Gary Epstein, "Auto-Obituary: The Death of the Artist in Henry Roth's *Call It Sleep*," *Henry Roth's Call It Sleep: 1934–1979*, ed. Bonnie Lyons, special issue of *Studies in American Jewish Literature* 5.1 (1979): 37–45.

32 Epstein 38, 39. In a somewhat strained reading of David's predicament, Bruce Robbins sees him "engaged in a process of vision and revision by which he tries to break out of the fragmented subjectivity to which his powerlessness condemns him. Unlike Prufrock, he succeeds. By the end of the novel he has touched power, if not controlled it." After claiming that David "permanently shifted the balance of power in his family," Robbins concludes: "Among the results of his research that can be generalized is the simple notion that power is dangerous but graspable, and not terminal." Bruce Robbins, "Modernism in History, Modernism in Power," *Modernism Reconsidered*, ed. Robert Kiely (Cambridge: Harvard University Press, 1983), 229–245.

33 Sherman 84, 90. Cf. Dorothy Seidman Bilik: "Leo represents Americanization and assimilation. But David is not really ready for apostasy," *Immigrant Survivors: Post-Holocaust Consciousness in Recent Jewish American Fiction* (Middletown: Wesleyan University Press, 1981), 20–35.

34 Helge Normann Nilsen, "A Study of the Protagonist in *Call It Sleep*," *Dutch Quarterly Review of Anglo-American Letters* 13.1 (1983): 28–41.

35 Girgus 96. And again: "Reborn on the street, [David] serves as a central consciousness for a chorus of American voices and identities" (107). For Melvin H. Bernstein, the novel's "sense of peopleness makes it a fiction without ideology but with an empirical theology," "Jewishness, Judaism and the American-Jewish Novelist," *Chicago Jewish Forum* 23 (Summer 1965): 275–282.

36 Diane Levenberg, "Three Jewish Writers and the Spirit of the Thirties: Michael Gold, Anzia Yezierska, and Henry Roth," *Book Forum* 6.2 (1982): 232–244.

37 For Diamant, "The long road marked by telegraph poles is the way to greater experience," and David's "experience and exploration of his environment constitute an investigation into the enormous power of metaphor" (337), which the critic sees as "a defensive tool against actuality" (345).

38 Wirth-Nesher goes on to say: "As in all works of fiction, [the

characters] are tied to real places which are, by the cartography of the imagination, transformed into illusory cities on maps of our own making" (109).

39   In the fall of 1987, when driven to his old East Side neighborhood for the production of a video, Roth directed the crew to this very corner. Looking out of the car window at the leveled debris behind the sagging metal fence, Roth smiled and with his habitual wry humor said, "Oops, we're late." The red brick building across the street where his old chum Izzy used to live was still extant, as was the building in mid-block where Reb Pankower held his *cheder*.

40   Morris Dickstein, "Call It an Awakening," *New York Times Book Review* 29 Nov. 1987: 1 +.

41   ". . . as long as I lived on Ninth Street, in the Lower East Side, I thought I was in a kind of ministate of our own. It never occurred to me that the world could be any different" (*Shifting Landscape* 66).

42   Quoted by permission; emphasis added. Roth had explicitly indicated this much as early as 1969: "I took the violent environment of Harlem . . . and projected it back onto the East Side. It became a montage of milieus, in which I was taking elements of one neighborhood and grafting them onto another"; cf. David Bronsen, "A Conversation with Henry Roth," *Partisan Review* 36.2 (1969): 265–280. In reiterating this clarification in 1977, Roth commented: "Anybody who knew [the East Side] would know that" (Friedman 32). Cf. also: "What I did was simply superimpose a later slum attitude on a Jewish slum, because probably if I had written it *honestly* it would have been one of those period pieces on the Jewish immigrant . . . with all the amusing asides and Jewish stories and Jewish characters with their quirks and so on and so forth," from an unpublished taped conversation, April 24, 1985.

43   Cf. Deborah Dwork, "Health Conditions of Immigrant Jews on the Lower East Side of New York: 1880–1914," *Medical History* 25 (Jan. 1981), 5. For much of the information in this and the following paragraphs, I am indebted to Mario Maffi, *Nel mosaico della città: differenze etniche e nuove culture in un quartiere di New York* (Milano: Feltrinelli, 1992).

44   Cf. Moses Rischin, *The Promised City: New York's Jews, 1870–1914* (Cambridge: Harvard University Press, 1962, 1977), 76–81.

45   Cf. Helen Smindak, "The Lower East Side Ukrainians," *The Quality of Life in Loisaida* 10 (July–August 1987): 15, 29.

46   Cf. Irving Howe, "Jewish Children, American Schools," *World of*

Our Fathers (New York: Harcourt, 1976), 274–277. Cf. Fiedler: "Though . . . David . . . goes to public school, that Gentile area of experience is left shadowy, unrealized" (104).

47 Marcus Eli Ravage, *An American in the Making: The Life Story of an Immigrant* (1917; New York: Dover, 1971), 88. Cf. also Howe 256–260.

48 *Shifting Landscape* 252. "Nature's First Green," a brief memoir of Roth's young days in Harlem, was originally published by William Targ as the first volume in his series of rare, hand-printed books. By urging him to develop this kind of memoir, Mr. Targ is to be credited with having given the writer a new impetus.

49 Blanche Gelfant, *The American City Novel* (Norman: University of Oklahoma Press, 1954), 3. Although in her seminal study Gelfant did not discuss *Call It Sleep*, which at that time was out of print and had been nearly forgotten, many of her insights into the use of the city by American writers are relevant to Roth's novel.

50 Henry Roth, *A Star Shines over Mt. Morris Park* (New York: St. Martin's, 1993), 27.

51 Marcello Pagnini, *The Pragmatics of Literature*, trans. Nancy Jones-Henry (Bloomington: Indiana University Press, 1987). Cf., in particular, Chapter 2, "Reception."

52 "There is, on the one hand, the relation between the text and the extratextual systems that form its context and to which it relates, and on the other the cooperation, occurring in the time-flow of reading, between what the reader is given on the page and his habitual orientations"; cf. Wolfgang Iser, *Prospecting: From Reader Response to Literary Anthropology* (Baltimore: Johns Hopkins University Press, 1989), 68–69.

53 The superimposition of diverse literary and nonliterary models is constant throughout *Call It Sleep*. For a discussion of textual constructs that in various combinations make use of biblical passages, Freudian symbolism, and *topoi* of the fairy tale, the novel of immigrant life and the novel of education, cf. Mario Materassi, "Il grande romanzo di Henry Roth" and "Sul modulo dell'insieme semantico in *Call It Sleep*," *Rothiana* 43: 155–167.

54 "Notice that she appears as a piece of technology, who is 'charged,' 'ironed,' and 'blackened' " (Wirth-Nesher 98).

55 " '[Y]ou can go all the way up inside her for twenty-five cents. For only twenty-five cents, mind you!' " (565). We may see in the Statue construct an example of *mise en abîme*. Present at the beginning and at the end of the novel, the Statue of Liberty encloses

David's story as the "horns of the harbor" (10) embrace the statue itself in a sort of telescoping of the relationship between individual and environment in the novel. Girgus saw "the changing persona [Roth] assigns to the Statue of Liberty" as symbolic of the "growing complexity of [David's] relationship to America" (106).

56 In the passage here referred to (*Call It Sleep* 401), a subtle allusion to e. e. cummings's poem, "I will be / M o ving in the Street of her," underscores the modernistic quality of David's visual experience.

57 *Call It Sleep* 133. David recurringly experiences instability, both optical and emotional. Cf. also: " 'The school – The school is over there now!' " (140); "You had to know everything and suddenly what you knew became something else" (178); "something might change again, be the something else that had been lurking all the time beneath the thing that was" (257); "Even Ninth Street, his own familiar Ninth Street was warped" (383); "Again the world sagged, shifted" (442).

58 For the concept of "actant" cf. A. J. Greimas and J. Courtès, *Sémiotique, dictionnaire raisonné de la théorie du langage* (Paris: Hachette 1979).

59 In a letter to this writer postmarked Dec. 21, 1961, Roth wrote that he found a connection between the change in the point of view at the end of the novel and his creative paralysis. He changed the point of view, he explained, "as a transition to the choral part; and probably, in retrospect, subjectively I might add, an indication that the form of the novel was being broken, along with the creative psyche of the novelist."

4

The Classic of Disinheritance

RUTH WISSE

BY the time Henry Roth began to write his novel *Call It Sleep*, the American immigrant story was already commonplace. The ominous Prologue in which Father, after a separation of two years, comes to pick up his wife and the child he has never seen from Ellis Island, compresses into a few brief pages the by-then-standard opening scenes of arrival in the new land, relying on our familiarity with the setting to realize that something new is being done with the theme. We are told that "there was something quite untypical" about the scene we are witnessing, and being in the position of the old peddler woman and the overalled men in the stern of the steamer *Peter Stuyvesant* who have seen enough immigrant reunions to know how such people conventionally behave, we realize along with them that this is a very curious meeting. Its oddity awakens our sense of mystery: How is this family different from other families that arrived in America? Or, how will this story of immigrants differ from those we have already heard? The story is different because the protagonist arriving from Europe with his mother is entering a much more dangerous new land than America. The little boy in the old-fashioned hat is beginning a new life in the hitherto unconstituted family of his mother and father, and as the fate of his hat gives warning, he will have to muster more than the usual capacities of mind and spirit if he is to survive.

Henry Roth's book about an immigrant child presents childhood as the archetypal immigration. Every child hopes to arrive in a friendly new land, a golden land, that will treat him with dignity and warmth. Happy families may be all alike at least in this respect, that the fortunate pairing of the parents is retroactively confirmed by their desired, beloved children. Children of happy families are made to feel that their arrival benefits the existing settlement. But children born into less than perfect unions can never do anything to alter the condition that produced them. Because they loom for their parents as reminders of rejection or lovelessness, they must look out for harm from the very persons who should be protecting them. Growing up is for them a frightful contest of wits, as they must try to avoid antagonizing their parents without knowing why they do so. Having never *earned* dislike through their misdeeds, they cannot fairly anticipate how or why they provoke punishment, yet they have to figure out the connections between cause and effect if they hope to avoid abuse.

Child and immigrant both are required to learn a new language, to adapt to new surroundings. The burden is on each to adjust to a world already complete without him. Children may appear to be the most adaptable of immigrants because they are anyway engaged in the process of adjusting to their surroundings, and are already exercising the required skills of observation, emulation, intellection. In addition, the child has the greatest incentive to learn because he is the most desperate immigrant, lacking the advantages of maturity and mastery in other areas that can sometimes help to compensate for physical and social disadvantage. Immigration is humiliating for adults because they are forced back into the position of children, and required to relearn what cost them so much effort the first time.

In one important aspect, however, the two conditions are dissimilar, for unlike the immigrant, the child can never select the home in which he must learn to live. The agony of David Schearl begins with his arrival into the troubled union that his parents have forged; compared to that, his conquest of America is a piece of (chocolate) cake.

David's headgear is unceremoniously stripped from him in the Prologue, along with any lingering notion of divine or ancestral grace. Thus, when we are joined to his consciousness in the opening sentence of Book I, the child is already aware that "this world had been created without thought of him." The observation holds true at every level, beginning with the physical. Too small to reach the faucet above him, he lacks the power to slake his thirst and must call upon his mother – "tall as a tower" – to do it for him. She helps him with the mechanics of the operation, assuring him that he will one day be big enough to do it himself. "Have little fear," she says, and indeed, were it only a matter of growing taller, David might look forward to mastering his environment in the natural course of time. The natural world, however, is not his only challenge. His mother expects something from her son in return for the water she gives him: a kiss with lips as cool as the water that wet them. This kiss alone has the power to erase, albeit momentarily, her "reserved and almost mournful air," but being part of the ritual she has forged between them, she will not ask for it directly, expecting her son, like a storybook hero, to recall or discover it on his own. As David's mother prompts him to find the propitiating formula to slake her thirst, so he will be required to solve the much more tangled riddle of the family before either of them, mother or son, can feel secure.

David's mother is his only teacher and protector in this early stage of his life. She answers his questions to the best of her ability, and is finely attuned to his moods, though rarely aware of their cause. Unlike Yussie's mother who hollers at her children, Genya Schearl cares tenderly for David, and speaks to him so poetically that we don't have to look very far beyond her conversation for the source of his own powers of expression. Yet her enveloping warmth has a darker side. Being under suspicion by her husband, and unfamiliar with the world beyond her door, she often has to exploit David's presence to save herself. Far from alleviating his fears, she adds to them by designating him as the mainstay of her love, a role he cannot reject without risking the loss of her protection. "Waltuh, Waltuh, Wiulflo-wuh," chant the little girls of the street chorus, vulgar counter-point to the lyricism of the mother in Roth's characteristic rhyth-mic movement from inside to outside the home. The young ladies pronounce themselves ready to die for this flower lover, and long before he knows anything about his mother's past, so reciprocally attuned is David to her yearning for love "some-where else," that upon hearing this evocation of the land of distant wildflowers, he is himself overcome with her longing for it.

The oedipal paradigm seems to fit the relations between this mother and son so closely that many a reader thinks he has discovered in it the key to the boy's hypersensitivity. But Genya's heart was driven wild in another land, another language, another landscape, and by another lover, not the boy's father. After her passion was brutally crushed by her Christian savior and reviled by her father, she became a pariah for whom exile is the logical consequence. Her personality was affected by this crisis, turning her inward, against her generous nature, and forcing her departure from home, into a strange marriage and a stranger land. The only home that Genya can subsequently provide for her infant son is exile, so that he must become the more alien the closer she binds him to herself. She is not simply the "typical" Jewish Old Country mother protecting and urging on her son, nor the classic type of emotionally thwarted woman whose maternity is charged with erotic fervor; she is also – and perhaps above all – an outcast who, despite having done no wrong in her own eyes, has forever forfeited the honor and trust of her familial community. David's father is likewise marked by unprosecuted charges against him, reinforcing the couple's sense of banishment. David's mother and father were driven from Europe not by historical forces of political oppression and economic necessity, but by their families, and the family they form is a reaction to the families that cast them out. This is one of the many ways in which Roth's story creates its own undertow in the generic rhythm of the immigrant novel: Genya and Albert are only accidentally part of a "Jewish" "mass migration" that was looking for opportunity in a freer land. Their anomalous presence in the optimistic immigrant tide increases their claustrophobia, and our sense of their entrapment.

Albert's frustrated rage is the counterpart of Genya's fierce longing for love. The day we join him, David is going somewhere alone with his father for the first time. On this awful trip the father reveals to the boy his capacity for murder while forcing him to keep it secret. Albert needs no persuasion by God to bring his son to the altar; he is quite ready to sacrifice the boy whom he blames as the cause of his impotence. Once David discovers the magnitude of his father's anger (though not its source), he forever after imagines Albert with hammer poised to strike, and knows that he cannot expect a staying miracle should he ever become the target of his father's fury. First by his mother, then by his father, David is given responsibility beyond his capacities to discharge, and without being able to appeal to the other parent for help.

Nor does the book offer its young hero any alternative source of guidance. Neither in public school – notably inconsequential in this account of David's development – nor from any of the other adults in the book can David learn what he has to know. This is the greatest difference between Henry Roth and James Joyce to whose narrative technique he is otherwise indebted: Joyce's young artists shake themselves free from a world of excessive teachings and tenacious authorities, seek out their surrogate fathers from among a host of candidates, then, as repositories of layered culture and national history go off to forge in the smithy of their souls the uncreated conscience of their race. Roth's denuded young artist has to work his way in perplexed solitude through stages of discovery without God or judgment, as the Jewish saying has it – *leys din veleys dayan.*

David discovers quite on his own that life is brutish and short. Sex reveals itself to him in a cupboard where traps are set for mice and rats, death in a terrifying black box that is being carried from the home of a neighbor. Shocked by the horror of these twin mysteries, he turns to his mother for help, but she cannot help him with the first and will not calm him regarding the second. Luter's pursuit of Genya alerts the child to the dangerous power of sexual attraction, and inadvertently, to his mother's capacity for deception. In response to his fears of mortality his mother offers him the emotionally unsatisfying (but artistically haunting) story about her grandmother that makes of death a seasonal matter in which human beings show dignity by recognizing their affinity with leaves. Deprived of the possibility of faith, David learns disbelief instead, distrust of both his mother and his father ("Don't believe. Don't believe. Don't believe. Never!").[1] The street reinforces the lesson from the home with the teaching that "Id ain' no Sendy Klaws, didja know?"[2] David is progressively stripped of trust in his parents and of the sustaining myths that once offered a measure of confidence to humankind. He does not so much overcome his fear of the "cellar" as defy it, "as though he had slammed the door within him and locked it."[3] By the end of Book I, the hardened little boy has lost his innocence without any compensating advantage of experience. In the language becoming current at the time that Henry Roth wrote this book, David the child immigrant is on his way to becoming an existential hero.

* * * * *

The arrival of Aunt Bertha into the Schearl household at the beginning of Book II forces information and conflict out into the open. Like the sweat that pours from her body, Bertha brings everything to the surface. It may seem ironic that she, of all people, introduces David to art, since the comic scene in which she drags the little boy around the Metropolitan Museum seems designed to debunk the great masterworks rather than exalt them. Yet her candor is necessary for David's passage from the cellar to the world of representation, for without her he could never have begun to penetrate the secret of his parents' marriage. As the only local link with the past, she is also the first person in the house who insists on knowing and speaking the truth. She, whose coarseness provokes Albert into questioning her kinship with Genya, actually moves her delicate sister to laughter, and by changing the balance of power in the household relieves David of some of his responsibility for his mother's happiness. Inevitably, her vulgar speech threatens the family's contract of silence, and in the way that literary realism tears the veil from human exploits – from villainy as well as love – she exposes some of the father's menace and the mother's erotic history.

Few detective novels unravel their mystery as suspensefully as this second section of *Call It Sleep*. Yoked to the intelligence of the child who has to elude his mother's watchfulness while pursuing the evidence of her tale in a language he does not know, the reader experiences David's urgency as the matter of life or death that it is for him. In this most moving, artistically exalting sequence of the book, the child's curiosity is satisfied at great expense. To solve a mystery is to know the truth, that his father's suspicions about the son's paternity are only biologically, not psychologically unfounded. As we discover later, when David spins out a "lie" for his *cheder* teacher, he thereafter joins his father in doubting his mother's true relation to him. Genya, whom we encounter as David's mother and Albert's wife, had already spent her romantic passion on a church organist, a man whom, given the chance, she would have followed into the world, and into the church. The clue to his mother's emotional life is the picture she hangs on the wall of their apartment. Unlike the masterpieces in the museum he is dragged to by his aunt as an act of cultural duty, this reproduction is personally meaningful, evoking for the mother the secret longing she carries within herself. By discovering the man who stole his mother's heart, the boy helps to clear up the tragic misunderstanding between husband and wife, but in the process he shatters the myth of the family – and of the "Jewish" family. David's later attraction to Leo, and his naive hope that he may be saved by the power of the cross, echoes the motif of his mother's life, before she had to settle for second best.

The existential hero, uprooted in body and spirit, is no longer able to benefit from accumulated family or tribal tradition. Unable to absorb the customs and lore of his society in the natural course of growing up, this child immigrant is part of a family that has used immigration as a means of escaping from the past. Thus, although much has been made of the power and richness of the narrative device of the simulated Yiddish spoken within the Schearl family, Yiddish functions in this book as an isolating rather than a socializing tongue. It underscores not the richness of the inherited Jewish civilization that the Schearls have in common with the millions of Jewish immigrants who surround them, and the culture that ties them to their coreligionists past and present, but the exquisite separateness of their existence, the way they are divided even from one another. At no point, not even in the Yiddish theater that Albert attends in his disappointing friendship with Luter, does this book introduce the possibility of a sustaining Yiddish or Jewish institution, let alone a meaningful Jewish way of life. To invoke once again the contrast with James Joyce, who felt the artist had to go into exile to gain some distance from the culture that claimed him too intensely, Roth's young artist, born into exile, must painstakingly piece together knowledge of his origins, even against his parents' attempts to obscure those origins. In telling his story he will be able to use neither the language of his home, nor that of the street, but a forged English that draws attention to its disjunctions. All that David learns reinforces the knowledge that he stands alone.

* * * * *

The experience of *cheder* in Book III, "The Coal," explicitly crushes any sentimental notion that the residue of a religious and cultural tradition can help compensate for the fissure caused by this mass migration and for the atomization of the metropolitan city. Everything surrounding the boy's Jewish schooling mitigates against the project – the father's ambiguous decision to make him "at least something of a Jew"; the mother's association of *cheder* with trying to escape her teacher's onion breath; Reb Yidel Pankower's debased authority and his attempt to shore it up with switches. When the schoolchild, against all odds, begins to feel that his life is leveling off miraculously thanks to the "increasing nearness of God," and believes that he may be able to find in the recalcitrant Hebrew text the source of truest Power, his attempt to gain that knowledge, by clambering through the window *into* the schoolroom, is thwarted by the teacher who was to have imparted it. The process of immigration has driven a permanent wedge between the children of the streets and the carriers of their heritage. In other circumstances Yidel Pankower might have found the ideal student in David Schearl and the sensitive boy a meaningful guide in this lonely old man. The *cheder* teacher is the only character in the book apart from David whose voice is rendered at least once from the inside, and given the complementary hunger of teacher and student, he alone had the potential of becoming the boy's spiritual father. Instead, the teacher's grotesque isolation from his pupils provokes one crisis after another, and finally triggers the bloody climax in the relationship between actual father and son.

Here a literary comparison may prove instructive. One of the richest depictions of an East European Jewish childhood is *Shloyme reb chaims* (translated into English as *Of Bygone Days*), written at the turn of the century by the foremost pioneer of both Yiddish and Hebrew prose fiction, Sholem Jacob Abramovitch, the pseudonymous Mendele Mocher Sforim. By the time Abramovitch-Mendele wrote this memoir, he recognized that the organic community in which he was raised was turning into an anthropological curiosity, that the greater personal freedoms he had sought as part of a gradual process of change had been part of a much larger, irreversible cultural and social revolution. His memoir intimates that the Jewish child's emerging self-consciousness signifies the breakdown of the collective consciousness of traditional Jewry with its strengths as well as its weaknesses.

Not surprisingly, David Schearl's imagination is fired by the very same chapter of Isaiah that once enflamed the imagination of young Shloyme, son of Reb Chaim. It is not surprising because Chapter 6 of Isaiah is one of the most remarkable dramatic passages of the Bible. Its images of the Lord on a throne high and exalted, the fiery angels calling each to the other "Holy, holy, holy is the Lord of Hosts," and the lone prophet in the Temple crying, "Woe is me, for I am lost, for a man of unclean lips am I" form part of Jewish daily liturgy (with Jews rising to their toes in emulation of the exalting angels). Shloyme is the same age as David when he discovers the passage:

He began to draw mental pictures of God surrounded by ministering angels with wings, and to wonder about all kinds of mysteries that were pecking away at his brain, demanding an explanation. He didn't feel comfortable asking questions about these matters, as they didn't pertain to the subject of his lessons. Once he did try to put the problems before his teacher, his face burning as he spoke. But Lipe Rubens merely shook his head with a little smile as if to say: go on, now. Sometimes he asked bearded elders about the things that were bothering him, but he always got the same angry answer: "Hold your tongue! Your business is to obey the rules as they appear in the books, to study, and to pray; if you don't, God will punish you in the next world with whips of leather and whips of fire."[4]

Blessed with a devoted teacher, Lipe Rubens, whom his father had chosen for him with exquisite care, Shloyme is nevertheless confined to rote learning and moral instruction. In both these works about Jewish children, the inadequacy of traditional education suggests the larger dissatisfaction with a Jewish way of life that is thought by the author to be stifling individual development. But Abramovitch-Mendele, the adult author, knows and profits from the text of Isaiah at least as much as his teacher, and in drawing attention to the punitive pedagogy of his elders he reminds us of the biblical glory that is the true heritage of the Jews, theirs to claim and to hold. There is no such touchstone of glory for Roth, for whom the disintegration of tradition is the true lesson of America, and David Schearl's only heritage. From *cheder* David learns what does *not* stand behind him, namely the splendor of old from which he can no longer hope to draw inspiration, meaning, and power. In the new world, there are still men of unclean lips, but no faith to sear their souls.

Section III of *Call It Sleep* takes place in the months preceding the spring festival of Passover, and ends on the eve of the holiday. Schematically organized to heighten the irony of Jewish observance in a faithless world, this part of the narrative is almost programmatic in its juxtaposition of religious possibility and local corruption of it. On the eve of the Sabbath an old woman pays David to light the stove for her in a scene that seems designed to demonstrate hypocritical circumvention of Jewish law. In preparation for the seder, the family celebration that commemorates the exodus of the Jews from Egypt, the *cheder* boys are being taught one of the concluding songs of the Haggadah, a philosophically resonant tale of innocence and guilt that begins with the purchase of a goat and ends with God slaying the Angel of Death. The correspondence between the teacher's punitive pedagogy and the aggression in this song are more than coincidental, and no one reading this passage could imagine that the boys will enjoy their family's holiday any more than they do the experience of learning the song. Most notably, David's first real exposure to Jew-baiting takes place on the very eve of the festival of freedom.

> It was Monday morning, the morning of the first Passover night. One was lucky in being a Jew to-day. There was no school.

When David tries to perform the ritual burning of the *khometz* in the street on this fortunate day, he is humiliated by the Hungarian janitor. A little later, when he is chased down by a small gang of gentile boys near the river, he denies being Jewish to avoid punishment. These encounters with anti-Semitism are relatively mild compared to what Jews had grown accustomed to in Europe, particularly in the dangerous season of Passover-Easter, but David has no knowledge or pleasure that might have compensated him for being a Jew. The sufficient irony of David's initial perception that one was lucky in being a Jew on Passover because "there was no school" is compounded by both his experience at the hands of anti-Semites and his failed experiences as a Jew. All that David anticipates as he approaches his door on Passover eve is that his mother will give him clean underwear, so that his ordeal on the street will not precipitate a yet more unpleasant ordeal at home.

Roth demythifies the Passover holiday, the Jewish family, the immigrant experience – the enveloping categories once thought to shape and therefore to claim the individual. His dismantled Jewish tradition forms part of the novel's overall psychological-philosophical worldview that liberates the solitary self from the nightmare of history, beginning with his own family history. Many of Roth's fellow Jewish immigrants underwent a similar process of emptying themselves of their past, without David Schearl's anguish or his creator's ability to describe the process. Roth was telling the story of a generation that assumed it was becoming more culturally advanced by freeing the individual from the constraints of his origins. But part of the genius of this book is that it reveals so much more than it sets out to tell. The more David "frees himself" from the civilization that formed him, the more he becomes depleted and exhausted. The same process that liberates him from the burdens of his inheritance also strips him and leaves him disinherited. The triumph of the modern self over its oppressive circumstance is achieved at the cost of a sustaining human community.

In contrast to generations of children who become adults by acquiring useful information, skills, and sustaining rituals from their parents, family, and community, David Schearl learns to function autonomously by stripping away layers of false hope and false mythology. The existential child does not pine for the greater harmony and enveloping security of an earlier time but accepts his finite situation and struggles to shoulder it. By the beginning of Book IV David "felt secure at home and in the street – that was all the activity he asked." His independence has yet to be put to the test, and when it is, in this final section of the novel, he earns his right to be considered an existential hero. Because the story is so closely confined to the boy's fears and doubts, we are in danger of forgetting how often and how bravely he manages to overcome them. There is something unassailably strong in the child's character: The book's comparison in stature to *Moby-Dick* rests as much on David's grit as it does on the author's narrative scope in telling his story.

As David makes his way outward from the cocoon of family into the streets and beyond, to stand exposed, finally, to the full range of voices that make up America, his autonomy grows with every loss and punishment he suffers. His involvement with Leo recalls both Genya's infatuation with a Christian lover and Albert's hungry reach for a male friend, and David's ability to absorb the lessons of disillusionment at such an early age suggests that he has already outstripped his parents in experience. Both Genya and Albert suffered dire punishment at the hands of their fathers, but neither triumphs over the ordeal as does David. When the boy gives his father, suspected of patricide, the weapon he knows his father can wield, he changes the balance of power between them forever. At the point of testing, David subverts the patriarchal role in the Sacrifice, offering himself to the father without waiting for the father to sacrifice him. In thus challenging Albert he strips the ogre of his menace to reveal the wretched man beneath, while liberating himself from guilt. Through this unflinching readiness to assume the assigned tasks, the boy untangles the riddle of family, deconstructing the past so that all may live in humbled present-day reality. David's ultimate test of power – with a milk dipper for Excalibur – earns him the cherished peace he has been seeking since he came to consciousness.

I am not certain this novel gains from Chapter XXI of Book IV in which we hear an American chorus as David accepts his final "dare." One could justify the device structurally and thematically, or as a small tour de force of Joycean homage, or in the number of creative ways that critics have done. But I have always felt here the author's strain to prove the largeness of his work, as though he were trying to do justice to the extraordinary achievement of his young protagonist. Perhaps, to the contrary, Henry Roth needed this change of pace because the intensity of the narrative would otherwise have been too heavy to bear. Whatever its creative genesis, the artistic result of the passage is to draw attention to its universalizing technique, and away from the universality of its hero. By this point in the narrative, David has long since been established as a "ward" of the city, its deracinated, isolated, uncommonly plucky new offspring.

The power of the novel and the power of the boy derive from a common source. Just as David knows that the world was created without thought of him, so the author was born into a Babel of cultures, none of them comfortably his own. Roth did not have the choice of Jewish writers before him of writing in a Jewish language. By the time he was brought to America Yiddish was reserved only for inside the home and Hebrew remained for him a dumb mystery. He was confined to English, a language spoken around him in so stunted a form as to make Eliza Doolittle's seem professorial. He further lacked the sustaining tools of art, such as a nurturing tradition for the individual talent, a social climate of shared cultural values, a familiar or inspiring landscape. These limitations he accepted as the beginning of his task, and tried to make deprivation work for him. Under the crazy quilt of languages he discovered what people try to conceal through language; tunneling through the received ideas of his home and native culture, he set the individual consciousness about as free as it can get.

But the effort proved so draining that the sleep of half a lifetime seemed hardly enough to restore child and author to purposeful energy. His achievement left hanging the question, to what purpose the Herculean effort? Child and adult author had taught themselves to live without most of the things others live for. When an earlier generation of East European authors asked, "For whom do I toil?" the largely rhetorical question implied that the context of creative labor was an implicit community that merited such exertion whether or not there was any response to the artist in kind. Roth's novel unwittingly reveals how little is left for the existential artist after he has freed himself from an implicit community. Child of a loveless family, Jew without Jewishness, American master without an ennobling myth of American culture, Roth and his hero have entered the emptied world that Jean Paul Sartre conceived in his philosophy, and it is not surprising that he expressed his existential selfhood the same way Sartre did, by abdicating his moral freedom in favor of the Communist ideal. At that point in his life, Roth might as well have called it sleep. His masterful novel illuminates like no other study of its time how the impulse of self-empowerment could result in the need for self-enslavement.

NOTES

1   Concluding words of Book I, Chapter XIV, p. 114.
2   Book I, Chapter XVI, p. 141.
3   Ibid.
4   Mendele Mocher Sforim, "Of Bygone Days," in Ruth R. Wisse ed., *A Shtetl and Other Yiddish Novellas* (Detroit: Wayne State University Press, 1986), p. 296.

5

Henry Roth in Nighttown, or,
Containing *Ulysses*

BRIAN McHALE

LITERARY history, in its collective wisdom, seems to have settled on a descriptive epithet for *Call It Sleep*. Roth's novel, we have grown accustomed to hearing, is "Joycean." Robert Alter has described it as "together with *The Sound and the Fury* ... the fullest American assimilation of Joyce" (1988: 34; see also Alter 1994: 3). The *Columbia History of the American Novel*, speaking with the voice of canonical authority, pronounces it "arguably the most Joycean of any novel written by an American" (Elliott 1991: 394–395). Roth's aesthetic kinship with Joyce was noticed as early as 1935 by the novel's first reviewers (see Ribalow 1960: xii–xiv). Roth himself has gone on record as acknowledging Joyce as his "master" in matters of novelistic technique, while simultaneously repudiating the creative cul-de-sac into which, he alleges, Joyce's aesthetic ideology led him (Roth 1987: 189, 266–267 and passim). Nevertheless, although many commentators have applied the "Joycean" epithet to *Call It Sleep* – usually honorifically, occasionally not – few have taken it seriously enough actually to explore the relationship (if any) between Roth's poetics and Joyce's.[1]

Robert Alter is one of the rare exceptions to this general pattern. In an exemplary review article of 1988, he juxtaposed passages from Joyce and parallel passages from *Call It Sleep* with a view to substantiating the alleged "Joycean" qualities of Roth's novel. Alter recognizes the presence of both the earlier Joyce of *A Portrait of the Artist as a Young Man* and the later Joyce of *Ulysses* in Roth's text, but, he contends, it is especially the technique of *A Portrait of the Artist* that pervades *Call It Sleep* (1988: 34). In this chapter I propose to follow Alter's lead, but in a different direction. I propose, like him, to establish the "Joycean" credentials of Roth's novel – which is to say, in effect, its *modernist* credentials – but with reference to *Ulysses* rather than *A Portrait*. If, in so doing, I end up rehearsing some of the most familiar principles of Joyce's modernist poetics, this is because I have thought it preferable, on the whole, to err on the side of obviousness.

In point of fact, the supposedly "obvious" proves to be singularly *un*obvious when it comes to Joyce's alleged "influence" on modernist fiction generally. One has only to raise the question of Joyce's intertextual presence in modernist writing to run up almost immediately against the paradoxical status, simultaneously normative *and* transgressive, of *Ulysses*, this founding text of modernism. For at the same time that *Ulysses* establishes, or at least consolidates, a particular modernist poetics of fiction, it also scandalously transgresses the limits of that poetics (see McHale 1992: 42–58). Consequently, modernist novelists like Roth, writing in the troubled wake of *Ulysses*, have been compelled not only to find ways of adapting Joycean poetics to their own uses, but also, paradoxically, of "taming" Joyce, ways of regulating the rule-giver. In this double sense "Joycean" texts, Roth's conspicuous among them, "contain" *Ulysses* – they both *absorb* the poetics of this foundational modernist text, and seek to *restrain* its transgressive (postmodernist?) wildness.

I

When I speak of *Ulysses* as "foundational" and "normative" for a certain modernist poetics of fiction, I am ascribing to it the function of a "paradigm" in something analogous to Kuhn's (1962) sense of that term; or the function of "initiator of a discursive practice" in something analogous to Foucault's sense of *that* term (1977: 133–136); or, finally, the function of a "model" in precisely the sense of Even-Zohar's polysystem theory (1990). In its function as a model, *Ulysses* makes available for contemplation and imitation the preferred elements (themes, topics, types, styles, "realemes" in Even-Zohar's sense, etc.) and rules for their combination which together identify a particular strain of modernist practice. If one calls this strain "Joycean" modernism, one is not speaking tautologically but *metonymically:* The name "Joyce" and the epithet "Joycean" are metonymic figures for the entire poetics of which *Ulysses* is the model. *Ulysses*, the text by James Joyce, eventually entered the canon of twentieth-century Western literature, and Joyce himself the inner circle of canonical authors, but as a *model, Ulysses* entered the active canonized repertoire of modernism, circulating among literary producers and consumers, enabling the former to produce new texts in the canonized "Joycean-modernist" mode, and the latter to recognize, interpret, and evaluate those texts.

If we are seeking to substantiate a claim, such as Alter's, that *Call It Sleep* represents "the fullest American assimilation of Joyce," or the *Columbia History's*, that it is "arguably the most Joycean of any novel written by an American," then we might proceed by documenting evidence of Joyce's direct influence on Roth. If we did so, however, we would only have succeeded in illuminating a relatively trivial aspect of the relation between Roth and Joyce, and would have left unexamined the more interesting relation between Roth's text and the Joycean model of modernism. To investigate that relation, we need first to establish some of the central features of the model realized in *Ulysses*, and then identify their presence in *Call It Sleep.*

There is no space here to give anything like an exhaustive account of the *Ulysses* model (but see Beebe 1974, Fokkema and Ibsch 1987). For present purposes, we will have to make do with a very partial model indeed, the complexity of modernist poetics reduced to a mere handful of its most salient features.

Let us consider only the following features of the model:

1 the presentation of consciousness (of one or more characters) as a screen on which the complexity of modern urban experience registers
2 variation in narrative technique and dominant motifs from section to section of the text
3 a network of motifs spanning the entire text, counterposing a centripetal (integrative) force to the centrifugal force of variation from section to section
4 a mythic subtext, or parallel (superior) ontological stratum

Presentation of consciousness

In *Call It Sleep*, the registering consciousness is that of the child protagonist, David Schearl. In a sense, his consciousness merges the two principal Joycean models of interior life in *Ulysses*, the model associated with Stephen Dedalus and the one associated with Mr. Bloom; his style of registering the urban experience is a composite of their respective mind styles.

"If David is a Jewish Ulysses," writes Murray Baumgarten, "he is also a Yiddish Stephen Daedalus [sic]" (1982: 34–35). Indeed, David's affinity with Stephen Dedalus, rather than with Bloom, has impressed most commentators. Moreover, it has almost invariably been *A Portrait of the Artist as a Young Man* (1916) that is cited in this context rather than *Ulysses*. What David shares with Joyce's Stephen, it has long been recognized, are his "epiphanic" experiences of ordinary reality, that is, those moments in which (in the words attributed to Stephen in the earlier draft of *A Portrait of the Artist* entitled *Stephen Hero*) one glimpses a "sudden spiritual manifestation . . . in the vulgarity of speech or of gesture or in a memorable phase of the mind itself" (Joyce 1956: 211). An "object achieves its epiphany," according to Stephen, when "its soul, its whatness, leaps to us from the vestment of its appearance" (218). Such epiphanic moments recur throughout *A Portrait of the Artist*, but they also occur for Stephen in *Ulysses*, notably at the close of each of the novel's first three chapters ("Telemachus," "Nestor," "Proteus").

David, too, experiences intimations of the spiritual in ordinary speech, gesture, objects, or combinations of objects: in an arresting phrase spoken by his mother, in the conjunction of carriages and confetti, in the burning of a celluloid doll, in a children's rhyme heard in the street (a failed epiphany, in this case), and so on.[2] Often these epiphanies have the same structure, and sometimes even involve some of the same elements, as Stephen's in *Ulysses*.

Thus, for example, a crucial epiphany for David is the moment when, lulled into reverie by the sunlight glinting off the East River, he is abruptly recalled to reality by a whistle from a crewman aboard a passing tugboat (III.vii.248). Much later that same whistle, recurring in an entranced memory or dream state, will reawaken David to life from his near death by electric shock (IV.xxi.431). Alter has associated David's East River epiphany with Stephen's, in a *A Portrait of the Artist*, of a girl wading in the Liffey (Alter 1988: 35). Even closer, it seems to me, are two seaside epiphanies of Stephen's in *Ulysses*, elements of which seem to have been recombined to form the epiphanic moment of *Call It Sleep*. In one of these epiphanies, Stephen believes himself to have been hailed by a voice from the sea, presumably that of a swimmer, only to discover that what has caught his attention is the cry of a seal (Joyce 1934: 24). In the other, he is jarred out of solipsistic reverie by the apparition of a sailing ship, "her sails brailed up on the crosstress, homing, upstream, silently moving" (Joyce 1934: 51). Roth seems to have retained key elements of these two Joycean epiphanies – water, ship, visionary reverie, and a sound that recalls the dreamer to reality – and to have resynthesized them in David's epiphanic moment by the East River.[3]

But if David is, like Stephen, the "Artist as a Young Man" (or "Young Boy," as Alter specifies, 1988: 33), and attuned to epiphanies of the spiritual in the ordinary, he is also, like Mr. Bloom, a marginalized citizen of a modern metropolis. An observer and outsider, an urban wanderer, David is moreover, also like Bloom, a specifically *Jewish* wanderer – the modern city-dwelling Jew, as Ulysses, "Jewlysses."[4] Like Bloom, David responds to his condition of civic marginality, and to the insupportable pain of his home life, by developing defensive patterns of evasion and self-effacement, patterns that structure not only his physical behavior but also his mental interaction with his environment. He also shares with Bloom an avid, promiscuous curiosity about the world around him, an appetite for the minute particulars of urban experience. In particular, David shares Bloom's willingness to speculate about objects, words, and conditions which he has never experienced or about whose meaning or use he is ignorant, for instance, wreaths on the doors of gentile houses (I.viii.58), oysters and other *treif* foodstuffs (III.iv.226), or the source and circulation of the city water supply (I.i.17).[5]

Hence the characteristic ebb and flow of engagement and withdrawal, approach and avoidance that David's interior monologues share with Bloom's. Here is a representative sample of Bloom's mind style:

> – Mrkganao! the cat cried.
> They call them stupid. They understand what we say better than we understand them. She understands all she wants to. Vindictive too. Wonder what I look like to her. Height of a tower? No, she can jump me . . . Cruel. Her nature. Curious mice never squeal. Seem to like it . . . Wonder is it true if you clip them they can't mouse after. Why? They shine in the dark, perhaps, the tips. Or kind of feelers in the dark, perhaps . . . Why are their tongues so rough? To lap better, all porous holes. Nothing she can eat? He glanced round him. No. (1934: 57–57; my ellipses)

What dictates the shuttling rhythm of Mr. Bloom's rapidly shifting attention here – from inside to outside, from perception to reflection to speculation – is in part his responsiveness to the world around him, but also in part the operation of his self-censor, abruptly lowering the shutter on thoughts too painful to pursue, or even fully to acknowledge. The pronoun "she," in this passage as throughout the opening pages of the "Calypso" chapter, from which it comes, refers ambiguously to Bloom's cat and his wife Molly, still upstairs in bed at this hour. Thus Bloom's characteristic speculations about his cat conceal (from himself, if not from the attentive reader) reflections on his wife's perspicacity ("They understand what we say better than we understand them"), her supposed capacity for cruelty, and her appetitiveness.

Now compare a sample of David's mind style:

> He looked up. They were both gone – the two cages on the first floor fire-escape. A parrot and a canary. Awk! awk! the first cried. Eee – tee – tee – tweet! the other. A smooth and a rusty pulley. He wondered if they understood each other. Maybe it was like Yiddish and English, or Yiddish and Polish, the way his mother and aunt sometimes spoke. Secrets. What? Was wondering. What? Too cold now. Birds go south, teacher said. But pigeons don't. Sparrows don't. So how? Funny, birds were. In the park on Avenue C. Eat brown. Shit green. On the benches is green. On the railings. So how? Don't you? Apples is red and white.

Chicken is white. Bread, watermelon, gum-drops, all different colors. But – Don't say. Is bad. But everybody says. Is bad though. (II.vii.174)

Here, I submit, we detect the same rhythm of approach and recoil, curiosity ("So how?") and self-censorship ("Don't say. Is bad."), openness and defensive shuttering that characterizes Mr. Bloom's interior discourse.

Variation in technique and motifs

When Joyce revealed the inner structure of *Ulysses* to Stuart Gilbert, with a view to assisting (but also controlling) his text's future interpreters, he identified a different narrative technique and a different set of dominant motifs for each chapter. For the first nine chapters, there is perhaps less actual variation in technique than Joyce led Gilbert to believe, but from about Chapter 10 on the uniform "initial style" of the first nine (see Lawrence 1981) is abandoned and we do indeed encounter a different technique in each chapter: multiple or dual perspectives ("Wandering Rocks" and "Nausicaa" respectively), imitations of musical forms ("Sirens"), parodies of popular ("Cyclops") and literary ("Oxen of the Sun") styles, dramatic form ("Circe"), catechism or question-and-answer ("Ithaca"), and so on.

As for dominant motifs, according to the chart Gilbert compiled under Joyce's tutelage, each chapter (with a few exceptions) possesses its own organ, its own art, its own colors, and its own symbols. Thus, for instance, woven into the fabric of the "Calypso" chapter one could expect to find such motifs as the kidney (organ), economics (art), the color orange, and the symbol of the nymph, whereas the "Nausicaa" chapter yields the eye and nose (organs), painting (art), the colors grey and blue, and the symbol of the virgin, and so on (Gilbert 1952: 41). Taking their cue from Gilbert (ultimately, that is, from Joyce himself), analysts of *Ulysses* have dutifully documented the presence of these motifs, as well as others that Joyce did not mention to Gilbert, but which also vary in much the same way from chapter to chapter.

Variation of technique is much less conspicuous in *Call It Sleep*, in fact all but subliminal, so that one would be justified in

81

wondering how conscious Roth could have been of producing this "Joycean" effect of formal variety. Nevertheless, it is possible to demonstrate a more or less systematic variation in dosage and function of different modes of speech and thought representation – the basic building blocks of Roth's technique – from book to book.

Thus, the free indirect mode predominates in Book I, where it is used almost exclusively to represent David's interior discourse.[6] Free indirect discourse is also conspicuous in Book II, but here it has a different function, namely the representation not of interior discourse but of *spoken* discourse, and not of David's speech but that of others – his mother and father, especially his Aunt Bertha and her suitor, Nathan Sternowitz. The shift from interior discourse to uttered speech (to the aural channel generally) is perhaps signaled in the opening paragraph of Book II, when David reflects on the differences between Brownsville and the Lower East Side, to which his family has just moved: "Here in 9th Street it wasn't the sun that swamped one as one left the doorway, it was sound – an avalanche of sound" (II.i.143). In Book III, free indirect discourse tends to be replaced in representations of David's inner life by direct interior monologue, that is, by a "classic" stream-of-consciousness technique such as one finds in the "Proteus" or "Penelope" chapter of *Ulysses*. Finally, though all these techniques can be found combined in Book IV, the formal center of gravity in this book shifts decisively to direct spoken discourse, especially in the climactic chapters XIX through XXII.

Although there is in Roth's text no system of motifs comparable to the one anatomized in Stuart Gilbert's famous (or notorious) chart, there are nevertheless different keynote symbols for each book of *Call It Sleep*. Some of these are identified by the titles of the respective books: the cellar (Book I), the picture (II), the coal (III), the rail (IV). Other motifs emerge from the text itself as it unfolds. Thus, for example, for Book I, apart from the keynote symbol of the cellar, one distinguishes a set of ancillary motifs including the hammer (I.ii), the rattrap (I.vii), the carriage (I.ix), and so on; or at least, one does so if one is well versed in the protocols of modernist reading.

More distinctively, one can also identify for each chapter of *Call It Sleep* a different key *language* and a correspondingly different *confrontation of languages*. As Hana Wirth-Nesher (1991) has established, Roth's is a multilingual novel, but the different languages that compose its heteroglossic mix are not evenly distributed among its four books, nor are all the various confrontations among them equally salient in every book. Thus, the novel's prologue serves to establish Yiddish as the linguistic norm of the text as a whole (from the point of view of its characters), but a Yiddish represented here by "translation" into a rather formal register of standard English. The key language motif of Book I is the confrontation between this Yiddish norm and the American English of the streets, including the substandard, almost impenetrably dialectal English spoken by the Jewish immigrants themselves. This tense English/Yiddish confrontation manifests itself in a number of episodes, including the early one in which David's father coaches him in the English to be used with the father's employer (I.ii) and, crucially, the episode in which David, having wandered away from home, cannot make himself understood to his English-speaking fellow citizens (I.xii,xiii). The functional distribution of the two languages – Yiddish for "indoors," for the family circle, English for "outdoors," for the street, for interacting with outsiders and strangers – is perhaps captured symbolically in a striking image when, straddling the threshold of his tenement house, David reflects on the impossibility of holding both the inside (i.e., the Yiddish-speaking world of the family) and the outside (i.e., the English-speaking world of the street) in mind simultaneously:

He wondered why it was that one could be half in the street and half out and yet never be able to picture the street and the inside of the house together. He could picture the street and the yellow wall of his house, but not the inside. (I.xvi.132)

By contrast, the key language of Book II is Polish, and the crucial episode is the one (II.ix) in which David's mother and his Aunt Bertha slip back and forth between Yiddish and Polish without being aware of it, so deep are they in conversation, while David (who knows no Polish) eavesdrops. Book III introduces another language into the heteroglossic mix, namely Hebrew, the sacred language David has begun learning to read at the *cheder*, and around the confrontation between the *mameloshn* (Yiddish) and the *fotershprakh* (Hebrew) this book revolves (see Wirth-Nesher 1991: 453–455). In Book IV the system of dominant languages varying from book to book breaks down, or perhaps the dominant becomes *language in general*, for here all the key languages of *Call It Sleep*, as well as other registers and varieties that have not figured importantly in the text before, mingle in the linguistic uproar of the climactic final chapters.

Network of motifs

Variation in technique and motifs from chapter to chapter, the tendency for each chapter to acquire its own distinctive formal and thematic "fingerprint," would seem to present obstacles to the formal unification of the text as a whole, particularly in the absence of a strong narrative line (which *Ulysses*, a "day-in-the-life" novel, conspicuously lacks). Nevertheless, *Ulysses* is recognized as the model of a formally integrated text. If this is so, then the effect of integration must be attributable in large part to the operation of another class of motif which, recurring in changing contexts throughout the text, functions not to distinguish one chapter from another but rather to bind the text's disparate parts together into a whole.

Some of these recurrent integrative motifs are purely verbal: key words (e.g., "metempsychosis," "parallax"), recurrent phrases or intertextual quotations (e.g., from *Hamlet, Don Giovanni,* Yeats' "Who Goes with Fergus?"), and the like. Others are objects or persons in the world of *Ulysses* (e.g., Bloom's potato and cake of soap, Stephen's ashplant, the sandwichmen advertising Hely's stationer's shop, Parnell's brother).[7] Integrative motifs of *Ulysses* tend not to function singly but in combination, forming motif-complexes, e.g., the "Oriental" motif-complex associated with Bloom, or the Shakespearean motifs (especially from *Hamlet*) associated with Stephen.

This same strategy of countering the centrifugal, disintegrative tendencies of the text by deploying a set of recurrent motifs can be observed in *Call It Sleep*. Here the integrative motifs include, for instance, motifs of light and darkness: the darkness behind the cellar door versus the light of the street beyond (e.g., I.i.20; IV.ii.268), the metaphorical light and heat generated by the father's apocalyptic violence (I.x.83), the gaslight on the mantle (I.xv.118), the light produced by the burning doll (II.ix.205–206) and the lightning storm (III.iv.234), the light explosively released by the short-circuited third rail (III.x.253; IV.xxi.419–422) and the abrupt darkness that ensues, and so on. Sexual motifs abound, from the moment when David guiltily notices the "shadow between [his mother's] breasts" (I.ix.64) to the moment when he inserts the phallic milk ladle (with its "grotesque armored head," I.xxi.414) between the "grinning lips" (413) of the sunken rail. A complex of christological and messianic motifs accumulates around the figure of David, of which the crosses of the telegraph poles (simultaneously Christian and phallic) near the beginning of the book (I.xii) and the image of the Sacred Heart that so fascinates and puzzles David near its end (Iv.x) are only the most obvious.

This last example of a motif-complex suggests another dimension of the integrative function of motifs in the "Joycean" model of modernist fiction. These recurrent christological motifs of *Call It Sleep* not only help to bind together the successive parts of the text along the axis of its linear unfolding; they also (like the Greek key words "metempsychosis" and "parallax," and many other motifs of *Ulysses*) indicate the presence of a second, parallel plane of organization, a parallel (higher) reality or mythic subtext.

Mythic subtext

Since at least as early as 1923, when T. S. Eliot called attention to it, readers have been aware of the "mythical method" (Eliot's phrase) in *Ulysses*, that is, of the presence and (especially) the function of the "continuous parallel" sustained between the contemporary world and events in the novel, on the one hand, and the world and events of the *Odyssey* on the other.[8] Eliot's point, corroborated many times over since 1923, was that the *Odyssey* parallel did not merely function as some kind of scaffolding for the text, useful in the construction process but otherwise negligible, but rather served to guarantee the ultimate unity and meaningfulness of *Ulysses*. It did so by superimposing on the chaotic surface of everyday contemporary reality a superior reality plane, something like the literary equivalent of the sacred realm in a traditional two-tier (sacred/profane) ontological system (see Pavel 1986). Literally subliminal (or super-liminal?), this second plane was accessible only to those who already possessed the interpretive "key" or formula, something along the lines of the reading instruction, "Read the narrative as a continuous parallel with the *Odyssey*." Otherwise its presence was revealed only in coded fashion, through various motifs that "infiltrated" the contemporary world from the mythic subtext and that, from this perspective, could be seen to function as the exposed tips of the mythological iceberg.

In *Call It Sleep*, the function of mythic subtext is performed not by Greek mythological literature but by the Judaeo-Christian messianic myth, the presence of which is signaled by the text's pervasive christological and messianic symbolism.[9] The scriptural David, in Christian exegesis, prefigures Christ, and David Schearl is associated here not only with his scriptural namesake (see, e.g., I.ii.26) but also with a whole series of typological prefigurations of the Messiah, including Moses (I.xv.12), Isaiah (the most overtly "messianic" of the prophets, at least in the Christian perspective; see III.iv.227, 256–257 and passim), and others. Finally, in the novel's climactic chapters David's identification with Christ, anticipated as early as the episode of the cruciform telegraph poles in I.xii, is consummated in his (presumably) redemptive near electrocution.[10]

II

When a text achieves canonized status as a model for the production of further texts, the features of its poetics are not only abstracted and formularized, but also typically simplified in the process (see Even-Zohar 1990: 21–22). This is conspicuously the case with *Ulysses*, which entered the modernist repertoire of models in a severely reduced state, literally cut in half. It is the poetics of roughly the first half of *Ulysses* that became normative for modernism – that is, the chapters in what Joyce called his "initial style," from "Telemachus" through "Scylla and Charybdis," together with the perspectivist chapters ("Wandering Rocks," "Nausicaa") and the final stream-of-consciousness chapter, "Penelope." However, since the text of *Ulysses* also gained admission to the canon in its own right, and not just its model, the novel's heterogeneous and nonnormative later chapters survived in the literary system's long-term memory, to be reactivated at a later date, when the transgressive poetics of *Ulysses'* second half served to supply fresh models for *post*modernist fiction (see McHale 1992: 42–58).

Roth's practice in *Call It Sleep* largely corroborates this analysis. For the most, Roth's narrative poetics is oriented toward the normatively modernist first half of *Ulysses*. Only once does his text shift from the normative model to a poetics resembling that of *Ulysses'* second half. This shift has always been perceived, by readers of *Call It Sleep* as well as by Roth himself, as a transgression of the text's own norms, or (Roth's word for it) a "rupture" (see Roth 1987: 76, 181; for the corroborative testimony of readers see, e.g., Levin 1960; xlviii; Guttmann 1971: 54). The point where this rupture occurs is the episode of David's near electrocution and rescue in IV.xxi.

The very look of this episode on the page – its spacing and typography – signals immediately that we have before us something quite distant from the poetics of Roth's earlier chapters. But its distance from the norm of *Call It Sleep* (which is also, let me repeat, that of the normatively modernist chapters of *Ulysses*) is at the same time a measure of its proximity to what is arguably the most "abnormal" chapter of *Ulysses*, namely "Circe." As in "Circe," the electrocution episode imitates the look on the page of a dramatic text, with speeches and what appear to be italicized stage directions – except that Roth, unlike Joyce, suppresses the indications of speakers, so that we are forced to guess who among the characters delivers which line of dialogue. Identifying the speakers, however, proves to be easier than it might at first appear, most of the speakers in the "play-script" passage of IV.xxi (roughly, pp. 413–431) having already been identified by name and situation in the early pages of the chapter (409–412) if not earlier, in chapter XX. Thus identifying speakers in the latter part of chapter XXI is mainly a matter of working backward to the more explicit indications of speakers in its earlier part.

Moreover, the stage directions prove not to be stage directions at all, but a form of interior discourse ("psychonarration," as Wirth-Nesher correctly specifies, 1991: 456), representing what is passing (consciously? unconsciously?) in David's mind. But then again, many of the stage directions in "Circe" also appear to represent what is passing in some character's mind, so on closer scrutiny that difference, too, dwindles.

Like "Circe" in another way (see Perl 1984: 196–197), the electrocution episode is recapitulative and, as it were, encyclopedic, recollecting and recombining, in the space of a few pages, all the principal motifs around which the novel's earlier chapters had been organized. It recapitulates, among others, all the integrative motifs identified above: motifs of light and darkness, sexual motifs, christological and messianic motifs. Motifs of light and heat recur here, for instance, in O'Toole's phallic metaphor of the cutting-torch (I.xxi.416), in Bill Whitney's story of setting the bed afire (416), and in the electrocution itself. Sexual motifs occur in Mary's obscene story of sexual humiliation and revenge (413–417), in O'Toole's obscenity-packed discourse, in the image of the "red cock" (417), and in the unintended sexual innuendo of the "kindly faced American woman" urging her immigrant interlocutor to "go all the way up inside" the Statue of Liberty (415). Christological motifs include routine oaths ("Jesus!," "Christ, it's a kid!," "fer Jesus sake!," 420), allusions to the feeding of the five thousand (417) and Peter's denial of Christ (418), and the crucifixion imagery of David's interior discourse (425). In particular, the psychonarrative discourse of David's (un)consciousness recapitulates, as if systematically, all his episodes of epiphanic experience throughout the novel: the epiphany of the cog from the clock (see I.i.21–22), of his mother's phrase "eternal years" (I.ix.69), of the conjunction of coffin, carriages, and confetti (I.ix.70), of the whistling tugboat crewman (III.vii.248), and so on.

Here for once, following Joyce's lead, Roth appears to have
ventured beyond the limits of normative modernism into the
transgressive space of *Ulysses'* second half, the space of the
"other" *Ulysses*. I emphasize "*appears* to have ventured beyond,"
for whether this is really so, and what the consequences of such
a transgression might be, can only be determined after we have
first reviewed the strange case of *Ulysses'* "other half."

III

Shortly after entering Nighttown, the red-light district in which
the "Circe" chapter is set, Mr. Bloom is forced to dodge out of
the path of a motorized sandstrewer, bearing down on him on
the streetcar tracks (Joyce 1934: 428).[11] His abrupt course adjust-
ment, a sprightly gesture of evasion and self-preservation, can be
read emblematically as a physical acting out of the constant,
ingenious micro-evasions and micro-adjustments that constitute
the very fabric of his interior life (see above). But if his gesture
of evasion characterizes Bloom himself, it also characterizes an
entire modernist poetics.

Marshall Berman (1988: 160) identifies such swerves and
dodges of creative evasion, needed for survival in the city streets,
as among the "paradigmatic gestures of modernist art and
thought," possessing a lineage stretching back as far as Baude-
laire's *Paris Spleen*, and enshrined in popular culture in the original name of the Brooklyn baseball team – the Trolley Dodgers,
later shortened to the Dodgers (and later still translated to the
West Coast).[12] The necessity of adapting constantly to the risks
and incitements of the modern city – to the ubiquity of the urban
crowd, the speed and density of urban traffic, the saturation of
the cityscape with advertising and commercial solicitations –
breeds in modern city dwellers a certain mental (even more
than physical) agility and volatility. This distinctively modern
volatility of consciousness is captured in the restless interior
discourses of *Ulysses*, not only in Bloom's interior monologues
but in Stephen's and Molly's as well.

Such volatility of consciousness has as its corollary, at least as
far as modernist poetics of fiction is concerned, the ultimate

stability (in a certain sense) and reliability of the world *outside* consciousness. The sandstrewer may be speedy, its abrupt appearance on the scene may be alarming and unanticipated, but it is reliably *there,* forming a part of the material world outside Mr. Bloom's consciousness with which he has to contend. And this corollary holds true even of interior monologues more radically detached from immediate reality than Bloom's. Even in the case of Stephen performing epistemological thought experiments on Sandymount Strand, or Molly musing in bed after midnight, the swerves and dodges of volatile consciousness are projected against the backdrop of a relatively stable "real world," one that we (as resourceful modernist readers) can reconstruct with a fair degree of confidence (see McHale 1992: 44–46, 64–66). Indeed, if the world outside consciousness were *not* reliably "there," we would have no stable background against which to gauge the relative motion of consciousness, and our sense of its volatility would consequently be lost.

This principle of volatile consciousness, with its corollary of ontological stability, underwrites and animates the poetics of all the normatively modernist chapters of *Ulysses.* Borrowing the title of one of the most volatile among them, let us call this the Proteus principle.

As it turns out, Bloom's emblematic encounter with the sandstrewer is one of the few events in the "Circe" chapter that one can convincingly assert "really" happened.[13] For by the time we accompany Mr. Bloom into Nighttown, we have already left the normative modernist poetics of the novel's first half far behind, and are deep into the transgressive "other half" of *Ulysses.* Here in "Circe" we are often in doubt about who is "really there" in Nighttown apart from Bloom and Stephen – are the girls from the beach, Gerty MacDowell, Edy Boardman, and Cissy Caffrey, really there? Blazes Boylan, is he really there? Is the man in the mackintosh? – and we are seldom able to distinguish confidently between "real" events and alcoholic hallucinations. Elsewhere a stable backdrop to the restlessness of consciousness, here the world of *Ulysses* dissolves into restless plurality (see Perl 1984: 196–211).

Apparitions flicker in and out of existence: Stephen's dead

mother and Bloom's father, mother, grandfather, and son Rudy, all long dead, appear and mingle with living characters (some of whom may very well not "really" be there themselves). Characters abruptly change their costume, their sex (Bella Cohen becomes Bello, Bloom becomes a woman), even their species (a beagle metamorphoses into an apparition of the late Paddy Dignam; Simon Dedalus materializes as a buzzard). Alternative (fantasized? hallucinated?) spaces open in the fabric of reality: A courtroom materializes and then "recedes" (Joyce 1934: 488); figured wallpaper in Bella Cohen's music room unfolds and expands into a countryside. Inanimate objects – Bloom's cake of soap, Lynch's cap, Bella's fan – acquire language, and speak for themselves. In doing so they become, in effect, realized synecdoches, and thus join a larger category of realized figures of speech – metaphors, idioms (dead metaphors), and so on – that "infiltrate" reality from the level of discourse throughout this chapter. Thus, for example, when one of the whores, rejecting Bloom's advice to quit smoking, uses the idiomatic expression, "Make a stump speech out of it," Bloom is immediately seen and heard making a (literal) stump speech (469).

Even more disturbing to ontological stability than the infiltration of reality by literalized figures of speech is infiltration from the level of the text's mythic subtext. Thus, for instance, the nymph in the picture hanging above the Blooms' conjugal bed descends from her frame to confront Bloom on his own level of reality. A surrogate for the nymph Calypso, she properly belongs to the novel's system of "continuous parallels" between contemporary reality and the world of the *Odyssey*. The nymph's presence as a character amounts to a kind of ontological short circuit, an illicit telescoping of reality planes.

Here in "Circe," in other words, as in the "other half" of *Ulysses* generally, the modernist poetics of volatile consciousness and stable world has been superseded by a different principle, that of ontological volatility. If we have agreed to call the underlying principle of the modernist chapters the Proteus principle, then it follows that we should call the animating principle of the novel's "other half" the Circe principle.

Not only is the world of "Circe" itself volatile, but the "Circe"

chapter can be seen as the locus from which emanates the ontological restlessness that disturbs the other chapters of the novel's
second half. It is, in a sense, the very epicenter of ontological
disturbance in the entire text. Most, if not all, the various techniques of ontological disturbance that typify the other transgressive chapters can be found, either recapitulated or antici-
pated, in "Circe."

Newspaper headlines like those that interrupt the narrative
in the "Aeolus" chapter; nonsense coinages and onomatopoeic
expressions like those in "Sirens"; parodies of various sub- and
paraliterary genres and registers (court reporter's style, parlia-
mentary style, medical discourse, American revival-sermon style,
etc.) such as one finds in "Cyclops"; catalogues and inventories,
typical of "Cyclops" and "Ithaca"; samples of incompetently "ele-
gant" writing of the kind that abounds in "Eumaeus" – all these
strategies for troubling the linguistic surface of the text and dis
rupting the "world-making" function of language are recapitulated or anticipated in "Circe" (see Attridge 1988: 127–157, 158–
187; McHale 1992: 48–55). One even encounters pastiches of
archaic and high literary styles of the kind elaborated at such
length in "Oxen of the Sun," but here placed incongruously in
the mouths of Nighttown whores. In "Circe," one might even
say, all these techniques of transgression seem most "at home,"
for here they can be seen most clearly in relation to each other
and to the overarching umbrella of the Circe principle of mutability and metamorphosis.

Mr. Bloom's characteristically modernist dodges and evasive
maneuvers, so finely adapted to the challenges, mental and
physical, of modern urban life, do not serve him nearly so well
in the volatile world of "Circe," which is to say the world of
Ulysses' "other half" in general. Here Joyce's techniques no
longer seem (as they did in the novel's first half) to represent the
situation of consciousness confronting the modern city, but quite
a different situation. It is perhaps something akin to what Fredric
Jameson has called "reality-pluralism," "a coexistence not even
of multiple and alternate worlds so much as of unrelated fuzzy
sets and semiautonomous subsystems whose overlap is perceptu-
ally maintained like hallucinogenic depth planes in a space of

many dimensions" (1991: 372). The city to which the Circe principle seems to correspond is not so much Bloom's Dublin, 1904 – or even Joyce's Paris, 1922, for that matter – as a city Joyce himself would not live to see: a centrifugal city, dispersed into a cloud of suburbs and satellite cities, the city center itself "renewed" as a series of elite enclaves or self-contained micro-worlds; a city less real than its electronic doubles and entertainment-industry simulations, volatilized, leaving behind it no more than a residue of the "real" city as a home for society's human discards. In "Circe" Joyce seems somehow to have antici-pated the postmodern city.

Joyce's prescience in seeming to anticipate, so far in advance of historical developments, the postmodern condition of reality-pluralism confirms again the "untimeliness" of *Ulysses,* which critics such as Colin MacCabe have remarked (1978: 109). If *Ulysses* is paradigmatic for modernist poetics, a founding text of literary modernism, it seems also (in its "other half") to overlap the entire subsequent develop of modernist poetics to land some-how on the far side of it. Precociously postmodernist, apparently in defiance of the logic of literary history, *Ulysses* now seems, at least in the eyes of contemporary "postmodernizing" readers, a founding text of postmodernist poetics as much as it ever was of modernism.

IV

Unleashed in the Nighttown chapter, the Circe principle seems to threaten the norms of modernist poetics from within, and at the very moment of their inception, or at least of their regulariza-tion. Later modernists, writing after Joyce and in the tradition of Joycean poetics, have sought by and large to evade or domesti-cate the Circe principle of limitless ontological volatility. Drawing back from the brink of what (from our perspective) appears as Joyce's precocious postmodernism, they have tended to practice a variety of policies of containment.

A case in point is John Dos Passos' Joycean novel of city life, *Manhattan Transfer* (1925). Traces of the "Circe" chapter appear everywhere here, but dispersed and bracketed within various types of discursive framing, as it were quarantined to prevent their contaminating the rest of the text. Thus, for instance, the stage directions of "Circe," the site *par excellence* of metamorphosis in Joyce's chapter, recur here in the form of heavily figurative cityscapes in which the city appears as malleable, fluid, metamorphic; but these cityscapes are physically distinguished from Dos Passos' narrative, set as italicized headnotes to the text's various chapters, *para*-textual, rather than fully integrated. Insofar as Circean mutability is permitted to penetrate the narrative proper, it is restricted to a small number of fixed, recurrent situations or narrative contexts, in effect Circean *topoi* – episodes of drunkenness, euphoria, delirium, imminent death, etc. – all of them carefully subjectivized to prevent their being mistaken for the "real world."[14]

Even more revealing, perhaps, is the case of Malcolm Lowry's *Under the Volcano* (1947). Here the principle of mutability and metamorphosis has been generalized to the entire text, to an extent that surpasses even *Ulysses* itself, yet at the same time that principle has been naturalized and recuperated more completely than anywhere else in the tradition of Joycean poetics. The key to this apparent paradox is the figure of Lowry's protagonist, the drunken Consul, whose presence simultaneously licenses and unproblematically contains the text's restless mutability. If apparitions flicker in and out of existence, if gaps appear in the narrative record and chronology is confusingly foreshortened, if objects and beings undergo fantastic metamorphoses, they are all explained in the distortions in the Consul's perception of the "outside world," induced by his alcohol consumption.[15] The Consul's function, in a sense, is to motivate the world's apparent volatility in *Under the Volcano*, and to neutralize it by rendering it merely subjective and idiosyncratic. He is the very figure of containment.

In the context of these later modernist policies of containment we can locate the electrocution episode in *Call It Sleep* (IV.xxi). In this episode Roth directly invokes the "Circe" chapter of *Ulysses*, but, having done so, promptly seeks, like Dos Passos before and Lowry after him, to contain and tame its poetics of ontological volatility.

As we have seen, the electrocution episode echoes "Circe" in a number of ways: in its playscript form, its uproar of voices, its plumbing of the depths of the protagonist's mind, its recapitulation of motifs and epiphanic moments from earlier chapters, and so on. In documenting such parallels, one does no more than corroborate the generally "Joycean" credentials of *Call It Sleep* and, reciprocally, the paradigmatic role of *Ulysses* for modernist poetics. At one point in this episode, however, the relation of the later text to its predecessor is more intimate and direct than merely the relation between a text and the literary model of which it is the realization. This point corresponds to the crisis when David, having inserted the milk dipper into the slot of the electrified rail, spectacularly short-circuits the system, producing a violent release of subterranean energy. Symbolically, it is as if, in shorting out the street railway's electrical system, David had also somehow short-circuited the intertextual system of *Call It Sleep,* allowing Roth's text and its Joycean intertext to coincide briefly and explosively in the same textual space.

The equivalent crisis in *Ulysses* is the moment when Stephen, seeking to drive off the accusing ghost of his mother, shatters the gas chandelier in the whorehouse parlor with his walking stick (momentarily transformed into Siegfried's magic sword Nothung):

STEPHEN
Nothung
(He lifts his ashplant high with both hands and smashes the chandelier. Time's livid final flame leaps and, in the following darkness, ruin of all space, shattered glass and toppling masonry.)
THE GASJET
Pwfungg!

(Joyce 1934: 567–568)

Now compare the "stage directions" recounting what happens when David short-circuits the electrified rail:

He kicked – once. Terrific rams of darkness collided; out of their shock space toppled into havoc. A thin scream wobbled through the spirals of oblivion, fell like a brand on water, his-s-s-s-s-ed – (IV.xxi.419)

It is hard, I submit, not to see Roth's sentence, "Terrific rams of darkness collided" etc., as literally a rewriting, the reinscription in Roth's text of the equivalent sentence from "Circe," "Time's livid final flame leaps," etc.[16] Roth duplicates Joyce's apocalyptic imagery, making a few lexical substitutions (e.g., "havoc" for "ruins") but generally preserving the key words of the original ("darkness," "space," "toppled/toppling"). Scrutinized, every detail here, incidental ones included (e.g., the onomatopoeic "his-s-s-s-ed," the "brand"), reveals unmistakable traces of Joyce's presence.

But having just this once allowed Joyce's intertextual presence to break through to the surface in this way – to well up from underground, as it were, like the energy released by David's short circuit – Roth's text seems to recoil. This recoil or textual withdrawal from too intimate an engagement with the Joycean intertext is complex. It comprises at least two aspects, one of *resistance* to Joyce's influence, the other of what I have been calling *containment*.

The aspect of textual resistance can perhaps best be understood in terms of the oedipal model of literary relations given currency by Harold Bloom's theory of the "anxiety of influence." According to this model, Roth's very existence as a literary artist can be seen to depend on his identification with his literary precursor and father figure, Joyce; yet precisely this identification with the powerful precursor constitutes the greatest threat to Roth's artistic identity and integrity. Joyce's influence, on this account, both enables and compromises Roth's independence; hence the anxiety. This oedipal analysis seems borne out by Roth's own repeated, anxious repudiations of Joyce in the years since he broke his long public silence around 1960 (see Roth 1987: 110, 170, 184, and passim). It is also borne out, at a different level and in another way, by the unresolved oedipal conflict between son and father in *Call It Sleep* itself, which from this perspective appears to have been mirrored in, or doubled by, the author's relationship with his literary precursor.

Roth's anxious relation to his precursor emerges clearly when, having directly invoked Stephen's crisis in the "Circe" episode as an analogue of his own protagonist's crisis, Roth proceeds to

undo the parallelism he has contrived. He does so systematically – too systematically, indeed, for in *exactly inverting* the key
axes and oppositions of Stephen's crisis his narrative reveals the
presence of the Joycean original more transparently than if it
had replicated Joyce's structure point for point. Thus, where
Stephen "lifts his ashplant high," swinging it *overhead* to shatter
the chandelier, David thrusts his milk ladle *downward* into the
slot of the rail. Where Stephen's intemperate action plunges the
music room into *darkness,* David's produces glaring *illumination.*
Stephen, after breaking the gas chandelier *indoors,* flees *outdoors*
into the street, there to be accosted and knocked down by a
drunken soldier. David, conversely, suffers a beating *indoors* at
the hands of his enraged father, then flees *outdoors* where he
short-circuits the electrified rail; and so on. The transformations
are systematic enough to be reduced to a formula: To recover the
Joycean original from Roth's version, merely rotate every *direction* 180 degrees and replace every *quality* by its opposite. This
would in effect produce a photographic negative, an X-ray photograph, of the episode's textual resistances to "Circe."

Resistance to the textual precedent of "Circe" attests to the
strength of Roth's *individual* anxiety of influence vis-à-vis his
powerful precursor. Roth's strategies of containment, on the
other hand, reflect a *collective* situation, that of all later modernists confronting the intractable double nature, simultaneously
normative and transgressive, of their founding text.

In reinscribing the apocalyptic imagery of "Circe" in his own
text ("Terrific rams of darkness collided," etc.), Roth left an opening, as it were, through which the poetics of "Circe" might have
entered *Call It Sleep.* Some readers have thought that they de-
tected in the electrocution episode a poetics of ontological plurality and volatility such as one finds in Joyce's chapter (see, e.g.,
Lesser 1981: 164). Closer inspection shows, however, that this is
not really the case. Whatever is metamorphic and mutable in the
imagery of this episode has been safely confined to David's interior discourse (his psychonarration), and not permitted to con-
taminate the "outer world" of *Call It Sleep* as it does the world of
"Circe." "Containment" here is not even a metaphor, but applies
literally to the special typographical conventions of this episode,

whereby David's hallucinations appear in italic type, inset from the rest of the text, justified on the left margin but not on the right, and even (for part of the episode, IV.xii.424–431) enclosed between parentheses. The effect is to produce a kind of textual enclosure, a boxed-in space or series of spaces within which (as in the italic headnotes of Dos Passos' *Manhattan Transfer*) the Circe principle is allowed free rein. But the walls of this textual enclosure are never breached. Nor, for that matter, are the ontological boundaries between the level of discursive figures and the level of world, or between the real world and the plane of mythic archetypes. Nothing equivalent to the materialization, in "Circe," of the nymph Calypso (or her photolithographed proxy, at any rate) occurs in *Call It Sleep*, and the messenger angels of Roth's messianic subtext remain *discursive* angels only – figures of speech, not characters in the world (see I.ix.70, I.xi.121, III.viii.252). Finally, there is here none of the "ripple effect" of Joyce's "Circe." No trace of the Circe principle, even in Roth's attenuated and subjectivized version of it, is allowed to spread beyond the confines of Chapter IV (xxi) to any other chapter of the book.

Thus, Roth invokes the Circe principle of *Ulysses*, but immediately displaces its ontological volatility into the realm of *consciousness* (or in this case, perhaps, unconsciousness). Like other later modernists – Dos Passos in *Manhattan Transfer*, Lowry in *Under the Volcano* – he contains the Joycean poetics of reality pluralism by subjectivizing it. Roth, in other words, retreats from the Circe principle to the Proteus principle, from transgression to normative modernism.

Or, one might say, he retreats to the poetics of trolley dodging – that is, to that response to the challenges of modernity of which Mr. Bloom's evasion of the sandstrewer is emblematic. Roth's modernism, the modernism of volatile consciousness, corresponds to a historically specific experience of the modern world, of moder*nity*. Marshall Berman (who is my guide in such matters) identifies this as the nineteenth-century experience of modernity: the experience, that is, of those for whom the confrontation with the modern involves the memory of the traditional and *pre*modern, so that their world is *doubled* (Berman 1988: 17; and cf. Jameson 1991: 307–308). Berman is right, it seems to me, in everything but the chronology, for there have been many who have experienced this confrontation with the modern across the gap of the premodern in our own century – immigrant populations, for instance, whose experience of the modern metropolis is shot through with the memories of the rural and traditional life of, say, the *shtetl* they have left behind. This is the experience of Roth's protagonists, the Schearls; it was Roth's own experience (see Geismar 1960: xxxviii–xxxix).

This experience equips such people to become *modern* in a certain way; it equips them to become trolley dodgers, creative evaders, Leopold Blooms, "Jewlysses." If they are artists, like Henry Roth, it may equip them to become modern*ists* (this distinction is also Berman's, see 1988: 345–346 and passim). But it may not equip them to pass to the next historical phase of the experience of modernity, the experience of the world as fragmented, multiple, speaking a plurality of incommensurable languages (Berman 1988: 17). This is something like the sense of the world that Jameson seeks to capture through his concept of "reality-pluralism," though he associates this latter not with a historical phase of modernity but with *post*modernism – unless we choose to regard postmodernism as the response to a late phase of modernity (as Jameson himself rather tends to do; see Jameson 1991: 302–313), in which case the difficulty disappears.

This second-phase modernity of restless plurality and incommensurability – "of unrelated fuzzy sets and semiautonomous subsystems," says Jameson – is the world of "Circe." It is not a world in which even Mr. Bloom feels at home, though he passes through it; it is not David Schearl's world, except subjectively, for a brief but wrenching moment. It is not a world, evidently, that Henry Roth was willing or able to countenance outside of a kind of neutralizing containment field – not that any of his fellow later modernists, Dos Passos, Lowry, or anyone else of their literary generation, was any more willing or better able to do so than he.

NOTES

1   Apart from "Joycean," the other category that has often been applied to *Call It Sleep* is "proletarian" (or "ethnic" or "immigrant")
novel. Walter Rideout (1956: 186) called *Call It Sleep* "the most
distinguished single proletarian novel," and Roth has confessed to
Leonard Michaels that when he was working on *Call It Sleep*, "I
thought I was writing a proletarian novel" (Michaels 1993: 20). On
the other hand, the Left critical establishment of the time was
divided over the question of Roth's "proletarian" aesthetic credentials, with the anonymous reviewer in *New Masses* dismissing *Call It
Sleep* as "introspective and febrile" – code words, presumably, for
"bourgeois modernist." (See Rideout 1956: 189–190 for an account
of Roth's initial reception among reviewers on the Left.) The recent
Columbia History of the American Novel, reflecting on the vexed question of how best to categorize *Call It Sleep*, has sought to finesse the
problem by appealing to its reception history: "The vicissitudes of
Call It Sleep's reception reflect the novel's unusual combination of
high modernist structure . . . and ethnic themes, a combination
that continues to embarrass our terms of critical inquiry" (Ferraro
1991: 394–395). It does not, evidently, embarrass them to the point
of preventing *Call It Sleep* from turning up in the *Columbia History*'s
chapter on "Ethnicity and the Marketplace," where the emphasis
falls unmistakably on its ethnic and proletarian themes rather than
on its modernist or Joycean structure.

2   Roth 1991: 69, 70, 205–206, 23. Henceforth all references will be
to this edition (which is paginated identically with the 1964 Avon
edition), and will be incorporated parenthetically in the text, thus:
(Book.chapter.page).

3   Somewhat more abstractly, David also shares the epistemological
skepticism that is the theme of Stephen's introspective reflection
on Sandymount Strand when he (David) muses: "How could you
hear the sound of your own feet in the dark if a carpet muffled
every step you took? And if you couldn't hear the sound of your
own feet and couldn't see anything either, how could you be sure
you were actually there and not dreaming?" (I.i.20). Compare
Joyce (1934: 38; my ellipses):
Stephen closed his eyes to hear his boots crunch crackling wrack and shells.
. . . Am I walking into eternity along Sandymount strand? . . . Open your
eyes now. I will. One moment. Has all vanished since? If I open and am for
ever in the black adiaphane. *Basta!* I will see if I can see.

See now. There all the time without you: and ever shall be, world without end.

4   This somewhat queasy pun is Roth's own, and one he applies self-mockingly to himself (Roth 1987: 219); but it might as well have been Joyce's.

5   This last instance seems specifically to echo a famous passage from the "Ithaca" chapter of *Ulysses* devoted to the Dublin municipal water supply (1934: 655).

6   Not all the commentators on *Call It Sleep* appear to have been aware of free indirect discourse (FID), and as a result the text has occasionally been misconstrued. By now, the literature on FID in poetics is voluminous; recent book-length studies include Cohn 1978, Banfield 1982, and Fludernik 1993.

7   A few are ambiguous between verbal and object status, notably the "man in the mackintosh," who appears both "in person" and (as "M'Intosh") as a verbal error.

8   The "mythical method" that Eliot discerned in *Ulysses* is also the method of *The Waste Land*, so that in this respect the modernist model for *Call It Sleep* is double, a composite of Joyce and Eliot. Evidence for the role of *The Waste Land* in this composite paradigm is especially easy to find in IV.xxi (see Wirth-Nesher 1991: 456), where a number of phrases (e.g., "the very heart of silence," 411; "the outstretched figure in the heart of the light," 421) seem indebted to passages from Eliot's poem. See also Roth's own acknowledgment of Eliot's importance for him at the time he was writing *Call It Sleep:* "I would say that Eliot was the major influence on my life" (Roth 1987: 191).

9   Alter has argued that Roth's use of myth in *Call It Sleep* has less in common with Joyce's allusive method than it does with the kind of "mythic drama" – hyperbolic language, apocalyptic implication – typical of American writers like Melville (Alter 1988: 36). I do not see these as mutually exclusive alternatives; nevertheless, it does seem striking that, according to his own account of his "discovery" of Joyce, Roth adopted *Ulysses* as his model precisely because it offered him a variable (modern, urban) alternative to the American tradition of "mythic" adventure stories (Roth 1987: 198–199).

10 Apart from the "global" features of the Joycean model that *Call It Sleep* shares with *Ulysses*, there are also a number of local affinities and filiations that might be traced – for instance, between Chapter IV.xvi of *Call It Sleep*, where the point of view shifts temporarily to Reb Pankower, and the opening of the "Wandering Rocks" chapter

of *Ulysses*, where the narrative perspective lingers with Father John Conmee for a number of pages, before parting from him to circulate among his fellow Dubliners; or between the final paragraph of *Call It Sleep* and the ending of the "Penelope" chapter of *Ulysses*, when Molly Bloom's interior monologue fades into silence as she (presumably) falls asleep. A still closer analogue for the end of *Call It Sleep* might be found, however, in the final paragraphs of "The Dead," the last story in Joyce's *Dubliners* (1914).

11 A sandstrewer is "an electric tram car designed to clean mud and refuse from the rails and to sand them" (Gifford and Seidman 1988: 455). Near the beginning of *Call It Sleep* IV.xxi, too, a motorman must use his bell to warn a pedestrian off the tracks (412) – corroborative evidence of the intertextual relation between this chapter and "Circe," if any were needed.

12 In John Dos Passos' *Manhattan Transfer* (1925) – another candidate for the title of "most Joycean of any novel written by an American" – failure to adapt to the demands of the modern city is regularly symbolized by traffic mishaps: Gus McNeil's milk van is hit by a trolley (Section I, chapter ii), Phil Sandbourne is knocked down by a car crossing Fifth Avenue (II.iii), and so on.

13 Moreover, our conviction of its "really" having happened derives not from anything in the "Circe" chapter itself, but from corroborative evidence to be found in a later chapter ("Eumaeus," Joyce 1934: 598).

14 In the later trilogy, *U.S.A.* (*The Forty-Second Parallel*, 1930; *Nineteen Nineteen*, 1932; *The Big Money*, 1936), Dos Passos would develop the quarantine strategies of *Manhattan Transfer* in the direction of even more complete systematicity. In place of the chapter headnotes of *Manhattan Transfer* he would designate one particular recurrent formal unit of *U.S.A.*, the "Camera Eye" sections, as the site of (subjectivized) metamorphoses; see, e.g., "Camera Eye" 28 and 39 (from *Nineteen Nineteen*), 44 and 46 (from *The Big Money*). The same Circean repertoire of narrative *topoi* – drunken delirium or euphoria, the moment of death, etc. – would be retained from *Manhattan Transfer*.

15 More troublesome, at first glance, are the insistent archetypal motifs – wheel, pariah dog, carrion birds, tempest, and shipwreck, especially various christological motifs – that seem to percolate up to the surface of the text from its (typically modernist) mythic subtext. But these too, it turns out, can be prevented from disrupting the text's ontological stability unduly, and by the same

strategy. For the Consul, a student of occult correspondences, engaged in interminable research for a book on traditions of secret knowledge, is a connoisseur and collector of such manifestations of mythic archetypes, so that their insistent recurrence can safely be regarded as his subjective projection, reflecting his vision of things rather than the actual structure of "reality."

16 Alter (1988: 36) claims to find in this passage echoes, not of Joyce's language in "Circe," but of Melville's characteristic metaphors and apocalyptic hyperbole. Although nothing prevents Roth from having two (or more) models for the same passage, I wonder whether Alter's preference for the Melville model here isn't a way of "redeeming" his author from too close an identification with the Joyce model. In other words, by choosing to place Roth in an American context (that of Melville), Alter may be seeking (however unconsciously or unintentionally) to *dis*place him from the Joycean context, where he runs a risk of being overwhelmed by his great predecessor, reduced to the status of a mere epigone. If so, then Alter's interpretive move would appear to mirror, at the level of commentary, Roth's own *resistance* to Joyce, at the level of the text; see below. Nor is Alter the only commentator to have reacted defensively to Joyce's perceived encroachment upon Roth's literary identity and integrity; see also, e.g., Levin 1960: xlviii.

WORKS CITED

Alter, Robert. "Awakenings. Review of Henry Roth, *Shifting Landscape* and *Call It Sleep." The New Republic* 198, 4 (Jan. 25, 1988): 33–37.

Alter, Robert. "The Desolate Breach Between Himself and Himself. Review of Henry Roth, *Mercy of a Rude Stream,* Vol. 1: *A Star Shines over Mt. Morris Park." New York Times Book Review* (Jan. 16, 1994): 3, 29.

Attridge, Derek. *Peculiar Language: Literature as Difference from the Renaissance to James Joyce.* London: Methuen, 1988.

Banfield, Ann. *Unspeakable Sentences: Narration and Representation in the Language of Fiction.* London: Routledge and Kegan Paul, 1982.

Baumgarten, Murray. *City Scriptures: Modern Jewish Writing.* Cambridge, Mass. and London: Harvard University Press, 1982.

Beebe, Maurice. "Ulysses and the Age of Modernism," in Thomas F. Staley, ed., *Ulysses: Fifty Years.* Bloomington and London: Indiana University Press, 172–188.

Berman, Marshall. *All That Is Solid Melts into Air: The Experience of Modernity,* 2d ed. New York: Penguin, 1988.

Cohn, Dorrit. *Transparent Minds: Narrative Modes for Presenting Consciousness in Fiction*. Princeton: Princeton University Press, 1978.

Eliot, T. S. "Ulysses, Order, and Myth," reprinted in *Selected Prose of T. S. Eliot*, ed. Frank Kermode. London: Faber and Faber (1975 [1923]), 480–483.

Elliott, Emory (ed.). *The Columbia History of the American Novel*. New York: Columbia University Press, 1991.

Even-Zohar, Itamar. "Polysystem Theory." *Poetics Today* 11, 1 (1990): 9–26.

Fludernik, Monika. *The Fictions of Language and the Languages of Fiction: The linguistic representation of speech and consciousness*. London and New York: Routledge, 1993.

Fokkema, Douwe, and Elrud Ibsch. *Modernist Conjectures: A Mainstream of European Literature*. London: C. Hurst, 1987.

Foucault, Michel. "What Is an Author?" in Donald F. Bouchard, ed., *Language, Counter-Memory, Practice: Selected Essays and Interviews*. Ithaca: Cornell University Press, 1977 (1969), 113–138.

Geismar, Maxwell. "A Critical Introduction," in Roth 1960, xxvi–xlv.

Gifford, Don, with Robert J. Seidman. *Notes for Joyce: An Annotation of James Joyce's "Ulysses,"* 2d ed. Berkeley, Los Angeles, London: University of California Press, 1988.

Gilbert, Stuart. *James Joyce's* Ulysses: *A Study*. New York: Knopf, 1952.

Guttmann, Allen. *The Jewish Writer in America: Assimilation and the Crisis of Identity*. New York: Oxford University Press, 1971.

Jameson, Frederic. *Postmodernism, or, the Cultural Logic of Late Capitalism*. Durham NC: Duke University Press, 1991.

Joyce, James. *Ulysses*. New York: Modern Library, 1934.

Joyce, James. *Stephen Hero*, ed. with introduction by Theodore Spencer, rev. ed. John J. Slocum and Herbert Cahoun. London: Jonathan Cape, 1956.

Kuhn, Thomas S. *The Structure of Scientific Revolutions*. Chicago and London: University of Chicago Press, 1962.

Lawrence, Karen. *The Odyssey of Style in "Ulysses."* Princeton: Princeton University Press, 1981.

Lesser, Wayne. "A Narrative's Revolutionary Energy: The Example of Henry Roth's 'Call It Sleep.' " *Criticism* 23, 2 (1981): 155–176.

Levin, Meyer. "A Personal Appreciation," in Roth 1960, xlvi–li.

MacCabe, Collin. *James Joyce and the Revolution of the Word*. London: Macmillan, 1978.

McHale, Brian. *Constructing Postmodernism*. London and New York: Routledge, 1992.

Michaels, Leonard. "The Long Comeback of Henry Roth: Call It Miraculous." *New York Times Book Review* (Aug. 15, 1993): 3, 19–21.

Pavel, Thomas. *Fictional Worlds.* Cambridge, Mass.: Harvard University Press, 1986.

Perl, Jeffrey M. *The Tradition of Return: The Implicit History of Modern Literature.* Princeton: Princeton University Press, 1984.

Ribalow, Henry U. "The History of Henry Roth and *Call It Sleep,*" in Roth 1960, xi–xxv.

Rideout, Walter. *The Radical Novel in the United States, 1900–1954.* Cambridge, Mass.: Harvard University Press, 1956.

Roth, Henry. *Call It Sleep.* Paterson NJ: Pageant Books, 1960.

Roth, Henry. *Shifting Landscape: A Composite, 1925–1987,* ed. and with introduction by Mario Materassi. Philadelphia, New York, Jerusalem: Jewish Publication Society, 1987.

Roth, Henry. *Call It Sleep.* New York: Farrar, Straus and Giroux, 1991.

Wirth-Nesher, Hana. "Afterword: Between Mother Tongue and Native Language in *Call It Sleep,*" in Roth 1991, 443–462.

6

Roth's *Call It Sleep:* Modernism on the Lower East Side

KAREN R. LAWRENCE

It seemed to me obvious that everywhere, even in Hitler Germany, to be outside of society and to be Jewish was to be at the heart of things. History was preparing, in its Jewish victims and through them, some tremendous deliverance and revelation. I hugged my aloneness, our apartness, my parents' poverty, as a sign of our call to create the future. . . . At the same time I had a sense of unreality, of doubleness, almost of duplicity, about the daily contrast of my personal life, my friends, my life in Brownsville, with those literary personages in mid-Manhattan who were so exciting and unreal to me . . .

Alfred Kazin, *Starting Out in the Thirties,* 47–48

IN describing his own experiences starting out in the thirties, Kazin captures something of the ambivalences and attachments hauntingly represented in Roth's *Call It Sleep,* a novel whose revival in the sixties owes much to Kazin and Leslie Fiedler. In his book, which begins in 1934, the year *Call It Sleep* was published, Kazin documents the literary milieu of New York in the thirties – conversations with John Chamberlain (daily book critic at the *Times*) and Malcolm Cowley and Otis Ferguson at *The New Republic,* a heady mixture of the literature and leftist politics that so preoccupied New York intellectuals. He was awed by these men, and acutely aware of his difference from them, particularly in terms of their sense of privilege; they were "so plainly with the haves, with the people who so mysteriously sat in positions of power" (48). Eagerly participating in debates about the relation between literature and social argument, Kazin scrutinized his own relation to power. A socialist who was nevertheless suspicious of ideologues, he summed up his own position:

"I was a literary radical, indifferent to economics, suspicious of organization, planning, Marxist solemnity and intellectual system-building; it was the rebels of literature, the great wrestlers-with-God, Thor with his mighty hammer, the poets of unlimited spiritual freedom, whom I loved – Blake, Emerson, Whitman, Nietzsche, Lawrence" (4).

In placing Jewish experience at both the margins and the center of political and literary events, in seeking to join the reality of Lower East Side streets with an Anglo-American prophetic tradition – which itself draws profoundly on Old Testament images and rhythms – Kazin captures the hybrid forces that propel the poetic grittiness of Roth's powerful novel. (Perhaps it is more accurate to say that both Kazin and Roth recognized the grittiness in the prophetic tradition of Blake, Whitman, and Lawrence.) Kazin's memoir, even more than his excellent foreword to the 1991 edition of Roth's novel, suggests the exhilaration and conflict symptomatic of immigrant Jewish children of artistic and intellectual sensibility, like the child, David Schearl, in Roth's novel, and Roth himself, as well as implicitly accounts for the novel's shifting place in modern literature. *Call It Sleep* records both David's and Roth's attempts to forge what Joyce's Stephen Dedalus calls "the uncreated conscience of [his] race," and, by this I mean a Jewish-American "conscience." As he moves from home to street to *cheder*, David is haunted by the image of the Hebrew prophets and seeks to fulfill the promise of biblical prophecy in his everyday life. Stylistically, Roth's prose combines the bardic tones of an eloquent, high English (which, like the King James version of the Bible is already a translation from an original, in this case, the Yiddish in which the characters think and speak) with the almost comic English street slang spoken with a Yiddish accent. Although Roth's novel is less obviously a portrait of the artist than Joyce's, there is a sense that David's struggle mirrors Roth's labor to produce his novelistic vision. Both "visions," David's and Roth's, fundamentally address questions about being inside and outside traditions and languages. *Call It Sleep* implicitly raises the following set of questions: How can one be a Jewish writer, an American writer, a European modernist? How can the novel craft a myth of uniqueness, a weighty, idiosyncratic interiority (a hallmark of modernist fiction in the teens and twenties) without surrendering social and material reality, particularly the recognition of what Voloshinov calls "intonation," the differently inflected ordinary language of different groups? How can the "visionary figures of speech" and "verbal refinement" of an internationalist modernism be mobilized in a poetry of the Lower East Side?[1] A discussion of *Call It Sleep* is important at this moment because the novel's writing and its fate in literary history speak to our continuing reassessment of the aestheticism, internationalism, and "politics" of that twentieth-century literature we call modernist.

Kazin's reading of *Call It Sleep* in his introduction to the 1991 edition sublates the conflicts he so insightfully explores in his record of the thirties; his reading seems firmly rooted in the aesthetics he describes in Roth's novel – it is a modernist reading of a modernist novel. "It is a work of high art, written out of the full resources of modernism. . . . We can see now that the book belongs to the side of the 1930s that still believed in the sacredness of literature, whether or not it presumed to change the world" (ix–x). Praising the novel for privileging the potentiality of character over the determinism of environment, he says, "Jews are generally so conscious of the pressure of history that it was a notable achievement for Henry Roth, coming out of the Lower East Side at a time when it was routine for people to dream of transforming 'conditions', to put character ahead of environment" (xiii). Here Kazin implicitly invokes the messy debate over the role of politics in literature that affected the reception of Roth's novel (it was condemned in *New Masses* for being "introspective and febrile," Ballou, 27) and, according to Roth's own testimony, proved such a burden to him as a Marxist writer once *Call It Sleep* was completed. (In an interview with Leonard Michaels in 1993, Roth cites the conflict between his artistic goals and his politics as one of the reasons he failed to produce a second novel for sixty years: " 'You're supposed to write, your ink is supposed to be a weapon in the class struggle,' " Roth told Michaels. " 'That's where my second novel foundered,' " Michaels, 20.) For Kazin, however, these conflicts seem to be subsumed aesthetically in an image of Joycean aesthetic refinement: "Anyone who recognizes Joyce's immense achievement in *Ulysses* will recognize his influence on Roth. In *Ulysses*, Dublin exists through the word-by-word progression of the subliminal consciousness. This is the mental world that is most ourselves, for nothing is so close to us as our inner thinking. The sources of this interior world remain mysterious as their effects are most inspiring" (xiv). Here Kazin's criticism falls squarely within a modernism rooted in an insistence on the primacy of consciousness and myth of uniqueness (a "belief," as Vince Pecora and Michael Levenson have shown, increasingly besieged and defensively maintained amidst the perilous "fate of individuality" in the twentieth century). Kazin ends his essay by saying of David, "He is on his way to becoming the artist who will write this book" (xx). The transformation of protagonist into author, as art transcends life's sordid details, and the reference to Roth's use of epiphanies, cast Roth in a particular Joycean mold crafted by Richard Ellmann in his biography (a plausible, though only partial view that Joyce often encouraged). But what does it mean to say that "nothing is so close to us as our inner thinking" in a book in which inner thinking is represented in a poetic and literary English already "translated" from a Yiddish largely unheard in the text?[2] Or, to put it another way, isn't Kazin's recourse to a perfectly interiorized thinking all one's own a wish to imagine words so pure that they do not circulate, a wish to purify the dialect of the tribe by keeping it at home? As even David's overprotective mother recognizes, this desire for an interior free of the bombardments of the world outside is an impossible dream.

In the rest of this chapter, I attempt to address some of these broad questions in relation to the "forging" of David's consciousness in the language of the text, an image I choose deliberately for its technological, mythic, and literary resonances. Just as the specter of Daedalus's workshop haunts Stephen's attempt to forge the uncreated conscience of his race in the "smithy of [his] soul," so the image of the Greek myth and Joyce's redaction haunt Roth's own "forgery," so conscious of its own belatedness.[3] What is the relationship between the hammering out of meaning in the precise and eloquently literary prose of the text, which largely represents the developing consciousness of the sensitive child, and the brutal threat of his father's hammer, a tool that bludgeons as it shapes? For *Call It Sleep* acknowledges the way words are, to quote Hartman, both "balm and venom," both wounding and healing (122). In addition, the novel attempts to connect bardic investments to social (and familial) investments. In Roth's urban, immigrant, American novel Thor's hammer, the tool of the artist, is also the symbol of Albert Schearl's terrible and violent power over his son and the sign of the father as laborer in turn-of-the-century New York. An anachronistic cattle handler, alienated by the drudgery of his work in the "promised land," David's father is, nevertheless, a part of the network of power that surges through the neighborhoods of New York City. David struggles to convert this threatening patriarchal power into the power of words, to convert the wrathful hammer into an instrument of precision and creativity. In doing so, he seeks a language of vision (Isaiah's language) whose power derives from rather than transcends the social world. The coal that touches Isaiah's lips is juxtaposed with the coal in David's cellar, fuel of the tenement as well as the visionary consciousness. As he throws the milk ladle (tool of his father) into the "crack" between the tracks ("In the crack, / remember. In the crack be born," David thinks to himself, 411), he forges his own version of enlightenment, creating a vision of power so terrifying and beautiful that it threatens to break him apart (just as the stichomythic hallucinatory prose breaks the narrative apart, disrupting representation). Through the literally shocking power of the public utilities David's hallucinatory vision is quickened into life.

What binds the hybrid strains of poetry, myth, mysticism, and social realism in Roth's novel is an oedipal pattern established in the first pages of the novel, already inscribed within the circuit of social forces outside the family. The "subliminal consciousness" that Kazin finds so Joycean is represented from the beginning as an interiority shaped by the titanic powers of maternal and paternal voices. Yet these voices are not mythic and familial only. They are to be understood, I would argue, in terms set forth by Deleuze and Guattari in *Anti-Oedipus,* as part of a libidi-

111

nous circuit of desire which connects man to the "machines of the universe" (Mark Seem, *Introduction to Anti-Oedipus,* xxiii). In a critique of Freud's analysis of the Schreber case, Deleuze and Guattari point out that the "sadistico-paranoiac machines" of Schreber's father "play no role whatever in the Freudian analysis." "Perhaps it would have been more difficult to crush the entire sociopolitical content of Schreber's delirium of [sic] these desiring-machines of the father had been taken into account, as well as their obvious participation in a pedagogical social machine in general" (297). Deleuze and Guattari see Oedipus as an idea in the mind of the paranoiac father, who "Oedipalizes the son" (275). Their description of the father's role in the Oedipus complex resonates with Albert Schearl's hatred of his son in Roth's novel and its relation to his own infantilized role as an immigrant. The psychic pattern already bears social investments:

And the child does not wait until he is an adult before grasping – underneath father-mother – the economic, financial, social, and cultural problems that cross through a family: his belonging or his desire to belong to a superior or an inferior 'race,' the reactionary or the revolutionary tenor of a familial group with which he is already preparing his ruptures and his conformities. (278)

In the final phallic gesture that, paradoxically, leads to David's penetration by power – a *sparagmos* and rebirth – this pattern finds its strange completion. The electrical charge of the family drama that the reader experiences in the early sections of the novel is climactically subsumed. The psychosexual is revealed as part of a larger circuit of power that animates the familial drama. David forges his vision by dangerously tapping the power system itself at a moment in which the oedipal gendering of power is destabilized, as David both penetrates power and is penetrated by it. The power coursing through David's veins and the language of the narrative have their sources in the refining fires of the prophetic books of the Bible (Isaiah's coal) *and* the system of public utilities; somehow this nexus of forces inspires the *fiat* that climaxes the novel. This is the Blakean terrible beauty that, like the Tyger, is forged in the furnace of a poetic imagination itself shaped by social forces. These social forces, fearful and yet thrilling, are specifically American forces as well. Again, Alfred Kazin captures the excitement of this image of "America, the power-house." In *New York Jew* he writes: "America, as even its most provincial visionaries had known, would soon be the greatest power instrument in history – we all went to make up that instrument" (14–15).

Thus psychic, social, poetic, even mystical strains in the novel are united in a concern, even obsession, with the relation between language and power, in the family and beyond. Specifically, interiority in *Call It Sleep* is constructed and mediated through paternal cursings and maternal blessings. The pitch of ordinary family speech acts and gestures is tuned up to a register of maledictions and benedictions, revealing the impact words have on psychic life. David is defined by these voices as Roth explores the relation between language and violence (one is reminded of his reference to ink as "a weapon in the social struggle"), language and healing, language and prophecy. Like Stephen Dedalus, whose "strange name seemed to him a prophecy" (*A Portrait of the Artist as a Young Man*, 168), David Schearl longs to hear the call of his destiny; amid the cacophony of voices that compose the ineluctable modality of the audible (to borrow from Joyce), David desires to purify speech into prophecy, to become another Isaiah, whose lips, touched by purifying coal, can speak the truth. But although Stephen feels the prophecy of a name that enables him to disown his biological father and adopt a mythical one, David cannot escape the wounding words of a father who believes his own paternity may be a legal fiction. David's very name, which means "beloved" in Hebrew, is a misnomer on the lips of the father; Albert continually substitutes other names for David; he refers to him as "the prayer," an English translation of the Hebrew word "kaddish," or prayer for the dead.[4] As Hartman says, "Like oaths and commandments, to which they are akin, [Curse and Blessing] seek to bind the action of those to whom they are addressed, yet unlike oaths or commandments they are resorted to when legal instruments are not appropriate or have failed" (130–131). The parents seek to "bind the action" of the son, to fix his identity; the self-arrest that climaxes the end of the novel is in part David's attempt to wrest control of himself, to fix himself apart from his family's fixations.

The first pages of the Prologue introduce the way maternal and paternal voices inflect the duality of language in its power both to hurt and to heal. Touching her husband's arm David's mother speaks her first words "timidly": " 'And this is the Golden Land.' " These words are followed by the simple narrative declaration, meant to suffice for the rest of the narrative, "She spoke in Yiddish." The narrator goes on to say "The man grunted, but made no answer" (11). In this scene, the mother's voice is a balm which tries to cover over the violence of the father's gestures, glares, and snarls. She apologizes to her husband (we do not yet know what for, but the action will be characteristic) and in response, "his brusque glance stabbed and withdrew" (11). He "rebukes" and "snaps" (12), she gently sympathizes and cajoles. How differently is the same Yiddish (mother) tongue inflected! "The harsh voice, the wrathful glare, the hand flung toward the child frightened him" (15). David's first recorded act in the novel is to burst into tears. The still unnamed mother and son cling together seeking refuge; the repeated use of the father's name, "Albert," produces him as the "other," the intruder.

Genya's first words, "And this is the Golden Land," echo the Prologue's epigraph: "(I pray thee ask no questions/this is that Golden Land)" (9). Her language repeats the gesture of the lady of Liberty, a promise of refuge. "The child and his mother stared again at the massive figure in wonder" (14). David's mother is his new colossus; his reality is confirmed between her legs, confirmed by the intensity of his attachment to her. Although *A Portrait of the Artist* initially records Stephen's perceptions of the world as gendered: "his mother had a nicer smell than his father" (7), the mother quickly fades as a shaper of Stephen's consciousness, her role displaced onto the women who become the artist's sexual and aesthetic muses. In contrast, David is like Paul Morel in D. H. Lawrence's *Sons and Lovers*, who rushes home to narrate the day's occurrences to his mother, as he thinks, "nothing was real until he told it to his mother." For Lawrence, as for Roth, the son's discourse needs the sympathetic ear of the mother.

This sympathy functions as narrative principle. Although David's consciousness is produced by his father's repressiveness (in Foucauldian fashion) as well as his mother's support, the early sections of the book establish the importance of the mother/son dyad that counteracts the sadistic carping of the father. David's consciousness is umbilically tied to maternal receptivity, as evidenced in his interior speech as well as the intimacy of their spoken dialogue. Although one is never free of the sense that this sympathy can silence if allowed to remain oceanic, the richness of David's consciousness depends on the enabling sympathy of his mother's voice and gaze, ear and eye. (Indeed, one can say that this ear and eye allow the narrative itself to continue, as if this receptive maternal audience were a surrogate for the reader, who follows David's course with all the attention of the mother.) For David, "reality" passes through the circuit of his love for his mother and hers for him. In the book, as in life, this is an enabling foundation; in the book, as in life, the child's is an exorbitant desire that can never be fulfilled:

"They will be coming soon," she said. They! He started in dismay. They were coming! Luter. His father. They! Oh! The lull of peace was over. He could feel dread rising within him like a cloud – as though his mother's words had been a stone flung on dusty ground. The hush and the joy were leaving him! Why did Luter have to come? (71)

David's internal weather materializes from these maternal gestures; the metaphors in the above passage capture the vulnerability of the ear that hears the sounds of rejection beneath ordinary statement. But this sensitivity is also nurtured by David himself, as he cultivates his own role as *audience* – overhearing adult speech (like the profoundly disturbing and mysterious dialogue between Bertha and Genya, which promises to disclose the secrets of the mother's body). The following record of David's consciousness reveals how his reality is constructed in this way, as he watches his mother react to his father's taunting jokes about Luter's wife hunting:

"All I hope is he doesn't blame my married happiness for his marriage!" He uttered the last words with a peculiar challenging emphasis.

115

David who was watching his mother as she stood above her husband serving him, saw her bosom swell up slowly as though responding to minute increments of pain, and then without response, exhale tautly her muted breath and look off blankly and resigned. David himself knew only one thing – that the relief Luter's absence afforded him was as sharp and fervent as a prayer, and that every wordless nerve begged never to see the man again. (115)

"(I pray thee ask no questions/this is the Golden Land)" – the injunction of the epigraph hangs over the narrative, as does the double meaning of the word "pray," whose politeness masks the intensity of the wish, the prayer, for deliverance, for refuge. David wordlessly watches the painful scene between his parents, experiencing his intense relief at Luter's absence with the fervor of a prayer. The mysterious gestures of adult drama represented here both inspire and reflect David's sense of powerlessness, as he feels himself suspended helplessly between divine wrath and salvation.

In a provocative essay on *Call It Sleep* entitled "Modernism in History, Modernism in Power," Bruce Robbins dismisses the force of the oedipal drama as a narrow, private form of the more crucial sense of social powerlessness of child and immigrant. "The child's stream of consciousness flows with such violence, one might say, because he cannot make the tap water flow at all [Robbins is referring to an early scene in which David cannot reach the faucet and must ask his mother for some water]. The world seems to break up into private fragments only because children – and immigrants, for the son's helplessness stands for that of the entire family – cannot control its public forces" (229). Robbins goes on to say in a footnote that "David's adored mother swells to mythic proportions in her son's eyes not because humankind is condemned to reenact the myth of Oedipus but because it is she who answers the call for water, who represents to her helpless child the awesome powers of the world 'behind the walls of a house' " (230n). But there is something too rapid about this leap over the familial to the social, for David's Yiddish-speaking gentle mother is unlikely to represent power outside the house, as Robbins claims – after the intimate eloquence of Mrs. Schearl's [translated] speech in her own domestic world, it is a shock to experience the comedy of her broken English when she speaks to the police. Hers is like the power of a Mrs. Ramsay in Virginia Woolf's *To the Lighthouse,* represented in her children's consciousness in the "august shape of a dome." It is mother's milk, so to speak, that nurtures these early sections of the novel, providing a source of enrichment. The mother salves the wounds inflicted by the father's maledictions and tries to shelter David from the pain inflicted in the strange world of the streets. But the sanctuary of the mother's language, ear, and body is itself a social assignment. As Deleuze and Guattari point out, the oedipal drama is the form in which the libido comes to consciousness in a larger circuit of social investments of all kinds.

What Robbins's view of the family drama also omits is the way Jewishness (not just immigrant powerlessness) inflects the emotional tone of the oedipal paradigm. Roth's use of the myth is very different from that of many of his modernist predecessors and contemporaries; in its freighted emotional register of curse and blessing it is far removed from a more anthropological and structural use of myth, such as T. S. Eliot's in *The Waste Land* or Ezra Pound's in the *Cantos.* Nor does *Call It Sleep* import the kind of generic psychoanalytic myth that Roth himself describes in an interview in which he insists that when he wrote *Call It Sleep,* he knew Freud only through osmosis: "I was aware [of Freud and psychology] only in a diffuse, general cultural way. I heard about these ideas and terms in my literary, intellectual group but never went to the discipline of studying it myself" (Lyons, 169). This popular Freudianism might have produced the narrow, too-familiar representation of family life that Robbins belittles, but this is not the Oedipus that Roth produces narratively. In its representation of the wounding father-son relationship, Roth's writing, like Franz Kafka's in his diaries, Bernard Malamud's in *The Assistant,* Saul Bellow's in *Seize the Day,* captures a particularly searing paternal relationship that is found again and again in the works of Jewish writers. The libido comes to consciousness for David in the heightened emotional drama of Old Testament curse and blessing. (Perhaps one could say that Roth's is a modernism that imports a more Jewish Freud.) At the same time, Roth's novel enacts literally the immigrant Jew's desire to seize

American instruments of power, to connect with a network of power running through and beyond the family.

In the two final chapters of the novel, the maternal and paternal powers of David's parents are represented in the circuit of larger systems of power in two ways. First, in the penultimate chapter (XXI) the narrative eroticizes the whole urban environment, creating not so much a symbol as a diagram of libido circulating through the universe. In this climactic chapter, in which narrative itself breaks down in the contrapuntal voicings of David's unconscious and the noises of the street, sexuality becomes both cosmic and technological, as David's desire and fixations are placed in a libidinous circuit figured by the electricity running through his body:

> *Power*
> *Power! Power like a paw, titanic power,*
> *ripped through the earth and slammed*
> *against his body and shackled him*
> *where he stood. Power! Incredible,*
> *barbaric power! A blast, a siren of light*
> *within him, rendering, quaking, fusing his*
> *brain and blood to a fountain of flame,*
> *vast rockets in a searing spray! Power!* (419)

This is the cosmic sexuality that deconstructs the opposition between nature and culture, David's body blasted by a storm of electricity. It is at once myth and schematic. Again, Deleuze and Guattari's revisionary notion of desire bears on Roth's novel:

But our 'object choice' itself refers to a conjunction of flows of life and of society that this body and this person intercept, receive, and transmit, always within a biological, social, and historical field where we are equally immersed or with which we communicate. The persons to whom our loves are dedicated, including the parental persons, intervene only as points of connection, of disjunction, of conjunction of flows whose libidinal tenor of a properly unconscious investment they translate. (293)

I would quarrel with the use here of the diminishing word "only" as applied to familial drama (and so, I think, would Roth), but the idea of desire as nomadic and migrant, as linking the circuit of the subject's libido to that of larger forces, wonderfully describes David's climactic epiphany. At first David's search for the source of power is cast in purely phallic terms; he throws his ladle into the "crack" as if assuming the mantle of his threatening and titanic father:

> *[O]nly the steely glitter on the*
> *tracks was in his eyes, fixed there like*
> *a brand, drawing him with cables as*
> *tough as steel. A few steps more and*
> *he was there, standing between the*
> *tracks, straddling the sunken rail.*
> *He braced his legs to spring, held*
> *his breath. And now the wavering point*
> *of the dipper's handle found the long,*
> *dark, grinning lips, scrapped, and*
> *like a sword in a scabbard –*
>
> *. . . . .*
> *Plunged! And he was running! Running.* (413–414)

Power is figured as phallic penetration of the inviting and grinning "lips" of the female body, which seduce with the promise of a new language. But nothing happens. "No light overtook him. . . . Only/ in his ears, the hollow click of iron/ lingered. Hollow, vain" (414). The consummation fails. In the final transfixing moment, however, the circuit of power passing through him arrests David, transforming him into both penetrator and penetrated:

> *The hawk of radiance raking him with*
> *talons of fire, battering his skull with*
> *a beak of fire, braying his body with*
> *pinions of intolerable light. And he*
> *writhed without motion in the clutch of*
> *a fatal glory, and his brain swelled*
> *and dilated till it dwarfed the galaxies*
> *in a bubble of refulgence – Recoiled, the*
> *last screaming nerve clawing for survival.* (419)

This is more Leda than Icarus, more a female body being ravished than a male body hammering out its desires, more a terrible, wounding, orgasmic annunciation than phallic triumph. David suffers Isaiah's purifying vision: "(Coal! And it was brighter than the/pith of lightning and milder than pearl,)" (430) in a figurative death that subsumes the gestures of self-assertion and self-annihilation.

After terrible agonistic hallucinations in which David confronts his father's threatening visage in the mirror (scenes which, as Brian McHale discusses in this volume, draw heavily on the "Circe" chapter of *Ulysses*), a maternal silence seals the patriarchal wrath in what itself threatens to return David to a womb of stillness:

> *(. . . But as*
> *if all eternity's caress were fused and*
> *granted in one instant. Silence)*
> . . . .
> *(struck that terrible voice upon the*
> *height, stilled the whirling hammer.*
> *Horror and the night fell away.* (430–431)

Yet the narrative passes beyond this pre-oedipal soothing that is tantamount to death. A new embryonic consciousness is born from this nothingness: "(A spiked star of pain of conscious-/ness burst within him)" (431). This new identity passes beyond the familial sphere of maternal blessing and paternal curse. Both the literally astonishing visage of the father that arrests David's gaze in the mirrors of his hallucinatory self-projections and the soothing maternal caress that threatens to still the narrative forever give way to an identity that is both wounded and restored. Like Odysseus's scar, David's star of pain signifies both wounding and healing.

The electrifying arrest of both David and the narrative in the contrapuntal poetry of Chapter XXI gives way to the final, deliberately anticlimactic chapter in which "ordinary" narrative resumes, though transformed. In the final anticlimactic chapter (XXII) in which narrative emerges after its shocking arrest, the voices of interne and policeman replace the thundering voice of the father:

"There you are, sonny! There you are!" The interne's reassuring drawl, reached him through a swirl of broken images. "You're not hurt. There's nothing to be scared about."

"Sure!" the policeman was saying beside him. (431)

Here we find Roth's second technique for revealing the oedipal pattern in its social locutions. In this final chapter, policeman and doctor supplant the father and mother as lawgiver and healer. The indifferent, impersonal American system of power intercedes into the charged psychic and spatial interior of the family, the interior which served as both threat and haven: "In the kitchen, he could hear the policeman interrogating his father, and his father answering in a dazed, unsteady voice" (437). " 'Put him down on the bed!' The interne motioned impatiently to the bed-room. 'And listen, Mister, will you ask her to stop screaming' " (435). The register of the mother's overprotective solicitations and the father's overzealous rage modulates to the ordinary, indifferent language of prescriptions and policeman's questions. " 'He's written down the name of some medicine for us to get,' " David's father tells his mother. " 'Sit there!' " he tells her as he prevents her from going to get the medicine. But we are told, "His peremptory tone lacked force as though he spoke out of custom, not conviction" (440).

The power of parental language, both maternal and paternal, seems diminished; the identity of the Jewish child is no longer spoken directly in Yiddish curses and blessings. " 'Sleepy, beloved?' " David's mother asks at the end of the novel, translating his English name, "David," into its Hebrew meaning. " 'Yes, Mama,' " he answers. But what follows is a slumber that seals the spirit and closes the narrative with a vision very different from the comfort his mother proffers in her characteristic way. "He might as well call it sleep," the narrator says, destabilizing the kind of soothing closure the mother wants to offer to her child – the phrase is repeated in the final paragraph to emphasize the provisional nature of this naming and accounting with which the narrative achieves closure. "It was only toward sleep that ears had power to cull again and reassemble the shrill cry, the hoarse voice, the scream of fear, the bells, the thick-breathing, the roar of crowds and all sounds that lay fermenting in the vats of silence and the past" (441). Sleep is a metaphor for the mixture of vision, hearing, and intense recollection that marks the penultimate section. Roth takes pains to distinguish the representation of speech from the arena of Freudian dream work. When David awakes, he thinks, "Then it wasn't a dream. Where had he been? What done? The light" (432) – "dream" is too fixed a word, suggesting a too-neat symbolic equivalent, a psychic purgation.[5] But occurring as it does strategically at the end of the novel and in its title, this metaphor offers a provisional and concessive summing up of the book itself; "sleep" is a figure for the culling and reassembly that is narrative retrospection. The provisional quality of this final naming ("call it sleep") extends to the act of narrative closure. The end of *Call It Sleep* does not refine a wounding experience into a beautiful aesthetic that somehow transforms the pain of existence; instead, it suggests what Hartman calls in his wonderfully suggestive essay "the emblematic product of an imaginative faith" (153), one which troubles as it lays to rest.

But the question of the power of language to lay pain to rest cannot be divorced from the different languages and dialects in which the text speaks memory. And here we return to the issue of the "smithy" in which the "conscience of the race" is created. Hana Wirth-Nesher points out that the multilingualism of Roth's novel (its use of Hebrew, Yiddish, Aramaic, and English) ties it to a tradition already existing within Jewish literature, even in ancient times (444). Loss and dislocation are endemic to this tradition; the Yiddish which functions as a Keatsian, unheard melody in the text is an emblem of this loss. As suggested by Eavan Boland's poem, "Mise Eire," this kind of loss is experienced in other immigrant or colonized traditions as well:

> a new language
> is a kind of scar
> and heals after a while
> into a passable imitation
> of what went before.
>
> (Eavan Boland, "Mise Eire")

Yet the pain of the loss of Yiddish underlying this "passable imitation" in Roth's novel is balanced, at least in part, by the rich possibilities of rediscovering Isaiah in the new world, Whitman's song with a Lower-East-Side intonation. It is important that David's epiphany and Roth's narrative are both punctuated by a cacophony of street voices; at the end of Chapter XX, it seems that these goading, daring voices inspire his vision:

The small sputter of words in his brain seemed no longer his own, no longer cramped by skull, but detached from him, the core of his surroundings. And he heard them again as though all space had compelled them and were shattered in the framing, and they boomed in his ears, vast, delayed and alien. (409)

In Roth's Jewish American version, prophecy is both a calling and a shouting, in a blend of the sublime and the mundane. In *Call It Sleep* the God of Isaiah is, as Stephen Dedalus says in *Ulysses*, a "shout in the street." It is appropriate to see David's visions as a Joycean epiphany of sorts, a moment of "sudden spiritual manifestation," as Stephen defines it in *Stephen Hero*, but it is crucial to retain the *dual* nature of Stephen's elaboration of this manifestation, which may be "in the vulgarity of speech or of gesture or in a memorable phase of the mind itself. He [Stephen] believed that it was for the man of letters to record these epiphanies with extreme care, seeing that they themselves are the most delicate and evanescent of moments" (211). Roth's Joyce is a Joyce who fuses the vulgarity and the memorable phase. David's orgasmic enlightenment (which, as I have already pointed out, is deliberately written beyond in the final anticlimactic chapter) is at the same time witnessed from the outside by a myriad of ordinary gazes:

The street paused. Eyes, a myriad of eyes, gay or sunken, rheumy, yellow or clear, slant, blood-shot, hard, boozy or bright swerved from their tasks, their play, from faces, newspapers, dishes, cards, seidels, valves, sewing machines, swerved and converged. (419)

Hartman says of modernist poetics that it "gave up nothing of literature's bardic daring despite the doubts and subversions of enlightened thought" (145). "One might as well call it sleep. He shut his eyes" reads the final line of Roth's novel, a modernist ending that concedes the imperfect nature of the logos and its inability to purify dialect. Nevertheless, closure follows its own concessive summoning up in the narrative – "He shut his eyes." Perhaps the most sadly ironic footnote to the sealing slumber of the final section of Roth's novel is its unfortunate efficacy: For more than fifty years the slumber continued, sealing up the words and the wounds of Roth's experience.

NOTES

1 I borrow this description from Geoffrey Hartman's "Words and Wounds," a very suggestive chapter of *Saving the Text* that resonates through my discussion of Roth (145).

2 See Hana Wirth-Nesher's discussion of this mediation in the "Afterword" to the 1991 edition.

3 At the 1981 James Joyce conference in Albuquerque, New Mexico, Roth spoke of Joyce's powerful and daunting influence; *Ulysses*, he said, liberated novelists to see that one's subject could come from one's own neighborhood. As he put it in an interview with Bonnie Lyons in 1985, "What I gained was this awed realization that you didn't have to go anywhere at all except around the corner to flesh out a literary work of art – given some kind of vision, of course" (168). In a 1984 essay included in *Shifting Landscape*, however, he invokes Joyce as a powerful model but says Joyce turned his "dazzling virtuosity" into "a mausoleum to lie in" (267).

4 Albert Schearl's substitution of this word "kaddish" for David's name seems to signal a resentment at the son's longevity and ultimate replacement of the father. How differently the nickname is inflected in Kazin's description of his own father's use, curiously enough, of the same name for his son: "[H]e would shyly but with unmistakable delight introduce me around as his *Kaddish*. 'Meet my *Kaddish*.' Meet the son and heir who will see me to the grave and say the last prayer over me" (*New York Jew*, 287).

5 See Wayne Lesser for an extended discussion of the "referential indetermination" of this metaphor (168). Lesser says "The final metaphor does not allow for the prefiguration of the world in object-to-object terms; it does not sustain the belief that language can be deployed to grasp the nature of things in figurative terms" (172).

WORKS CITED

Ballou, Robert O. Review of *Call It Sleep.* In *New Masses,* 12 Feb. 1935: 27.

Boland, Eavan. "Mise Eire." From *Outside History: Selected Poems, 1980–1990.* New York: W. W. Norton & Company, 1990, 78–79.

Deleuze, Gilles, and Felix Guattari. *Anti-Oedipus: Capitalism and Schizophrenia.* Trans. Robert Hurley, Mark Seem, and Helen R. Lane. Minneapolis: University of Minnesota Press, 1981.

Hartman, Geoffrey. "Words and Wounds." *Saving the Text: Literature, Derrida, Philosophy.* Baltimore: Johns Hopkins University Press, 1981, 118–157.

Joyce, James. *A Portrait of the Artist as a Young Man.* London: Penguin Books, 1976.

Joyce, James. *Stephen Hero.* New York: New Directions, 1944.

Kazin, Alfred. Introduction. From *New York Review of Books,* reprinted in *Call It Sleep.* New York: The Noonday Press – Farrar, Straus and Giroux, 1991, ix–xx.

Kazin, Alfred. *New York Jew.* New York: Alfred A. Knopf, 1978.

Kazin, Alfred. *Starting Out in the Thirties.* Boston: Little, Brown, 1962.

Lawrence, D. H. *Sons and Lovers.* Middlesex, England: Penguin Books Ltd., 1981.

Lesser, Wayne. "A Narrative's Revolutionary Energy: The Example of Henry Roth's 'Call It Sleep.' " *Criticism* 23.2 (Spring 1981): 155–176.

Levenson, Michael. *Modernism and the Fate of Individuality: Character and Novelistic Form from Conrad to Woolf.* Cambridge: Cambridge University Press, 1991.

Lyons, Bonnie. "Appendix." In *Henry Roth: The Man and His Work.* New York: Cooper Square Publishers, Inc., 1976, 159–176.

Michaels, Leonard. "The Long Comeback of Henry Roth: Call It Miraculous." *New York Times Book Review* 15 Aug. 1993: 3–21.

Pecora, Vince. *Self and Form in Modern Narrative.* Baltimore: The Johns Hopkins University Press, 1989.

Robbins, Bruce. "Modernism in History, Modernism in Power," in Robert Kiely, ed., *Modernism Reconsidered.* Cambridge: Harvard University Press, 1983, 229–245.

Roth, Henry. *Call It Sleep.* New York: The Noonday Press – Farrar, Straus and Giroux, 1991.

Roth, Henry. *Shifting Landscape: A Composite, 1925–1987.* Mario Materassi, ed. Philadelphia: Jewish Publication Society, 1987.

Seem, Mark. Introduction to Deleuze and Guattari, *Anti-Oedipus*, xv–xxiv.

Wirth-Nesher, Hana. Afterword. "Between Mother Tongue and Native Language in *Call It Sleep*." Reprinted in *Call It Sleep*. The Noonday Press – Farrar, Straus and Giroux, 443–462.

Woolf, Virginia. *To the Lighthouse*. San Diego: Harcourt, Brace, Jovanovich, 1927.

"A world somewhere, somewhere else."

Language, Nostalgic Mournfulness, and Urban Immigrant Family Romance in *Call It Sleep*

WERNER SOLLORS

> Despising
> For you the city, thus I turn my back;
> There is a world elsewhere.
> Shakespeare, *Coriolanus* III.iii

> Only at nightfall, aethereal rumours
> Revive for a moment a broken Coriolanus
> T. S. Eliot, *The Waste Land*

The solution to my difficult situation seemed to be that "world elsewhere" of Coriolanus, the world of the arts, the world of art, in which Eda Lou Walton figures so much because she gave me the opportunity to enter the world of the artist of that time, the detached artist.

> Henry Roth to Mario Materassi

The second novel . . . would have treated of just that theme: the youth's search for the world elsewhere: how the immigrant urchin who had lost the primacy of his ghetto haven and jettisoned faith . . . won another haven, a superior one, he thought, in the world of letters, in the world of art. Not to be. Shortcircuited. Aborted.

> Henry Roth, "Itinerant Ithacan"

I am grateful to Hana Wirth-Nesher for inviting me to write this essay, Tanya Ponton and Breda O'Keeffe for their energetic and resourceful research assistance, to Steve Love at the Hilles Library, Harvard University, to the Interlibrary Loans Office at the Zimmerman Library, University of New Mexico, to William M. Roberts at the University Archive of the University of California at Berkeley, to Thomas Berman at the University Archives of New York University, to Nancy Kandoian, Map Collections, and Stephen Crook, Henry W. and Albert A. Berg Collection, both at the New York Public Library, for their help in finding sources, to Daniel Aaron, Sacvan Bercovitch, Jules Chametzky, Dorrit Cohn, Jennifer Fleischner, Oscar Handlin, Karl Kroeber, Mario Materassi, Joel Porte, Marc Shell, and Doris Sommer for discussions and suggestions, to the Clark Fund at Har-

HENRY Roth's novel *Call It Sleep* (1934) has been justly praised as a twentieth-century masterpiece. Yet it has also been enmeshed in confusing categorizations. The novel was written by a young communist and was part of the controversies surrounding proletarian art; yet it was appreciated at a time when modernist experimentation seemed no longer compatible with communism.[1] It was developed with evident psychoanalytic interest by an author who claimed not to have read Freud at the time of the novel's publication.[2] Authored by an immigrant from Polish Galicia (belonging to Austria-Hungary at the time of his immigration), the book was not easily viewed as part of general American modernism, since ethnicity and modernism are often taken to be antithetical terms. And although thematically a part of "immigrant fiction," a fact that would place Roth in the company of such ethnic writers as Anzia Yezierska or Michael Gold,[3] *Call It Sleep* may actually have closer affinities with modern poetry and experimental prose.[4]

It is understandable that the formally innovative novel by a Jewish immigrant would receive much attention for its ethnic themes on the one hand and its modernism on the other; what I should like to do here, however, is to take a fresh look at *Call It Sleep* as an outstanding example of their fusion into "ethnic modernism." The novel conveys literary life to the concept of the "second generation" in the interwar period in the United States, precisely because of the author's refusal to go for the narrowly authentic, the typical, and the ethnically representative appeal, making the book part of "interface literature." I focus on language, the prologue, second-generation family romance, Chapter XXI of "The Rail," and on Roth's association with the anthropologist and poet Eda Lou Walton, to whom *Call It Sleep* was dedicated. Some observations on the little studied manuscript of the novel are also made throughout, mostly in the notes.

vard University for research support, to Lauren Gwin for proofreading and comparing the quoted excerpts with the text, to James Berman, Andreas Karatsolis, and Irit Manskleid-Makowsky for their excellent papers and theses, and to Alide Cagidemetrio for extended explorations of Roth territory.

"Wot's dot – rosary – . . . Can I have?": Unstable language and mediation

In praising *Call It Sleep*, Robert Alter stated: "I see nothing in the conception or execution of this extraordinary book that could not be readily transferred to a novel about a family from some other immigrant group."[5] More pointedly, Stephen Adams deplored the fact that *Call It Sleep* has become "pigeonholed as a 'Jewish novel,'" so is not seen as "the essential American novel."[6] Adams opposed Leslie Fiedler's celebration of the novel as "a *specifically* Jewish book, the best single book by a Jew about Jewishness written by an American, certainly through the thirties and perhaps ever."[7] Going even further in Fiedler's direction, M. Thomas Inge argued that the novel's greatness stems precisely from what keeps *Call It Sleep* from being universal; it succeeds because of "its literal accuracy and fidelity to an experience which only a few Jews who have lived a similar experience can fully appreciate."[8] Who *are* the implied readers of *Call It Sleep?*

Hana Wirth-Nesher has shown how important Roth's language is in approaching this question. Roth, like "all writers dealing with a multilingual and multicultural reality," had to devise certain strategies in order to represent "foreignness." Among Roth's preferred choices is the aesthetic method of creating the illusion for general American readers that they are reading a *translation* – thus Yiddish, although it may be "home" for the characters, can be "an alien language for the reader." But is the implied reader always *expected* to be Jewish or know Yiddish or Hebrew or Aramaic? No, but "one does have to be familiar with Jewish culture to understand all of the motifs and to appreciate the artistic pattern."[9] The most intricate part of the pattern, the ending of the book, shows, Wirth-Nesher concluded, that to assimilate is to become the "other," or, in this case, to become English-speaking and to use Christian symbolism. I should like to extend Wirth-Nesher's argument – which she convincingly developed in a detailed and nuanced reading of language and biblical contexts, both Jewish and Christian – in order to account for certain other elements in *Call It Sleep*.

129

It is true that more than a few phrases of Yiddish and Hebrew are left untranslated in the novel, and that a pervasive and characteristic linguistic strategy of the book is represented by the sentences: " 'And this is the Golden Land.' She spoke in Yiddish" (6). This posits the narrator as multilingual if not omniscient, and the reader as one who needs the narrator's mediation in order to understand the characters' original language, lost in English translation. Yet it is striking in many instances in the novel that the narrator does not provide information to the reader in any systematic fashion, so that no stable relationship between "English" narrator and "Yiddish" characters is sustained. Let us start with Genya's reference to the Golden Land that echoes the mysterious motto of the "Prologue" – *(I pray thee ask no questions / this is that Golden Land).* In their combination, the opening reference to the "Golden Land" and the English sentence Genya really speaks in Yiddish suggest that there is a world made accessible by the narrator-as-translator but not fully recuperable in the medium of the English-language novel that constitutes the only text we have. The "Golden Land" is not mystifyingly obscure – a commonplace, it resonates with the image of the New World as Eldorado and with Emma Lazarus's "golden door" – but it seems to come from a specific origin (*that* Golden Land) that the reader is made to believe is obvious but that is withheld.[10] Roth may thus be said to reveal and hide at the same time and the narrator does not often – or at least not always – use his powers to intervene in order to make ultimate determinations and clarifications.

When he does intervene, it is with the rhetorical gesture of immigrant literature in which linguistic terms, names, religious beliefs, or specific customs are explained to readers who are thereby pushed into the role of outsiders. This is an eternal problem in ethnic literature with multiple audiences: How much can a writer take for granted, and how much does he have to explain without alienating or boring those readers who might not need such explanations? If the information is incorporated into the text it may seem redundant to many readers and run against the aesthetic principle of economy. As an alternative, footnotes or a glossary sometimes explain the vocabulary with-

out interrupting the narration or putting off the *cognoscenti*. The
first two volumes of Roth's second novel, *Mercy of a Rude Stream,*
A Star Shines Over Mt. Morris Park (1994) and *A Diving Rock on the*
Hudson (1995), contain such a glossary, whereas the first novel
incorporates *some* linguistic explanations into the text. In *Call It*
Sleep, Roth's general form of narration is derived from Abraham
Cahan's choice to represent the Jewish immigrants' Yiddish as
good English – for Roth a highly stylized language – and their
English as broken English, full of Yiddishisms.[11] This procedure
suggests an inner world of richness and lyrical expression, a full
range of feelings and words that might remain hidden to an
English-only reader were it not for the narrator's mediation. If
applied exclusively, this strategy would not seem to require the
explanation of many specifically Jewish terms since the most
"Jewish" world could then be representable by translation into
the fullest range of "literary English." In the "broken English"
sections, however, many Yiddish words do enter into the text, at
times with the humorous effect of a pun. Thus Aunt Bertha
relates her experience with a dentist:

I am going to lose six teeth. And of the six teeth, three he called
"mollehs." Now isn't this a miracle? He's going to take away a "molleh"
and then he's going to make me "molleh." (211–212)

Irit Manskleid-Makowsky pointed out that although the American reader is not excluded from this passage, since his experience
partly resembles that of David, the reader who knows Yiddish
reaches an additional level of understanding, since the English
equivalent of "molleh" ("molar") is here juxtaposed with the
Yiddish term "moil," denoting "a mouth" or "complete, full." By
pulling her tooth, Dr. Goldberg would make Bertha whole. The
joke is compounded by the narrator's comment that David does
not know "what 'molleh' might mean in English" though he
thinks he knows that in Yiddish the word has "something to
do with circumcision." This misunderstanding of "molleh" as a
reference to the "moil" who performs circumcisions[12] confers on
this unexplained passage a triple level of meanings that give the
English reader an understanding partly superior to David's but
also significantly less complete than the narrator's – or Bertha's.

Yet on other occasions Roth's narrator does offer some translations, and he does not fear to interrupt the narration (especially for the "knowledgeable" reader) by offering them as appositions, by "doubling" the original so to speak. This is sometimes the case in bilingual punning, and at times in confrontation with Christianity. There is, for example, another pun Bertha brings home from the dentist, which centers on two possible readings of the word "kockin" as English "cocaine" and Yiddish "to shit." Here the narrator explains the apparent paradox that in America "kockin" "will clear the mouth of pain" (211).[13] Similarly, the grocery man's exclamation "Christmas. Jesus Crotzmich" (262) might have stood alone as a Yiddish in joke, or as a hardly visible and unobtrusive signpost suggesting that English is not the whole world or that a Yiddish- (or German-) speaking reader would get more out of the text, although the English reader might also intuit that "Crotzmich" constitutes some sort of ironic comment on "Christmas." But the narrator – speaking through David's interior monologue – goes on to explain it as follows: "Crotzmich means scratch me. Jesus scratch me. Funny." In such instances the implied reader would seem to be English-speaking, since a Yiddish reader would already have gotten the joke. (How would such passages translate into a Yiddish edition of *Call It Sleep*?) Such explanations may also, however, make the reader search for meanings in many other names and words that are *not* translated, such as the family name Schearl which means "scissor" in Yiddish (and hence evokes circumcision), or Rabbi Pankower's first name Yidel which translates as "little Jew."[14]

This positioning of the text toward "outsiders" is even more apparent in Chapter VIII, "The Rail," when David "explains" things Jewish to his admired Polish-American and Catholic friend Leo Dugovka whom he considers part of a "rarer, bolder, more carefree world" and who has a "glamour about him" (414). David is trading acceptance by the fearless and "superior" Leo in return for describing Jewish ritual items as funny – even though Leo debases the Jewish sacred to the level of profanity.

When Leo had asked him whether Jews wore amulets on their persons, David had described the "Tzitzos" that some Jewish boys wore under their shirts, and the "Tfilin", the little leather boxes, he had seen men strap around their arms and brows in the synagogue – had described them, hoping that Leo would laugh. He did. And even when Leo had said of the "Mezuzeh", the little metal-covered scroll that all Jews tacked on the door-posts above their thresholds – "Oh! Izzat wotchuh call 'em? Miss oozer? Me ol' lady tore one o' dem off de door w'en we moved in, and I busted it, an' cheez! It wuz all full o' Chinee on liddle terlit paper – all aroun' an' aroun'." David had not been hurt. He had felt a slight qualm of guilt, yes, guilt because he was betraying all the Jews in his house who had Mezuzehs above their doors; but if Leo thought it was funny, then it was funny and it didn't matter. He had even added lamely that the only things Jews wore around their necks were camphor balls against measles, merely to hear the intoxicating sound of Leo's derisive laugh. (414–415)[15]

The exchanges between Leo and David are not symmetrical, but neither is the novel's linguistic situation of mediation and explanation. What is done for the reader who might not know "Mezuzeh," "Tzitzos," and "Tfilin" (all are put in quotation marks in the text – as is bar mitzvah [293–294]) is not done for the reader who might not know a rosary, perhaps because the reader – here imagined Christian or Catholic – is expected to know it.[16] Leo's scapular, too, though briefly described, is rendered only in his dialect (413, 439); and when David asks Leo for the "scappiler" (by pointing at it),[17] he is offered a rosary instead. Although David now asks, "Wot's dot – rosary – [. . .]?" (440), and some non-Catholic readers might be asking the same question, the narrator – unlike the case of the Mezuzeh – does not attach an instant explanation by apposition, though he does insert one a few pages later.[18] Leo "pulled out a broken string of two-sized black beads near one end of which a tiny cross dangled with a gold figure raised upon it like the one on the wall" (444). Leo adds that "it's real holy."

If many passages seem made for the English-speaking linguistic outsider, others clearly imply or favor a polyglot reader, not only when Hebrew or Yiddish phrases or sentences are given without translation, but also in the "English" text. For example, a linguistic insider may be invited on many occasions to read *through* the English text for the original that is buried but apparently not completely lost in translation. Irving Howe has illuminated such readings with the example of Genya questioning why David had not kissed her with the words "There! Savory, thrifty lips!" (229). Howe writes that this

> phrase may seem a bit "poetic" in English, but translate it into Yiddish – *Na! Geshmake, karge lipelakh!* – and it rings exactly right, beautifully idiomatic. Roth here continues the Jewish tradition of bilingualism, but in a strangely surreptitious way, by writing portions of his book in one language and expecting that some readers will be able to *hear* it in another.[19]

The novel contains many other examples of this nature, among them Albert's repeated question, "Where is the prayer?" and Aunt Bertha's inquiry, "How fares a Jew?" (420). The Yiddish may just glow through the English, as in Albert's question, "Do you still ask?" (11), or in Genya's statement, "it grows late" (54). In other instances, Yiddish may or may not be implied when an unfamiliar or defamiliarized English phrasing calls attention to itself, for example in Bertha's colorful idiom: "Will you vomit up past shame?" and "Go talk to my buttocks!" (519), or in the rabbi's exclamations, "All buttocks have only one eye" and "May your brains boil over!" (289). Roth's method contributes much to the poetic quality of the novel, calls attention to the language itself, and creates the illusion among readers that such phrases as "that golden land" must refer to a Yiddish source.[20] Yet precisely this "poetic" quality also permitted Roth to insert many literary phrasings that had their origins in Anglo-American modernist aesthetics rather than in Yiddish: Thus he lets Bertha say, "A bath-tub is a bath-tub" (248), as if she were Gertrude Stein. Roth also alludes to Eliot's "Jugjugjugjugjugjug" (333), "unreal" city (383), or "heap" – Roth calls it "swirl" – "of broken images" (586) of *The Waste Land*, invokes Joseph Conrad with the phrasing "heart of darkness" (582), or makes a Joycean pun as in the dialect rendition of "a whore master" as "a hura mezda" (562) in order ironically to suggest the Zoroastrian god of light, Ahuramazda.[21] When Aunt Bertha, in her enthusiasm for shopping in America and in her disappointment in the Schearls' bathtub, repeats the phrase, "Blessed is this golden land" (205) and says, "I thought when I came to this golden land, there would be something better to bathe in than a box full of stony burrs" (247), Roth may want the reader to recall the full myth of the Eldorado, originally a king who resembles a gold statue because he had gold dust blown on him and who bathes in a lake that turns golden – a tale applied to the New World.[22] Roth's invented motto of the "golden land" may allude not only to Yiddish poetry but also to Sir James Frazer's *Golden Bough* (1890).[23]

To go back to the example of Yiddish, one may distinguish quite heterogeneous approaches to suggesting linguistic differences in the novel. They may be represented as Yiddish, with or without English translation or explanation; or they may be represented in idiomatic or defamiliarized English (the central linguistic fiction of the novel); these modes of representation may also clash. For example, when Bertha offers David, in English, "a liddle suddeh vuddeh," he responds, "No, I don't want it" – and the narrator adds: "He answered in Yiddish. For some reason he found himself preferring his aunt's native speech to English" (419). In cases such as this, Roth – although adhering to the logic of his method – seems to be pushing the fiction of language representation to its limit, as the switch from the offer of "suddeh vuddeh," a defamiliarization of "soda water," to a perfectly intelligible standard English response is declared to be a switch from "English" to "Yiddish" (represented as English).[24]

Roth thus uses at least two methods of "translating" – one aiming for euphony in English, making the "strange" tongue familiar, and another making the tongue familiar to an English reader sound strange and, at times, strangely poetic. The linguistic situation is thus unstable, and the narrator, however much he may mediate here and there, is not a consistently positioned stabilizing center.

The corresponding instability of the implied reader is further compounded by the presence of other forms of bilingualism and code switching such as Hebrew/English (in the long excerpts from Isaiah 6 and Deuteronomy 32),[25] Aramaic mixed with Hebrew/Yiddish-rendered-as-English (in the *Chad Godyah* of Passover), Genya's and Bertha's "screen of Polish" (261) with the all-important word for love "lupka" (219)[26] and David's Yiddish, or the Italian/Yiddish exchange between butcher and sweeper:

"Verstinkeneh Goy!" [. . .] "Sonnomo bitzah you! I fix" [. . .] "You vanna push me? [. . .] I'll zebreak you het." "Vai a fanculo te! [. . .] Come on! Jew bast!" (328)

No explanations are offered here; and although a "general reader" might understand "Bambino! Madre mia" (572), this is less likely in the case of "Mannagia chi ti battiavo!" (327) or of Benny's words, "If I blyibm duh ywully ylyod, den he wonthye hilyt me so moyuch, myaytlybe" (488). As the narrator puts it, "In trying to divine Benny's meaning, one could forget all else" (488). Some passages of the novel may be inaccessible to readers of *any* linguistic background.[27]

The various linguistic situations do not always stabilize the point of view of the narrator and suggest to readers that, despite the intermittent acts of mediation, there remain unfathomable and mysteriously undecoded depths of language. After all, the novel represents a world in which a *child*[28] is being socialized, and of which that child has to make sense. What complicates the role of language in *Call It Sleep* is precisely the fact that the novel not only highlights linguistic divides between established adult languages with relatively fixed glossaries, but also follows the process of language acquisition through a complicated system of what Naomi Diamant has discussed under the useful terms decoding and encoding[29] that David develops. The narrator sometimes withholds generally available terms in order to present the child's particular idiom that is built up by analogies and associations. In contemplating the omnivorousness of non-Jews, David thinks of the following:

Ham. [. . .] And chickens without feathers in boxes, and little bunnies in that store on First Avenue by the elevated. In a wooden cage with lettuce. And rocks, they eat too, on those stands. Rocks all colors. They bust 'em open with a knife and shake out ketchup on the snot inside. Yich! and long, black, skinny snakes. Goyim eat everything . . . (303)[30]

The context permits us to decode "snot" in "rocks" as David's personal term for "oyster" (a word withheld by the narrator in order to approximate David's consciousness), just as the "snakes" are not identified as "eels."

The linguistic conventions governing fictional literature further complicate the language of the text so that tense variations may be solecisms – as in "I'm losted" (126) – or specific to the narrative form of the novel – as in the sentence, "Tomorrow came" (148).[31] In stream-of-consciousness ruminations it may be hard to determine what is sociolinguistic reference and what is aesthetic coding.

Nor is the alternation between narration and interior monologue always coded in an identical fashion. Some doubling in the text is, for example, due to the strategy of letting "objective" and "subjective" passages complement each other. This is the case in the memorable scene in which David sees his mirror image appear and disappear in shop windows:

Only his own face met him, a pale oval, and dark, fear-struck, staring eyes, that slid low along the windows of the stores, snapped from glass to glass, mingled with the enemas, ointment-jars, green globes of the drug-store – snapped off – mingled with the baby clothes, button-heaps, underwear of the dry-goods store – snapped off – with the cans of paint, steel tools, frying pans, clothes-lines of the hardware store – snapped off. A variegated pallor, but pallor always, a motley fear, but fear. Or he was not.

– On the windows how I go. Can see and ain't. Can see and ain't. And when I ain't, where? In between them if I stopped, where? Ain't nobody. No place. Stand here then. BE nobody. Always. Nobody'd see. Nobody'd know. Always. Always? No. Carry – yes – carry a looking glass. Teenchy weenchy one, like in pocket-book, Mama's. Yea. Yea. Yea. Stay by house. Be nobody. Can't see. Wait for her. Be nobody and she comes down. Take it! Take looking-glass out, Look! Mama! Mama! Here I am! Mama, I was hiding! Here I am! But if Papa came. Zip, take away! Ain't! Ain't no place! Ow! Crazy! Near! I'm near! Ow! (514–515)

The vivid and rhythmic narration clarifies the monologue that follows and that makes the reader care about how David is experiencing the loss of his self-image.[32]

Call It Sleep also gives us many social data that connect the feelings of young David with historical and social forces. Although Roth's goal seems to be to deepen the sociologically oriented precursor texts of ethnic literature by complicating the linguistic universe and by focusing on a single child's experience, and although he has stated explicitly that the materials of the novel were not put together "in order to give you a picture of the East Side,"[33] the narrative does call attention to the specific historical moment and cultural context in which its world is set, starting with the prologue.

Prologue at Ellis Island

The prologue is set in 1907, a peak year for immigration during which more than 1.28 million people came through Ellis Island. The steamer is named *Peter Stuyvesant* – after the Dutch governor who attempted to prohibit the immigration of the "deceitful race" of Jews to New Amsterdam in 1654 – and it is the last boat leaving Ellis Island on a Saturday afternoon in May.[34] Roth soon moves to the familiar rhetorical tradition of rendering a panoramic immigrant arrival scene that is somewhat unusual, however, in listing "the joweled close-cropped Teuton, the full-bearded Russian, the scraggly-whiskered Jew, and among them Slovack peasants with docile faces, smooth-cheeked and swarthy Armenians, pimply Greeks, Danes with wrinkled eyelids" (3–4). Roth's *pars pro toto* of the body parts alternates with inanimate objects and with names designating countries of origin – so that the three elements begin to interact and destabilize the national identity of the past without blending into the new category "American." This catalogue is a variation of a rhetorical tradition of Ellis Island scenes. Edward Steiner, for example, described the arrival of

Slavic women with no finery except their homespun, rough, tough and clean; carrying upon their backs piles of feather-beds and household utensils. Strong limbed men followed them in the picturesque garb of their native villages; Slovaks, Poles, Roumanians, Ruthenians, Italians, and finally, Russian Jews.[35]

Roth takes this tradition a step further by choosing "untypical" physical characteristics ("pimply Greeks"), by focusing on the end of the day when the immigrant march has already passed by, and by offering a negative catalogue of what the family on which he focuses does *not* carry: "no sheets tied up in huge bundles, no bulky wicker baskets, no prized feather beds, no boxes of delicacies, sausages, virgin-olive oils, rare cheeses" (5). This family will not leave typical objects for the Ellis Island museum.

The father, mother, and child are introduced as a family first, while the restrained third-person narrator closely observes their clothes: but instead of guessing a country of origin, the narrator surmises that the man must have sent American clothes to his newly arrived wife. Only the child's "outlandish" blue straw hat with a polka dot ribbon (5, 6, 10, 11, 12) suggests something "foreign" (5). Adopting the angle of an old woman selling oranges and of two smoking men in overalls, the narrator almost implies that everything observed so far has not been the full truth: "The truth was there was something quite untypical about their behavior." In sorting out their untypicality, the narrator goes through ethnically typified meeting scenes:

The most volatile races, such as the Italians, often danced for joy, whirled each other around, pirouetted in an ecstasy: Swedes sometimes just looked at each other, breathing through open mouths like a panting dog; Jews wept, jabbered, almost put each others [A: other's] eyes out with the recklessness of their darting gestures; Poles roared and gripped each other at arms length as though they meant to tear a handful of flesh; and after one pecking kiss, the English might be seen gravitating toward, but never achieving an embrace. But these two stood silent, apart. (5–6)

The narrator separates the story of this family from any ethno-typicality, defusing possible attacks on the book for presenting unpleasant or sordid aspects of Jewish life[36] and positioning *Call It Sleep* against the optimistic, and even enthusiastic tradition of writing up immigration scenes.

The stylistic equivalent of the focus on the family is dialogue in which we learn the names of father and son (Albert and

David), though significantly *not* that of the mother (Genya).[37] More of their story begins to emerge, accounting for at least one source of the man's anger – his wife did not recognize him and, in paying their fares, had given the child's correct age, though a lie apparently would have cut the fare in half. The phrase "brat's right age" (8) foreshadows Albert's anxiety about paternity. They pass the Statue of Liberty – such a standard feature of immigrant literature that Emma Goldman invented a sentimental arrival scene of teary-eyed rapture at the Statue's emergence from the mist, in her autobiography, *Living My Life* (1931), even though she had arrived in America before the Statue of Liberty was erected. In *Call It Sleep* it is described quite untypically:

And before them, rising on her high pedestal from the scaling swarmy brilliance of sunlit water to the west, Liberty. The spinning disk of the late afternoon sun slanted behind her, and to those on board who gazed, her features were charred with shadow, her depths exhausted, her masses ironed to one single plane. Against the luminous sky the rays of her halo were spikes of darkness roweling the air; shadow flattened the torch she bore to a black cross against flawless light – the blackened hilt of a broken sword. Liberty. (10)

This defamiliarization of the silhouetted Statue – only Franz Kafka's *Amerika* deforms Lady Liberty in a similar fashion – contains some of the key terms of the novel: brilliant light, the raised broken hilt of a menacing sword, and the cross. Whereas Mary Antin had helped to redefine the official meaning of Liberty to stand for a welcome to immigrants, Roth casts her as the war god Ares or the angel with the flaming sword ready to drive humans out of paradise.[38]

The prologue prepares the reader for a novel that does not follow this opening, though it significantly establishes a crossing, a migration, as the first action of the book. Roth stated that he added the prologue only after finishing the novel, because he felt "the need to introduce it, to put it into its historical context, and in a formal sense to prepare for the ending. . . . In its externalized treatment, the Prologue prepares for the externalization of the climax."[39] The bulk of the novel lies between these two points and it is very much focused on the internal.

"A World Somewhere, Somewhere Else"

Immigrant Nostalgia and the Second Generation

What follows the prologue is like a close-up after a crowd scene. It is four years later, and from the perspective of David's height, Mama looks "as tall as a tower" (15), evoking the view of the Statue of Liberty of the prologue. The mother is described as representing physical closeness and intimacy by the "faint familiar warmth and odor of her skin and hair" (17), but the father is seen in more grotesque or surrealistic but menacing close-ups: "He was pale, grim. The fine veins in his nose stood out like a pink cobweb" (24); or, later, "The ominous purple vein began to throb on his temple" (198); or, "always the thin inscrutable mouth, always the harsh pride of taut nostrils, heavy lidded eyes" (371).

David can hardly be considered "representative" of any social stratum. Yet perhaps because of his exceptional qualities – he is sensitive to a fault, fearful, dreamy, and easily traumatized – he also becomes an unusually rich center of consciousness that confronts the contradictory forces surrounding a second-generation immigrant location. Thus little David finds himself in a world that "had been created without thought of him" (15). This observation refers to the fact that the kitchen faucet can only be reached by adults, but it marks David's symbolic location, too.

David grows up in a situation of nearly permanent cognitive dissonance and approaches the modern urban environment through the lens of fairy tales (*Puss in Boots* or *Hänsel and Gretel*), handed down stories of the Old World, rhymes and verses (Hickory Dickory Dock and *Chad Godyah*),[40] and the Bible. The particular problem for him is that the concretely remembered world of his parents is inaccessible so that he has to recombine generalizable parts of the parents' past and bits of the contradictory environment into which they have brought him.

The *choc* of the parents' migration experience distances (and alienates) David forever from the parents' references. This is apparent in the smallest details, for example the ditty "Waltuh, Waltuh, Wiuhlflowuh" (22) that Brownsville girls sing in the gutter:

The song troubled David strangely. Walter Wildflower was a little boy. David knew him. He lived in Europe, far away, where David's mother said he was born. He had seen him standing on a hill, far away. Filled with a warm, nostalgic mournfulness, he shut his eyes. Fragments of forgotten rivers floated under the lids, dusty roads, fathomless curve of trees, a branch in a window under flawless light. A world somewhere, somewhere else. (23)[41]

This passage articulates the second (or the first *American*) generation's difficulty with nostalgia. Where can David's nostalgia – here triggered by an American song – be directed when his own place of birth is available to him only through his mother's narration and not through concretely remembered sensual experience? The mother's warm and living body, the goal of David's oedipal yearnings, is also the physical space designating his origins, a space all the more important to David since he does not directly know his geographic place of birth. In the world of objects, David's "warm, nostalgic mournfulness" has only fragments as its *telos,* a hill, or a tree.[42] (It is indicative of Roth's stylistic self-consciousness that the sentence starting with the word "fragments" is itself followed by a sentence fragment.) Even when his mother gently chides him, her reference is to a world that has to remain inaccessible to David: "You're like those large bright flies in Austria that can fly backwards and forwards or hover in the air as though pinned there" (450). Yet there are no dragonflies in David's Brownsville and Lower East Side. Much of the past is lost to him, making his nostalgia mournful for that loss.

David cannot possibly absorb the whole worlds of Veljish or Tysmenicz that are transmitted to him only in parts and by reverberation. Reflecting on the meaning of Santayana's dictum that piety is "reverence for the sources of one's being," Roth once asked: "Are these *selected* sources of one's being, or all the sources?" (*Shifting Landscape* 235). In the context of *Call It Sleep,* that choice hardly exists: David has access only to highly selected fragments of forgotten rivers that he sees, or imagines he sees, when he closes his eyes. His "nostalgia" thus becomes, paradoxically, *forward* looking, directed away from concrete and local sensual impressions and toward transportable abstractions such as the "flawless light" that he ultimately seeks to find through electricity. His parents' memories surround David mostly as *words* – in a tongue that is increasingly giving way to the language of the family's new surroundings.[43] Thus David at times inserts into the mother's tales New World materials and English words that call attention to their incongruousness. For example, when Genya tells David a story about Gypsies and bears and says that "Sometimes these gypsies take a bear along with them wherever they go," David interrupts her with a telling question informed by his knowledge of the fairy tale, "The Three Bears."

"Do they eat porridge?" He had said the last word in English.
"What's porridge?"
"My teacher said it was oatmeal and farina, you give it to me in the morning."
"Yes, yes. You told me. But I'm not sure. I know they like apples. Still if your teacher –" (45)

The fully explained term "porridge" marks the limit of the mother's authority over her own story.[44] The interaction of mother and son shows that in the immigrants' world, the child may at times become the teacher of the mother. The mother carefully tries to support the teacher's authority as it goes beyond the mother's own linguistic horizon. Genya is thus forced to ask David the classic child's question: "What is porridge?" Even in the most idyllic exchanges between mother and son there are signs of intergenerational estrangement intensified by language differences.[45]

Genya tells David in a "scolding, bantering whisper" when he is not interested in meeting Bertha's suitor: "Aren't you just a pair of eyes and ears! You see, you hear, you remember, but when will you know?" (228). This evokes David's sensory fragmentation as well as a child's way of perceiving without generalizing.[46] Genya's question, "when will you know," may raise hope for an ultimate gaining of knowledge, but it also points to the possibility that David will not and can never "know" what his mother "knows." As Richard Rodriguez argued, "The child cannot have a life identical with that of his mother or his father. For the immigrant child this knowledge is inescapable."[47]

David is strangely attracted to and afraid of images associated with death. He asks his mother what people do when they die, and her answer, "They are cold; they are still. They shut their eyes in sleep eternal years," stimulates his fantasy: "*Eternal years. The words echoed in his mind. Raptly, he turned them over and over as though they had a lustre and shape of their own. Eternal years*" (85). In existential stories of the Old World, Genya provides David with the materials for his poetic construction that builds up toward the climax of the novel. He supplements images that are connected by contiguity – coffins and "eternal years" (86) – with others that are associated by sound and other forms of similarity (snow, tongs/zwank, confetti and carriages at a wedding).[48]

Roth's narrator early on makes use of the semantic field that will lead to the electric explosion at the end. Thus David bounds before his mother "electrified with relief" (138). Though David's relationship with his father is of a different order, Albert provides similar foreshadowings: David sees his father's right hand in "the electric circle of his vision" (105), and he feels that his father radiates "so fell, so electric a fury" that he is terrified (164) and senses "the terrific volcano clamped within" (166). And earlier, when David goes to pick up his father's belongings, Joe describes Albert's anger: "Holy Jesus, he looked like he wuz boinin' up. Didja see de rail he twisted wid his hands?" (26). This is followed by a reference to "David and Goliath" (27) that sets up the oedipal drama of son and father. The father appears to be an Abraham towering over an Isaac to be sacrificed, a Vulcan- or Thorlike God, or a John Henry figure at his workplace:[49]

He held a hammer in hand, he would have killed somebody. David could almost see him, the hammer raised over his head, his face contorted in terrific wrath, the rest cringing away. (28)

He may seem all-powerful to David. Yet Albert, the lord of hammer and whip, is actually both strong and weak. He is weak as a man in relation to Genya, impotent at times, and he permits himself to sound like David for a moment (144); he has to send his little son to get his pay from his former employer; he trusts

Joe Luter; his anger covers up his fear and sense of guilt – that ties David to a generational drama he has yet to decode, and in which David is defined as "the prayer" who will say Kaddish for, and hence survive, the father – or even become responsible for his father's death. Thus Albert introduces David to Luter with the words: "And that over there . . . is what will pray for me after my death" (32). David's association with Albert's death also summons violent rejections of the son by the father: "He's no son of mine! Would he were dead at my feet!" (107). And turning toward Genya in David's presence, Albert casts his son as a virtual parricide: "A butcher! And you're protecting him! Those hands of his will beat me yet! I know! My blood warns me of this son! This son!" (107).

The images of intergenerational violence are all the more striking since the father appears completely changed in conversation with Luter, when he expresses his own predicament as a migrant memorably and even lyrically:

I think when you come out of a house and step on the bare earth among the fields you're the same man you were inside the house. But when you step out on pavements, you're someone else. You can feel your face change.(34)

There is a difference between going outdoors from inside and migrating from Galicia to New York City. Through his conversations with Luter, Albert retraces his steps as a migrant back to a point of origin he believes he shares with Joe; bucolic shepherding scenes with cattle appear as his central image of the past. Luter is thus permitted into the house and becomes, in David's mind, the successful adult rival for Genya's affections. Talking about David and Albert in the child's presence, Luter provides fodder for David's family romance. He asks David the charged question, "Where did you get that white German skin?" (48).

Genya, we remember, did not bring any typical Old World objects to Ellis Island, and David's straw hat must long ago have disintegrated on the bottom of New York harbor. Yet both Genya and Albert incorporate into their New York home items of nostalgia that turn out to be charged with deeper meaning. This is something that David senses. Unconsciously, both parents attach specific meanings to exchangeable and "inauthentic" products they purchase to satisfy their nostalgic needs, and there is a strange parallelism in the aesthetic representations Albert and Genya choose.

For the mother, it is a ten-cent reproduction of a generic country scene that she hangs up and that significantly gives a name to one of the four books of the novel. Can "The Picture" "of a small patch of ground full of tall green stalks, at the foot of which, tiny blue flowers grew" evoke the aura of Veljish to Genya and David?

"I bought it on a pushcart," she informed him with one of her curious, unaccountable sighs. "It reminded me of Austria and my home. Do you know what that is you're looking at?"
"Flowers?" he guessed, shaking his head at the same time.
"That's corn. That's how it grows. It grows out of the earth, you know, the sweet corn in the summer – it isn't made by pushcart pedlars."
"What are those blue flowers under it?"
"In July those little flowers come out. They're pretty, aren't they? You've seen them, yes, you have, fields and fields of them, only you've forgotten, you were so young." (227)[50]

The mother-son dialogue marks the distance of the urban boy not only from the place of his mother's youth but from *any* countryside: He has forgotten the country and cannot even identify corn. David finds himself staring at the picture, searching for hidden meanings behind what was "only a picture of long green corn and blue flowers under it."

And she had said that he had seen it too, real ones, long ago in Europe. But she said he couldn't remember. So maybe he was trying to remember the real ones instead of the picture ones. But how? If – No. Funny. Getting mixed and mixed and – (250)

The picture constitutes David's opening to and veil over "real" memories. It also elicits Bertha's ironic question, "Are you starting a museum?" (249), whereas Albert would have preferred a picture of "something alive," for example, a "herd of cattle drinking such as I've seen in the stores. Or a prize bull with a shine to

his flanks and the black fire in his eyes" (252). The father ultimately gets something in this genre, a plaque with bull's horns
that has a more threatening effect on David:

> Before him on a shield-shaped wooden plaque, two magnificent horns
> curved out and up, pale yellow to the ebony tips. So wide was the span
> between them, he could almost have stretched his arms out on either
> side, before he could touch them. Though they lay there inertly, their
> bases solidly fastened to the dark wood, there pulsed from them still a
> suggestion of terrific power, a power that even while they lay mo-
> tionless made the breast ache as though they were ever imminent, ever
> charging. (404)

David recognizes what he thinks is a cow – not from life but from
pictures and from a movie he saw with Aunt Bertha. Genya
responds with a laugh, "A cow, but a he-cow!" She explains that
"it reminded him of the time when he took care of cattle," and
significantly, her eyes wander "to the picture of the corn flowers
on the wall" (404). Both parents thus establish an equivalence
between the two purchased items. David is affected by the horns
and contemplates them:

> Somehow he couldn't quite believe that it was for memory's sake only
> that his father had bought this trophy. Somehow looking at the horns,
> guessing the enormous strength of the beast who must have owned
> them, there seemed to be another reason. He couldn't quite fathom it
> though. (405)[51]

Family Romance and Bilateral Line of Descent

David's relationship to his parents' city-bought fetishes continues
his oedipal view of the laughing mother as land, summer,
beauty, and fertility, and the scowling father as enormous and
unfathomable animal power; yet Roth's fictionalization of David's predicament – the city boy does not recognize corn and
cannot tell a cow from a bull – also brings his aesthetic close to
Eda Lou Walton's observation about urban writers who are

> not intimate with the ritual of the seasons, with the gold-green and flag-
> red spring, with lush, leafy and slumbering summer, with the bravado of
> fire-lit autumn, nor with the long hush of snowy winter. . . . They

have no associations with the names of flowers even if they know the memorable names (and some of them have denied this).[52]

Hence urban artists and immigrants may become interested in "country" as an abstraction. They may, for example, embrace anthropology as a way of understanding past folkways *in general,* and substitute a lost and mourned after realm of their own family experience by reading Frazer's *Golden Bough* and its comprehensive and global accounts of mistletoe, corn-spirit, magical coal, fertility and lightning myths from Galicia to Cambodia.[53]

Perhaps the very disconnection of second-generation immigrant urban writers from a specific rural life that they still heard about from their elders in fragmentary reverberation made these artists so receptive to the "mythical method" in art that T. S. Eliot advocated in his review of Joyce's *Ulysses.* The mythical method permitted artists to unite past and present and to incorporate the modern experience "within a larger whole of human experience throughout time" (as David Perkins put it),[54] letting modernism function as an equivalent for twentieth-century nostalgia, and as a perfect response to modernity, especially for urban immigrant writers. In fictionalizing David, Roth was clearly drawn to this response.

Bertha plays the *buffo* part in this drama, providing comic relief. Bertha is hardly uncritical of the New World, yet she prefers the restlessness and the noise of the city to the boredom of the country. In response to Genya's somber warning, "One grapples this land closer to one's self than it's worth," she retorts:

"Closer than it's worth? Why? True I work like a horse and I stink like one with my own sweat. But there's life here, isn't there? There's a stir here always. Listen! The street! The cars! High laughter! Ha, good! Veljish was still as a fart in company. Who could endure it? Trees! Fields! Again trees! Who can talk to trees? Here at least I can find other pastimes than sliding down the gable on a roof!" (201)

Bertha's phrase "still as a fart in company" certainly provides an alternative view to Genya's picture of Veljish. Both Genya and Bertha speak of America as the "golden land," but whereas for Genya this is a questioning term, for Bertha it can be the neophyte's enthusiastic blessing. In her hope to realize the myth of Eldorado, Bertha wishes to see America as the fulfillment of everything the immigrant could not be in the country of origin.[55] It is fitting that she is thrilled by shopping in New York and comments on the huge underpants she bought that "when I hold them at a distance upside down this way they look like peaks in Austria." For Bertha, purchasing cheap and large-sized underpants seems to take the emotional place of remembering the sublime view of the Carpathian mountains – and by bargain hunting in the American marketplace she can symbolically take revenge on the Old World class hierarchies: "Twenty cents, and I can wear what only a baroness in Austria could wear" (206).

Bertha and Genya are not only "worlds apart in temperament" (192), but in their combination they also suggest the ambivalence of immigrants toward embracing new environments and yearning for the past. Bertha lacks depth, yet she is the catalyst who makes Genya speak about her past secret. For Genya corn is associated with the romantic figure of Ludwig, the Christian organist with whom she was in love but who spurned her before she married Albert. When Ludwig gets married, Genya watches the wedding procession, as she confides to Bertha: "I hid in the corn-field nearby. [. . .] I felt empty as a bell till I looked at the blue cornflowers at my feet. They cheered me. That was the last I saw of him I think" (271). Genya has substituted an image of beauty for an experience of pain and loss and she repeats the substitution when she buys the picture. This lends meaning to her unaccountable sighs. David, who overhears the conversation, senses a connection though he does not get the full meaning (271). Genya's corn story also provides a link with the song of Walter Wildflower and with David's straw hat, and becomes part of his fantasy material of imagining the "organist" not only as the mother's first lover but also as his real father, making him an illegitimate child, a "benkart" (273).

For Albert the specific meaning of cattle is the story of his guilt for his father's death: Although Albert could have saved him when he was gored by a bull, he did not lift a finger (530). No wonder David notices a speech hesitation, a hitch, whenever Albert says "my father" (148). Albert's sense of persecution

would seem to derive from that trauma of the past, and his guilt
for his father's death becomes fear of his own son, fear that
another "prayer" will continue the drama and become a
"butcher."

This heavily charged family drama is accentuated by David's
own guilt feelings connected with sexuality and betrayal of family and ethnic group to his non-Jewish peers. In his childish
beginnings with sexuality he experiences a fairy-tale-like double
bind in "playing bad" with Annie. These "dirty" sexual games
draw on family language and would require David to play the
"poppa" (64–65). David's quest is for the purification of the "dirt"
inherent in the family story, for an escape from the darkness of
the cellar and the closet to the world of light. In his friendship
with Leo Dugovka, David feels a "bond of kinship" (407). This
cross-ethnic kinship looks all the more glamorous to David since
it starts with a rooftop encounter that appeals to his visionary
side. David instantly worships the blond and blue-eyed boy (407,
410) who is four years older (416) and not afraid (413). Leo flies
kites, is daring, and, David thinks, "There was no end to Leo's
blessings – no father, almost no mother, skates" (411). (Skates
are associated by the rabbi with non-Jews [508].) Their bond is
based on David's weakness and stems from all the charged areas
of his young life including family, sex, and faith. It leads David
right back into the darkness of the cellar. He reaps the reward of
the rosary only for letting Leo "play bad" with David's cousin
Esther and witnessing this momentous event while pretending
not to care and exploring the "Big-little-big-little-little-little-big-
busted" beads of the rosary against the background of gurgles
and whines (478).

David's forward-looking nostalgia for light intensifies with the
experience of the whiteness of snow: "Their monotonous descent
gave him an odd feeling of being lifted higher and higher; he
went floating until he was giddy. He shut his eyes" (68). The
quest for "flawless light" (23) seems abstracted from Genya's
story of the light among trees (155–156) – which, since it may
have a Jewish origin, also marks an early counterpoint to Leo's
bragging that "Christchin light" is "way bigger [. . .] den Jew
light" (437). The religious schooling in the *cheder* also strengthens

his wish for a cleansing transformation of the profane into the sacred that would reenact the power of Isaiah's coal.[56] Reading the sacred text about the seraph's coal that can cleanse dirty lips (305) focuses David's energies onto his attempt to seek a vision, to find purification, and to provoke a crisis that will resolve his generational impasse, his religious needs, and fuse fragments of the past with modern technology as a secular substitute for transcendence. David has a vision of hypnotizing brilliance at the edge of the river:

In the molten sheen memories and objects overlapped. Smokestacks fused to palings flickering in silence by. Pale lathes grew grey, turned dusky, contracted and in the swimming dimness, he saw sparse teeth that gnawed upon a lip; and ladders on the ground turned into hasty fingers pressing on a thigh and again smokestacks. Straight in air they stood a moment, only to fall on silvered cardboard corrugating brilliance. And he heard the rubbing on a wash-board and the splashing suds, smelled again the acrid soap and a voice speaking words that opened like the bands of a burnished silver accordion – Brighter than day . . . Brighter . . . Sin melted into light. (333)[57]

Afterwards David feels "as though he had seen it in another world, a world that once left could not be recalled. All that he knew about it was that it had been complete and dazzling" (334). The world elsewhere of the parents' past – represented for David by their fetishes – has been transformed into a mysteriously surrealistic and modern vision that can be experienced in the city. At this point the gentile boys Pedey and Weasel – to whom David denies his Jewishness – make him drop a sword-shaped zinc sheet on the live electric wire under the trolley tracks. Fascinated by the terrific light that is unleashed and consumes the "sword" with radiance (340), David now seems set on the project of seeking an illuminating experience on the streetcar tracks.[58] He breaks into the *cheder* in order to reread Isaiah and continues to build up associations between his idea of a sacred vision and the world of technology. The rabbi finds him and laughs hard at David's crazy idea that he has literally seen Isaiah's light on the East Side: "God's light is not between car-tracks" (346).

Later David interrupts the recital of the biblical verse, crying that his mother died "Long ago! Long ago!" (498). He calls his mother his aunt and, when asked about his father, says his father was an organ player in a church in "Eu-Europe" (500), a Christian! Asked "in what land" the mother met the organ player, David, misunderstanding the concrete land for the abstract country, answers: "In where there was – there was c-corn" (501).

David's fantasy marks the extreme position of a child who denies his literal origins: His mother died long ago, the one who seemed to be his mother is really his aunt, the one who appeared to be his father is not, his real father is in the Old World, is a Christian, and David is an illegitimate child suspended between religiously divided worlds. It is remarkable how close this fantasy comes to the ones Freud described. But we have to recall that David tells this story to the rabbi (who sounds "as though he were strangling"). It is Freud's family romance – but with the difference that the immigrant child was separated from the father, has no physical recollection of the meaningful world of the parents, and may perhaps develop a more exaggerated drive not toward Freud's exaltation of the actual father, but toward the creation of a vision that would symbolically fuse David's divided worlds. Vladimir C. Nahirny and Joshua A. Fishman suggested that there were several strategies available for the second generation. Most important, second-generation immigrants could attempt to create an invented *bilateral line of descent* that includes symbolic American and ethnic ancestors and that connects and fuses American and ethnic origins.[59] This notion has some relevance to *Call It Sleep*.

In the novel the themes of technological modernity and urban polyethnicity build up the American side of David's bilateral descent line, balancing his parents' country origins and Jewishness. The novel also offers an externalization of the problem of the second generation. In one of only two chapters in which David is absent from the novel, Roth inserts a general comment on the second generation, ironically as a rabbi's diatribe. The chapter starts as a joke with the reader who must at first assume

that the hurrying figure is David who so far has always been
the center of consciousness. Together with the chapter at Aunt
Bertha's house from which David is also missing (but which
lacks interiority), this chapter provides comic relief and a change
of pace.

Reb Yidel Pankower may not have a religious message,[60] but
he does offer a comprehensive, hopeless, and in itself quite com-
promised, denunciation of the "American" generation:[61]

A curse on them! He glared about him at the children and half grown
boys and girls who crowded the stoops and overflowed into the side-
walks and gutter. The devil take them! What was going to become of
Yiddish youth? What would become of this new breed? These Americans? This sidewalk-and-gutter generation? He knew them all and they
were all alike – brazen, selfish, unbridled. Where was piety and observance? Where was learning, veneration of parents, deference to the
old? In the earth! Deep in the earth! On ball playing their minds dwelt,
on skates, on kites, on marbles, on gambling for the cardboard pictures,
and the older ones, on dancing, and the ferocious jangle of horns and
strings and jigging with their feet. And God? Forgotten, forgotten
wholly. (507)

The rabbi's moralistic tone is seriously undermined by his admir-
ing attitude toward the pedagogic practice of Reb R'fuhl (a telling
name when pronounced in English), anchored again in the Old-
World context of Vilna boyhood experiences that the second, the
American, generation cannot possibly share, and that a general
American reader can be expected to resent:

That was a rabbi! No random cuff did you get from him when he was
vexed. No mild pinch on the jowl. Ha, no! When he was angered, he
flogged, and when he flogged he took their pants down and spread the
flap of their drawers – and all so slowly and with what sweet words. Hi!
Ha! Ha! that was a sight to behold! They remembered it those young
ones. Not the watery discipline that he enforced. That's what was ruin-
ing this generation, watery discipline. Hi! And he, himself a rabbi now,
he had held the culprit's legs while the straps sank into the white
buttocks. There was a kind of pleasure then in hearing another howl, in
watching another beaten, seeing the naked flesh squirm and writhe and
the crack of the buttocks tighten under the biting thongs. (508)[62]

The rabbi thus stands symbolically for the (problematic) position of the older generation vis-à-vis the younger one, and he makes the older position hardly more attractive when he lustily advocates physical punishment but sullenly denounces skating. He wishes to articulate the need for a religious transcendence of the low realm of physicality but his own pleasure in chastising young boys in the name of "piety and observance" returns the project of the sacred to the worst kind of the profane. Their perverted love of violence also connects the rabbi and the father. It is in response to the older generation's violence that David gets stronger. His misdeeds seem to converge on him, and at first, almost "giddy with terror and guilt," David dodges "behind his mother" (537). But he rises to the occasion when Albert gets violent toward his pregnant sister-in-law Bertha and her husband Nathan: Interceding when the father's bent arm hangs motionless in the air – Albert's familiar hammer, whip, John Henry, Vulcan, Statue of Liberty, and Abraham over Isaac pose – David says bravely "I-It was me, papa –" and gives his father the whip. Albert calls his son "alien" and "stranger" (543); to make matters worse, when David confesses his guilt toward Esther – which Albert interprets as further proof against his own fatherhood – the father whips David and finds the (unnamed) rosary on the floor (546).

The pace abruptly accelerates through the intensifying explosion of serial fragments and nouns including many of the key terms of the novel. David picks up a milk dipper and breathlessly approaches the trolley tracks with the statement, *"Now I gotta make it come out"* (556), and the "crack" (558) out of which the rebirth is to take place blends technological site, sexual allusion (441), and reference to the fissure between worlds (481) that David acutely experiences.

"The tracks lay before him – not in double rows now but in a single yoke." Fusion, Modernism, and the "World Elsewhere"

Chapter XXI of "The Rail" represents a celebrated modernist explosion, David's desperate visionary act and near electrocution. The chapter corresponds to the polyethnic panorama in the prologue, but with a dramatic stylistic difference. Roth's method in this chapter is an alternation between external scenes and italicized passages, set as prose poems, that continue David's interior monologue, like cinematic crosscutting.[63] The bantering vulgarities of the various characters on East 10th Street are juxtaposed ever more rapidly against David who is about to reach the third rail with his milk dipper.

> *And his eyes*
> "Runnin' hee! hee! hee! Across the lots hee! hee! jerkin' off."
> *lifted*
> "An' I picks up a rivet in de tongs an' I sez –"
> *and there was the last crossing of*
> *Tenth Street, the last cross-*
> "Heazuh a flowuh fer ye, yeller-belly, shove it up yer ass!"
> *ing, and beyond, beyond the elevateds,*
> "How many times'll your red cock crow, Pete, befaw y' gives up? T'ree?" (568)[64]

The thread of David's movement is used to separate such figures as the watchman Bill Whitney, Huskey O'Toole and Callahan in the saloon, the oiler Jim Haig, the trolley car motorman Dan MacIntyre, the prostitutes Mary and Mimi, streetcar passengers, peddlers, the radical orator, the Salvation Army singers, and a kind American lady who inadvertently makes a sexually suggestive remark about the Statue of Liberty (another explicit echo of the prologue). One of these outside voices comments, "Five hundred an' fifty volts" (579).

> *(As if on hinges, blank, enormous*
> *mirrors arose, swung slowly upward*
> *face to face.[65] Within the facing*
> *glass, vast panels deployed, lifted a*
> *steady wink of opaque pages until*
> *an endless corridor dwindled into*
> *night.)* (579–580)
> *"Eternal years," the voice*
> *wailed, "Not even he."* (580)

Yet despite the association of "eternal years" with death, David miraculously survives his near electrocution.

David's burnt foot (594) reinforces the Oedipus motif, but a preliminary recognition of intergenerational connectedness and even likeness also emerges as the result of the crisis of David's injury. In the last chapter the American policeman brings David home, and the son seems elated when he sees his father weakened: "That sense of triumph that David had felt on first being brought in, welled up within him again as he listened to him falter and knew him shaken" (593–594). Yet one can speak of a certain family reconciliation at the end. The father's recognition is unequivocal: "Yes. Yes," he was saying. "My sawn. Mine. Yes. Awld eight. Eight en' – en' vun mawnt'. He vas bawn in –" (594). The mother is ready to accept her share of the guilt, too, and admits that she let David listen to her and drove him away to protect him from Albert (597).[66] David, having enjoyed his power, now feels a sense of "vague, remote pity" (598).

In the last paragraph of the novel Roth uses three times the phrasing that gives the novel its title, and the passage is a masterpiece at sustaining ambiguity: What is the "it" of *Call It Sleep?* The novel itself (Klein 196)? a state analogous to physical slumber in which eyes and ears and other conscious faculties succumb to the automatic and the subconscious (Mooney 16)? "a vision that unifies his fragmented world" (Allen 447 in 1964 edition)? a "strategic retreat" (Samet 581)? a "psychic rebirth" (Saperstein 47)? death (Epstein 42)? a mystical experience or a redemption of sorts (Lyons 1976, 110–113)? "a turning point from which it is impossible to withdraw" (Sheres 77)? David's "resurrection as a Jew from a living death" (Girgus 107)? hope (Ferraro 121)? the victory over darkness (F. Roth 219)? peace (Walden 272) and the end to David's difference and to his conflicts (Forgue)? reaching manhood (Geismar xlv)? a fuller vision, an individual creative act (Immel 333) that makes "beauty out of the ugliness of David's world" (Freedman 155)? "a radical challenge to the text itself" (Lesser 172)? "oblivion, a perfect silence or nothingness – a mystic place beyond the concrete realities that are simply too much to bear" (Chametzky 24)? "a textbook example of an imaginary resolution" (Buelens 7)? or a "liminal state," "a point at which looking forward" may be more important than "looking back" (Berman 60)? Is it an indication, as Eda Lou Walton wrote, that "Roth's young hero conquers his environment" (Walton, *This Generation* 583)? And to conclude with two of Roth's own readings, does the phrase "call it sleep" refer to "an artistic accession or an assumption into artistry" (Roth in Lyons 1976, 167) or to "the end of that kind of creative life" (Roth in Freedman 155)? – a contradiction analogous to Coriolanus's proclaiming "a world elsewhere" only in haughty reaction to his banishment, so that "accession" also means "end."[67]

The ending is also the extraordinary realization of "a world elsewhere" that David experiences and that finds its aesthetic equivalent in the world of arts that Roth enters with the writing of *Call It Sleep*. The electric experiment within the text thus finds its counterpart in the aesthetic experimentation of the novel. If only for a moment – perhaps Roth thought of the Faustian moment that cannot last – David's electric vision of light, power, and modernity realizes the world elsewhere within the text; correspondingly, the modernism of the novel's form that reaches its highest point near the ending is Roth's successful attempt at rendering it. One may well view the end of *Call It Sleep* as an extended Joycean "epiphany," and David's act at the trolley tracks as a version of the "objective correlative," famously defined by T. S. Eliot as "a set of objects, a situation, a chain of events which shall be the formula of that *particular* emotion" to be expressed; "such that when the external facts, which must terminate in sensory experience, are given, the emotion is immediately evoked."[68] The ending is also an application of the "mythical method," since the construction of machines for mimicking "the clap of thunder and the flash of lightning" was part of Roman kingship rituals that were to prove the royal ancestry in Jupiter, and that Frazer associated with Romulus – one of the two sucklings of the Roman wolf that Bertha explicitly commented on in the museum.[69]

The ending brings together the central images of the novel, and bridges the dichotomies and ruptures – just as Hart Crane's "bridge" provided such a fusion. Cellar, picture, coal, and rail, sword, dipper, electricity, transcendent vision, and polyethnic setting all come together in David's action so that father and mother, parents and child, Old World and New World, vulgarity and the sacred, sexual imagery, cusswords, and metaphysical yearning, Christianity, Judaism, Zoroastrianism, and secularism, revolutionary action and betrayal, fear and triumph, coexist in one powerful surge of dangerous brightness that lasts for only a moment but holds in suspension all the tensions under which David suffered. He has found "a set of objects" in order to externalize his emotional dilemmas, but the balance that this act achieves is uneasy and momentary. At the end, David has become somewhat like father and mother, for better or worse. The "triumph" of the end is subdued.

The Itinerant Ithacan at the Eighth Street Crosstown Trolley Line

The "world elsewhere" in Roth's aesthetic may refer to yet another set of circumstances. Although he had originally planned to use materials of his own life from Brownsville to Greenwich Village, Roth ended *Call It Sleep* when David is only eight years old. According to Roth, the "very original conception of the book was to include my entire trajectory – from ghetto child to Greenwich Village, but finally I decided to leave David at his childhood."[70] Ever since 1934 readers have been looking forward to the novel that would reach the Village years, but Roth developed writer's block before finishing the sequel: "I had tried to write a second novel. This novel was to start where *Call It Sleep* ends and follow the progress of the immigrant child to the world of Greenwich Village; the ghetto youngster coming to awareness in the world of art. But I never managed to write this second novel."[71]

In two remarkable literary pieces of 1977, "Kaddish" and "Itinerant Ithacan," Roth did begin to fictionalize this process; and what emerges at the center of "the world of Greenwich Village" is the association of the writer "R" with the New York University professor of English and anthropologist Eda Lou Walton – who has been mentioned throughout this essay.[72] Roth writes in "Kaddish" that she permitted R to enjoy "his years on Parnassus, whose emblems were his English tweed jacket, his Dunhill pipe, and his private study looking out on a Greenwich

Village backyard," but that once the (ten-year) relationship – he is ambivalent whether he should call it "affair" – ended, "he would have to make retribution, multiple retribution for all the privileged years he had enjoyed" (*Shifting Landscape* 188–189). This suggests an intimate connection of the world of Mount "Parnassus" with Walton. His focus on dress style, almost a masquerade, and privilege seems connected to a sense of guilt, be it social, personal, or artistic, requiring retribution. Roth met Walton in the mid-1920s, when he was not yet twenty years old, and he explores "Eda Lou" 's milieu in "Itinerant Ithacan," as "R" is sitting

> in her one-room apartment where palpable city dust drifted down ubiquitously on furnishings, windowsills, and mantle piece, dust scuffed up from hectic Eighth Street, just above the window. So near the scraps of conversation outdoors, guffaw and repartee, so near the scrape of shod feet in passing, clash of crosstown trolley, blast of auto horn, brought into the room along with the normal drone of the city; sat there for the nth time, conning T. S. Eliot's "Waste Land." While in the obscure alcove in the rear of the apartment, stretched out on the bed with its sable velour covering, Eda Lou tittered girlishly in the arms of her young lover, the handsome and talented Lester Winter, R's chum since high school and now a sophomore at NYU. (197)[73]

The immigrant child and student represents himself as a migrant into the world of *The Waste Land* and as a new Dr. Jekyll.[74] The noise of the city streets near Eighth Street, and especially the "clash of the crosstown trolley" would seem to connect some of Eliot's imagery ("Trams and dusty trees") and the memory of the Lower East Side, while the erotic context transforms the hypnotized reader into Eliot's Tiresias of "The Fire Sermon" who has "foresuffered all / Enacted on this same divan or bed." The odd love triangle in which R plays the voyeur who does not look and memorizes *The Waste Land* instead is the repetition of another scene:

> Eda Lou had returned from a trip to Europe with a copy of Joyce's *Ulysses* which she had smuggled through customs. (And that too was something to note, that she could dimple with duplicity, decoy with her large brown eyes and genteel reserve; it was something to learn.) [. . .]

Eda Lou had brought the *Ulysses* along for Lester to read. But after an hour or two, he put the novel aside remarking that it wasn't necessary for a writer to strain for such bizarre effects simply in order to prove his originality. So R fell heir to the book. And while the lovers dallied, [. . .] R, unaccountably determined to exploit the opportunity, read the *Ulysses*. He read it doggedly, perplexedly, moiling through hundreds of close-printed and often baffling pages for a story. There was no story, and the meaning seemed to be the absence of meaning. (198)

Roth's "R" is always the intense reader, more open to Eliot or Joyce than was his rival (who is not yet openly acknowledged as such). *Ulysses* makes R recognize that any materials could be turned into "something noble, into a work of art" "by the alchemy of language," that the memories of the "tenement backyards of his neighborhood, the dingy cabbagy Fels Nap[h]tha soap mopped hallways, the battered brass letter boxes, qualified for alchemy" (198). R realizes in a flash that he need not follow Melville to the South Sea Isles or Mark Twain to the Mississippi, or Jack London to the Yukon in search of that world elsewhere: "It was all here, right here. It was the language that made the difference, that transmuted meanness into literature. Jesus! What a discovery!" (198–199). The Itinerant Ithacan Ulysses taught him that the world elsewhere was right where he was, in the noises of the Village and in the memories of the East Side.

This story of the initiation into *Ulysses* and *The Waste Land* suggests that the "accession" into the "noble" world elsewhere was partly freeing and partly frightening. Reading seems to be a sublimatory act that might make the reader a better artist and, ultimately, more eligible as a man, too. It would appear that in the long run R was chosen – by a "dark, petite, and grave" woman who is always described as a little duplicitous, whether in smuggling *Ulysses* into the country or in directly encouraging R during a momentary absence of Lester. Here and in other accounts Roth represents his old self as passive (at times rendered in the passive voice), a bystander, a spectator; and Walton is typically described in terms of "taking care" of Roth, of being "generous," or "generous to a fault." She is "maternal," their age difference of twelve years is always stressed; he describes her lifestyle as leading her to "any number of affairs, almost promiscuity, but not quite" (Lyons 1976, 160) and he inevitably casts himself as shy and naive, a child: "I am a terribly naive person" (*Shifting Landscape* 294); or: "I was naive, you see, I was protected. I was taken care of" (Freedman 153); or "I was so very shy! So it was she who said, 'I will support you' " (*Shifting Landscape* 295). Roth is "adopted" by an "older generation" and the result is a feeling of "gratitude," "dependence" (generating implicitly a quest for "independence" – or the wish to be "rescued" or "retrieved"), and "guilt," a sense of not being able to grow up, to mature. Maturity stands for independence, but also a job, family, children, normalcy.[75] Roth almost represents the writing of the novel – as was the reading of Eliot and Joyce – as if it were an exam, a test, or an initiation rite:

This whole novel was written on examination booklets they give you in New York University to take your examination. They have eight pages and this gives you a feeling of accomplishment. And I never wrote more than those eight – because I was lazy. You can see how it would take me four years to write this novel.[76]

Roth also speaks of being "admitted," or of an "assumption," into the world of the arts.[77]

Roth has stressed that in imagining *Call It Sleep* he took great liberties with autobiographical materials: For example, he wrote his sister out of the novel and made his father starker. Perhaps most intriguing are his comments about Genya. Roth stated repeatedly and startlingly that he split his mother into the figures of Genya and Bertha: "Actually, my own mother was the source of both of these contrasting female figures. I abstracted one side of my mother, rounded it out and created an aunt who in most respects is the antithesis to David Schearl's mother. The presence of Aunt Bertha seemed to give an aesthetic justification to the character of the mother as well."[78] This procedure invites rereading the novel for a division between attraction and repulsion, serious filial love and vulgar comedy, or for Genya as the good and Bertha as the bad mother. David's embarrassment of the older generation is highly focused on Bertha and thus deflected from Genya; one has only to think of the museum scene and remember that "aunt" may be a symbolic substitute for "mother."[79]

Yet there is more to the story than this. Genya was strongly inspired by Walton: "David's mother really borrows from the woman I was living with: a highly cultivated professor of English literature. This is Eda Lou Walton to whom the book is dedicated."[80] The composite figure of Genya is thus – according to Roth's accounts – a supreme embodiment of the wish for a bilateral descent. This also means that the Village is not just the neutral place from which a retrospective novel was written; it is directly inscribed into the text. The "maternal" quality of Walton, Roth's quest for "independence" while finding only "dependence," his search for "normalcy" as symbol of that "independence" make it possible to connect the aesthetic representation of Genya with Roth's rhetorical shaping of his image of Walton.[81] In reconstructing such contexts, I am not proposing a biographical approach to a great literary text. I am suggesting that there are interesting rhetorical analogies between *Call It Sleep* and Roth's later writings that suggest that it was only the Village aesthete Roth who is *not* represented in *Call It Sleep* who could give shape to the Brownsville child's consciousness. The world of the Lower East Side, culminating in the electric *choc* at the Tenth Street switch of the Eighth Street trolley, was remembered and recreated at the other end of the Eighth Street crosstown line. It must have seemed like magic that, from both points of view, the other world was only a trolley ride away, linked by rails.[82]

Since Georg Lukács, we have become accustomed to read historical novels not only for the time they represent but also for the time in which they were written.[83] Instead of looking at Roth's "ethnic" experience rendered in the modernism of *Call It Sleep,* we might also see the deep interconnectedness of the ethnic childhood of 1911 to 1913, the romantic and aesthetic tribulations of the Village, and the political situation of the early 1930s in the making of the novel. Thus Roth stated that *Call It Sleep* "violates the truth about what the East Side was then," described it as a "montage of milieus," and specifically suggested that the rise of anti-Semitism epitomized by Hitler influenced the scene where David denies his Jewishness to Pedey and Weasel (336).[84]

In other words, instead of looking at the novel as a "straight" representation, whether of Freudian family romance or of immigration, it may well be intertwined with, or a partial disguise of, another tale associated with the world of the arts and centered on Walton. The theme of the second-generation immigrant location may appear so clearly drawn only as it corresponds to a modernist position in representation. Roth's own retrospective accounts suggest that at the time he wrote *Call It Sleep* the worlds of childhood and young manhood, of ghetto experience and modernist aesthetics, defined each other, with the result that he managed to look at each world through the eyes of the other. Crossing worlds, the *Ur*-experience of the prologue, may be the central theme for the "detached artist" Roth, not fidelity to one world.

Perhaps it is from this vantage point that the unstable linguistic center of the novel makes sense and that the analogy of David's quest with that of the artist for a world elsewhere actually works. The fusion of ethnicity and modernism is so successful in this instance because both ethnic childhood and artistic modernism were strongly and simultaneously felt by the writer, each reminding him of the other – and thus doubly moving the reader. The following statement by Roth describes his project well and enriches the discussion about the novel's relation to the category "Jewish literature" that has been the subject of debate:

What I think American Jewish literature represents is the interface between the immigrant and the host society. What is being described is the feeling of what is happening as the process takes place, a process in which one culture begins to impinge, to enter into, or to permeate the other culture.[85]

We often read "ethnic" literature by freezing books to the ethnic origins of the author's birth. But what if the shaping force, the aesthetic of what we are reading about an ethnic past were so intricately shaped by another world (for example, one generated by interethnic love and reading) that it has little to do with the origins we are looking for? *Call it Sleep* may be a perfect case in point and it is not surprising that it has been praised both as "specifically Jewish" and as "essentially American." A truly outstanding example of the particular form of "interface literature" of cultures in contact that is ethnic modernism, the novel may present the deepest expression of second-generation art by merging East Side and Village origins so fully that it renders a powerful and haunting bilateral descent myth of Jewish immigrant childhood and American modernist initiation. Two worlds are connected in such a way that there was always "a world somewhere, somewhere else," different from and yet similar to the one inhabited *or* fictionalized. Perhaps in such dualisms the most successful works of ethnic modernism were produced, creating ethnic verisimilitude precisely by drawing emotionally on aesthetic sources rarely connected with – and perceived to be antagonistic to – the ethnic location. This process was also experienced as a deep crisis, a burnout, and a short circuit (metaphors close to the language of the novel's ending that Roth also applied to his life),[86] and as an intense experience for which such a price had to be paid that no new creative stage emerged for nearly half a century.

NOTES

1 See the anonymous *New Masses* review of 1935, the responses by Greenhood, Burke, and Seaver, the review by Gollomb, as well as the discussions in Rideout 186–190, Ledbetter, Klein 193–195, Lyons 1976, 16–19, Dickstein 79–80, Harris 86–90, and Roth, *Shifting Landscape* 188. In 1977 Roth said that *Call It Sleep* "is not a proletarian novel. Probably Mike Gold's *Jews Without Money* is a proletarian novel." Riese interestingly cast the proletarian discourse of the novel as the one that actually mediates between ethnic and modernistic discourses. Syrkin wrote that Roth had "the literary equipment of a major novelist, which can be said of no other American Jewish writer."

2 Roth to Jane Howard in 1965: "I don't know much about Freud and I never did. . . . If I'd known about things like Oedipus complexes I probably never would have written the book at all. I'd

have said, 'Shucks, why bother? Sounds just like a case history.' "
(Howard 76). By contrast, Roth described his own childhood to
Bonnie Lyons in terms of Freud's "Family Romances." He suggests
that his sister mattered little because of his egotism: "I so continually monopolized my mother's affection that I regarded myself as
the one and only child around – with the exception of my father.
My sister was his favorite. That I would say is a thumbnail sketch –
with all its Freudian meanings" (Lyons 1976, 159). Roth also told
William Freedman in 1972: "Of course, I knew about Freud, but I
only had a smattering of it. I knew only what almost everyone else
knew of Freud, and that wasn't a great deal. . . . I guess I must
occasionally have thought about the relationship in Freudian
terms, but I wouldn't say I was following Freud" (Freedman 155).
Alessandra Contenti argued that the extreme similarity of Roth's
representation to Freud's "family romance" – with its emphasis on
the child's fantasy of being an illegitimate or adopted child – makes
it likely that Roth had *not* read Freud since he would probably have
avoided such a precise correspondence (Materassi 106–107).

3   See Ferraro 90–94 and Dickstein 79. The reader gets a good sense
of Roth's poetic education by looking at Eda Lou Walton's anthology *The City Day* (1929) in which Roth is understatedly thanked for
"assistance in proofreading and other clerical help" (vii). It is a
collection organized in three parts, following the times of day. It
includes samplings from T. S. Eliot, e. e. cummings, Langston
Hughes, Amy Lowell, Hart Crane, William Carlos Williams, and
many other poets in a city world, among them David Greenhood
who was to defend Roth in *New Masses*. On Roth and Joyce, see
Lyons 1976, 117–123, and Manskleid-Makowsky 111–117; for excellent stylistic comparisons, Alter 1988, 34–36.

4   Roth has demanded that his novel be read in this way; and a Roth
concordance or, even better, a *Call It Sleep* hypertext might stimu-
late a fuller understanding of Roth's systematic method of building
up the novel on the principle of verbal recurrences and variations.
See, for example, Elèna Mortara's careful reading of the dark/light
imagery (Materassi 45–75); Materassi's pursuit of such recurrences
as "play" (Materassi 155–167), Guido Fink's analysis of the motif of
"sleep" (Materassi 143–154), or Lyons' close readings of the novel.

5   Alter 1969, 166.
6   Adams 43.
7   Fiedler 96.
8   Inge 49. See also Nelson 7. For detailed discussions of the novel's

"Jewishness" see Lyons 1976, 125–133 and Manskleid-Makowsky 47–93.

9   Wirth-Nesher, "Between," 298–300.

10 Wirth-Nesher, "City Codes," 178, cites the full text of a Yiddish poem in which a reference to the golden land appears.

11 For a meticulous discussion of the philological and syntactic features of "Yinglish"-speaking children and adults in *Call It Sleep*, see Immel 335–350 who, following Kleederman's unpublished dissertation, documents vowel omissions, substitutions of consonants and vowels, contractions, double negatives, added -ed endings to irregular verbs in the past tense ("tooked"), the use of present perfect instead of present tense, wrong prepositions, questions starting with "so" or ending with "no?," and other linguistic aspects of the novel.

12 Hebrew *mohel*. I am here following Manskleid-Makowsky 60–61, who also ponders the possibility that Bertha's sentence might mean "that by taking away a mouth the doctor would make her one" or "by taking her mouth he would make her more complete." In the manuscript of *Call It Sleep* in the New York Public Library, David's parents react to Bertha's pun: It causes "David's father to writhe and spit behind his newspaper in dry disgust, but even David's mother to wince slightly" (3?A, [p.4]). In the memoir "Weekends in New York" (1984), Roth describes studying a photograph of the Lower East Side "nostalgically" on which he "could make out the word *Mohel* in Hebrew lettering on a sign above the doorway of a tenement" (*Shifting Landscape* 274).

13 See also Manskleid-Makowsky 60 and Gollomb 552. The manuscript does not yet contain an explanation of "kockin," only the sentence, "And she laughed immoderately much to the annoyance of David's father" (booklet 3?A). See also Rabbi Pankower's advice, expounded with curled thumb and forefinger, "take yourself home, sit long in the privy and you'll have a clearer brow" (385).

14 See Pinsker 155, 150, and Kazin 17.

15 "Miss oozer" sounds out an English meaning opposite to the sacred significance of a *mezuzeh;* the sound effect of "Miss oozer" may also echo William Carlos Williams' "cross oozy" in his "Overture to a Dance of Locomotives" (Walton, *City Day* 106).

16 Gordon Poole has noted that such profane terms as "knish" (64, 398) and "tookis" (463) are not explained (Materassi 131), but neither is the sacred word "philacteries."

17 David's gesture connects his speech act with theories of language

according to which pointing represents a first or primal, mute state of gesture language, a form of expression "inseparable from the thing referred to." See Dougald McMillan, *transition: The History of a Literary Era, 1927–1938* (New York: Braziller, 1976), 179–203; here 196.

18 This betrayal also replicates the mother's affair with the organist; and it is significant that it is Leo who explains to David what an "orrghaneest" is (435).

19 Howe 588. This quality is much more pronounced in dialogue than in narration (Poole in Materassi 131).

20 Alter 1988, 36–37, noted the "Shakespearean dignity" in such English renditions of Yiddish as "The light before my eyes grew black!" for "es iz mir finster gevoren oif di oigen," and called attention to the Melvillean tone in exclamations such as Albert's "Nothing fulfills itself with me! It's all doomed!" – which is also very close to the complaint, "I can't accomplish anything; I can't succeed in anything," that Freud cites in *Beyond the Pleasure Principle* (21). Harap found that, in contradistinction to "the widespread use in entertainment and humor of Yiddish phrases as occasions for humor," Roth gives conversational Yiddish speech a seriousness which does not permit of risibility. Some examples: "No, they'll know the black hour [*shvartz yur*] hasn't seized me." "Woe me" [*veh's mir*]. "Your man [or husband] [*dein Mann*] is asleep." "The light before my eyes grew black" [*shvartz vor die eugen*]. "A black year befall you!" [*A shvartz yur off dir*]. "Shah! Be butchered" [*Sei geharget*]. "Where was learning, veneration of parents . . . deep in the earth" [*teefindrerd*]. "Do as I tell hammering the samovar" [*khoken mir a cheinek*]. Of course, as we have seen, Roth also uses the language difference for its comic potential. Immel 348–350 gave more examples; Sherman 87, however, found that these "rather awkward examples of translated Yiddish recall Hemingway's obtrusive efforts to capture Spanish in *For Whom the Bell Tolls.*"

21 Roth in Lyons 1976, 171. The phrase "a hura mezda" does not yet appear in the earlier answer, "What is a suitor?" (3?E), and in one of many notes and additions Roth wrote to himself at the composition stage of the novel, he associates the "jug a jug jug" to the "bed spring rhythm during copulation" (Notes Additions IV, items 56 and 57).

22 See Alexander von Humboldt, *Relation historique du Voyage aux Règions èquinoxiales du Nouveau Continent* (Paris: 1814–1824), vol. 8, 486–487, 674–718; A. F. Bandelier, *The Gilded Man (El Dorado)*

(New York: D. Appleton, 1893), 8–17; J. A. Zahm, *The Quest of El Dorado* (New York: D. Appleton, 1917), 9–36, with illustrations; and Constantino Bayle, *El Dorado Fantasma* (Madrid, 2d ed., 1943), 15–43. For a discussion of Chinese immigrant visions of the United States as "gold mountain" after 1836, see also Xiao-huang Yin, "Gold Mountain Dreams: Chinese American Literature and Its Socio-Historical Context, 1850–1963," Dissertation, Harvard University, 1991, 19–21. Genya tells Bertha: "It appears to me that you'll grow from green to yellow in this land years before I do" (202); and the novel contains several allusions to gold, including Bertha's gold crown (215) given to her by Dr. Goldberg (i.e. literally, "gold mountain"), the rabbi's address to David, "my gold" (290), the "golden lolling" (355), the "golden-skinned, smoked white-fish" that opens "like a golden volume" (359), the "gilded mortar and pestle" (459) on Kane Street, the golden crucifix on Leo's rosary (480), the rabbi's watch opening like a gold bivalve (505), the "trickle of gold" of a train on the bridge (559), and the "golden cloud of birds" (578). Hart Crane (66) referred to the "dream called Eldorado" in the "Indiana" section of "The Bridge" (1930). Wirth-Nesher, "Between" 303, notes the contrast between the "golden land" and "Bronzeville."

23 When *Call It Sleep* was published, Kenneth Burke defended Roth against an anonymous attack in *New Masses,* because Roth had captured "with considerable sympathy and humor, the 'pre-political' thinking of childhood, the stage of development wherein we follow much the same pattern of magic as Frazer outlines in *The Golden Bough.* The great virtue of Roth's book," Burke continued, "was in the fluent and civilized way in which he found, on our city streets, the new equivalents of the ancient jungle – a parallelism which culminates magnificently when the electric current in the car tracks takes the place of the lightning that struck down Frazer's sacred oaks"; Burke 21. See Frazer 607. Walton included an essay of Burke's in *This Generation. The Golden Bough* was referred to in the notes to Eliot's *Waste Land* and offers many possible contexts for *Call It Sleep.*

24 Such moments have affinities with romantic irony of the type Peter Szondi called attention to: the thematization of something *formal,* such as singing in an opera (as opposed to a play); see his *Theory of Modern Drama* (1965). See also Roth in Lyons 1976, 169–170. The novel gives a dazzling array of possible versions of the Brownsville street David calls "Boddeh": Bodder, Potter, Poddeh, Bodder, Body,

Pother, Powther, Bahday, and Barhdee Street (124–128, 135); and Genya says that it means "bath street in German" (37) – hence Riese supposes that it is really "Bade Street" (225). No street of *any* such name existed in Brooklyn, and neither did the supposedly neighboring "Oriol" and "Parker" streets (128). It is also telling that Roth regularly calls the neighborhood "Bronzeville" (and not "Brownsville") in the extant parts of the manuscript. By contrast, the topography of 749 East 9th Street appears to be quite precise.

25 Roth's manuscript includes a notebook in which he collected the appropriate Hebrew passages (second unnumbered notebook between 3?G and 3?H). For a suggestive discussion of a Hebrew/English passage, see Portelli 168.

26 In *Mercy of a Rude Stream* 102–103 Roth represents an incestuously toned scene between Ira and his mother around the word *lyupka,* and the word recurs on the following pages. The word *lupka* does not yet appear in the manuscript of *Call It Sleep,* and it may be Russian rather than Polish.

27 Unexplained multilingualism connects *Call It Sleep* to both immigrant literature and well-known tendencies in modern poetry from Eliot and Pound to the trilingual poems by Eugene Jolas (see McMillan 114–116).

28 Roth's decision to focus on the age from five to eight had its parallel in Eugene Jolas' *transition* essays on *Finnegan's Wake* as a work in progress, focusing on Joyce's adaptation of Richard Paget's recreation of children's language (McMillan 190). David's age has been made the subject of varying assessments. Yet the novel seems quite definite on that subject: He was, according to Genya, born on July 12, 1905 (18); according to Albert, who suspected an earlier birthdate that would make his paternity questionable, David is eight years and one month old at the end, set in the summer of 1913. Hence he is 21 or 22 months old in the prologue (though Albert wanted Genya to state the age as 17 months, and the Hamburg doctor guessed "over two years"), he is approaching his sixth birthday in "The Cellar," and he is seven in "The Coal" (282). In the manuscript, Roth settles on just such a chronology, also giving the mother's month of conception and the father's departure for America as November and December 1904 (Notes Additions VI, item 68). Even if readers took literally Albert's "foible" (282) of increasing David's age (see Altenbernd 680–681), they could not arrive at a significantly different age for David. Roth mentioned

that his own parents had a similar dispute about his year of birth; and David's birthdate would seem to constitute a compromise between the opinions of Roth's parents (Bronsen 265).

29   See Diamant 346.

30   The word "snot" was famously used in "snotgreen sea" at the beginning of *Ulysses*. Kleederman, a very careful reader of Roth, writes that the passage from "In a wooden cage" to "those stands" "is an example of a change of construction in midstream which gives the effect of discontinuity" (5). This analysis is based, however, on the Avon Press reprint, whereas the 1934 edition has a period after "elevated" followed by a capitalized "And." Another serious difference between the texts is the rendering of "sable fibres of the earth" (340) as "stable fibres" (A 253). For such reasons, I am citing from the first edition, second printing.

31   Dorrit Cohn, *Transparent Minds: Narrative Modes for Presenting Consciousness in Fiction* (1978; reprinted, Princeton: Princeton University Press, 1983), 99–140, describes and discusses "narrated monologue." See also Käte Hamburger, *The Logic of Literature*, trans. Marilynn J. Rose, 2d ed. (Bloomington: Indiana University Press, 1993), 72, for a discussion of fictional sentences of the type "Tomorrow was Christmas." Compare also Genya's direct "To-morrow will be Sunday" (7); and Roth's use of the pluperfect in order to render simple past events in narration: "Yesterday afternoon and the day before, she had been impatient with him, unresponsive to his questions" (166); Hamburger 73.

32   It is hard to believe that Freud's similar account of a child in *Beyond the Pleasure Principle*, published in English twelve years before *Call It Sleep*, would not have been on Roth's mind when he constructed his mirror scene: "One day the child's mother had been away for several hours and on her return was met with the words 'Baby o-o-o-o!' which was at first incomprehensible. It soon turned out, however, that during this long period of solitude the child had found a method of making *himself* disappear. He had discovered his reflection in a full-length mirror which did not quite reach the ground, so that by crouching down he could make his mirror-image 'gone' " (14–15). Freud is exploring "repetition" and its connection to the death instinct, themes hardly remote from the novel with its "sleep eternal years" and the policeman's comment on "Body" street, "sounds like the morgue" (128). See also David's related fear of not hearing his own footsteps (19).

33 Manskleid-Makowsky 110. Maffi 199–201 offers an excellent read-
    ing of *Call It Sleep* as a novel of the Lower East Side.
34 In contrast to Abraham Cahan's *Yekl,* Roth never articulates that
    this means traveling on the Sabbath. For Peter Stuyvesant see
    Selzer 10. See also Fink (in Materassi 77–85), Ferraro 94–100, and
    Immel 270–287 for detailed commentaries on the prologue.
35 Edward A. Steiner, *On the Trail of the Immigrant* (New York: Fleming
    H. Revell, 1906), 73–74. Steiner was also an immigrant from Aus-
    tria.
36 Yet see the review by Gollomb for just such an attack.
37 Her name seems to appear first on page 82, in her description of
    her grandmother's address to her, though she is earlier called Mrs.
    Schearl by Joe Luter (38). Whereas Aunt Bertha appears as such in
    the manuscript, the mother does not yet seem to have a first name;
    this suggests that "Genya," though common, may be a telling
    name, derived perhaps from Greek "Eugenia" or from the Russian
    "zhenya."
38 For references to Kafka – whose work appeared in *transition* in the
    1920s and whose *Amerika* was first published in 1927 – and other
    deformations of the Statue see Hamilton Holt, *The Life Stories of
    Undistinguished Americans As Told by Themselves* (1908; reprinted
    New York: Routledge, 1990), xx–xxi. Gordon Poole connected
    Roth's description of the Statue as a fear-inspiring paternal and
    maternal deity with the later imagery of *Call It Sleep* (Materassi
    122–125). Roth's description resembles the image of a boy flying a
    kite on a rooftop in Berenice Van Slyke's poem "East Side Kites"
    (Walton, *City Day* 89) – a poem thematically connected with Chap-
    ter VII, "The Rail." See also Hart Crane's line "Over the chained bay
    waters Liberty" in "To Brooklyn Bridge" (Walton, *City Day* 171) and
    his reference to the Statue in "Cutty Sark." For Mary Antin, see her
    book *They Who Knock at Our Gates: A Complete Gospel of Immigration*
    (Boston and New York: Houghton, Mifflin and Co., 1914), 25–26.
39 Freedman 156. Since Roth alluded to the "Prolog im Himmel" of
    Goethe's *Faust* (*Shifting Landscape* 178–182), the prologue at Ellis
    Island might also be a representation of the modern equivalent of
    the divine plane of action. If Roth had omitted the prologue, the
    novel's first sentence would have come closer to the opening of
    Ulysses. The move from the sociology of the prologue to the psy-
    chology of the novel also implies a choice, a selection of a nobility
    of sorts, from among the crowd, a theme supported by Luter's

remarks that David's hands are small "like those of a prince" (49), or by the resemblance of Genya's comb to a "crown" (82). Roth at some point planned five books (one giving more room to Aunt Bertha) and an epilogue "before school" for the novel, and he referred to "The Coal" as "first light" and "The Rail" as "last light" in the manuscript.

40 The use of such aesthetic childhood materials at the beginning of Joyce's *Portrait of the Artist as a Young Man* would seem to have provided a perfect model for Roth's needs, so that the adaptations here turned into exuberant ways of surpassing the model (333, 313–314); he also employed both an English nursery rhyme and the Jewish Passover verse.

41 "A world somewhere else" alludes – as the motto suggests – to Shakespeare's *Coriolanus* III.iii. 136, spoken as Caius Marcius "Coriolanus" haughtily goes into exile and pronounces his exilers banished. The phrase was made the title of Richard Poirier's study, *A World Elsewhere: The Place of Style in American Literature* (New York: Oxford University Press, 1966), a book that seems quite pertinent to, though it makes no mention of, *Call It Sleep*. Poirier invokes *Coriolanus* (6) and sketches the American writer's tendency to substitute for political or historical worlds environments that exist only in style.

42 Later in *Call It Sleep* David is "content yet strangely nostalgic" after kindling a fire (331); and Roth described his own nostalgia for a photograph in *Shifting Landscape* (274). In an interview Roth commented on the attention Irving Howe's *World of Our Fathers* received: "The interest in Howe's book almost corresponds to the reemergence of *Call It Sleep*. On the part of the Jews, it is nostalgia; on the part of non-Jews, curiosity" (Lyons 1979, 54). He opened another interview with the statement: "It's too bad I was not older when I was brought to America, so that I could recall the Old World and the original home of my mother and father." And he admitted to feeling nostalgia on returning to the – now Puerto Rican – Lower East Side (Bronsen 265, 276).

43 Immel 350 stresses the differences between adult and child language, noting that the parents' generation is linguistically still rooted in Europe whereas the second generation has to face the full force of cultural conflict. Yet such curses as Bertha's "May a trolley-car crack his bones" (209) are hardly "traditional" and may show the negotiation of tradition and modernity in the languages of both generations.

44 Since David has just mentioned that he saw three bears in a book (that his mother does not know), his association of bears and porridge obviously stems from the Scottish fairy tale "The Three Bears," in which all three bears complain in their various voices, "Somebody has been at my porridge!" Bettelheim discusses the tale in terms of a child's search for identity, desire to find out the sexual secrets of adults, and attempt to try out a father's, mother's, and child's place; he also focuses on the story's appealing depiction of an outsider while letting the insiders (the bears) win.

45 Generational polarization and the subversion of parental authority in immigrant families were concerns of Margaret Mead, who contributed the poem "And Your Young Men Shall See Visions" to Walton's *City Day* 95. She noted the American "expectation that the child will pass beyond the parents and leave their standards behind him" (Mead 41). Erik Erikson also argued that "psychoanalysis of the children of immigrants clearly reveals to what extent they, as the first real Americans in their family, become their parents' cultural parents" (Erikson 294).

46 This passage connects to the beginning ethnic panorama with body parts (3–4) as well as to the ending with its double phrasing: "It was only toward sleep that every wink of the eyelids could strike a spark [. . . .] It was only toward sleep that ears had the power to cull again and reassemble the shrill cry" (598). The repeated references to eyes and ears may also echo Isaiah 6:10: "Make the heart of this people fat, and make their ears heavy, and shut their eyes; lest they see with their eyes, and hear with their ears, and understand with their heart, and convert; and be healed" (the seraph to Isaiah), as well as the chapter "Shirat Haazinn" (Give ear), the song of Moses from Deuteronomy 32 that Roth cites in Hebrew (see Makowsky 90).

47 "An American Writer," *The Invention of Ethnicity,* ed. Werner Sollors (New York: Oxford University Press, 1988), 11.

48 Roth's method of building up free association is reminiscent of Faulkner's in the Benjy section of *The Sound and the Fury.* See also William James's "The Two Laws of Association" (William James 79–90) and Eda Lou Walton's description of "accumulative imagery," *City Day* 27, in which "several ideas and emotions in the impact of imagination are fused into one. It is a poetical progression of thought and a summation of that thought at the same time." Roth's notes in the manuscript indicate how consciously he built up recurrences and associations, e.g.: "Possibility of linking pincers

(or tongs) with sugar cubes and eternity" (unnumbered pink booklet, item 45).

49 Moses, Abraham, and Jacob (195 – Bertha's comment); for John Henry, see Erikson 298–306.

50 This section of *Call It Sleep* invites comparison with the Kiev-born Marya Zaturensky whose poem "Nostalgia" begins with the stanza:
>   That field so green, so green,
>   In the sun's graying gold
>   Once seen, now never seen,
>   O God, that path so green! (Walton, *City Day* 88)

The motif of the "blue flower" also goes back to the romantic quest for art in nature by Novalis and Eichendorf.

51 The reader might at this point think of "horns" in connection with Albert's fear of cuckoldry and doubt as to his paternity of David.

52 *City Day* 3. Walton also notes how this predicament can be resolved by the language of poets of the city. In their work: "a word of motion comes to express quiet, a word of field-flatness, to indicate pavement, a word of sunlight to picture streets electrically etched" (*City Day* 12).

53 Apparently without being aware of Burke's suggestions of 1935, Mary Redding read *Call It Sleep* for conscious and unconscious allusions to *The Golden Bough* and mentioned that Eda Lou Walton was reportedly enthusiastic about Frazer. Redding investigated such motifs as the corn-spirit, Vulcan, magical coal, impotence, and the "Fire-King" myth of Cambodia: "If the Fire King draws the magic sword a few inches from its sheath, the sun is hidden and men and beasts fall into a profound sleep; were he to draw it quite out of the scabbard, the world would come to an end"; Frazer 71, Redding 194. See also Lyons 1976, 119. T. S. Eliot praised Frazer for increasingly abstaining "from the attempt to explain." Eliot also compared Frazer's work with Freud's and found that *The Golden Bough* is "of no less importance for our time [. . .] throwing its light on the obscurities of the soul from a different angle; and it is a work of perhaps greater permanence, because it is a statement of fact which is not involved in the maintenance or fall of any theory of the author's."

54 David Perkins, "The 'Mythical' Method," *A History of Modern Poetry: From the 1890s to the High Modernist Mode* (Cambridge: Harvard University Press, 1976), 505–511. Here: 511, 509.

55 America was often perceived by immigrants as the fulfillment of

specific denials of the Old World; see, for example, the Swedish farmer in *The Life Stories of Undistinguished Americans* who is happy not to have to lift his hat to everyone in America. A utopian vision of America may thus be – as with Bertha's underpants – an upside-down version of the Old World. Bertha's restlessness and love of noise also affect her view of New York, and she finds the Upper East Side "quiet, as a forest" (195).

56　William Butler Yeats's poem "Vacillation," dated 1932, may have some bearing on *Call It Sleep*. It opens with the stanza:

> Between extremities
> Man runs his course;
> A brand, or flaming breath,
> Comes to destroy
> All those antinomies
> Of day and night;
> The body calls it death,
> The heart remorse.
> But if these be right
> What is joy?

This may be the first allusion to Isaiah's coal; yet it is in the seventh stanza that the theme of Isaiah's coal is connected with that of modern art:

> *The Soul.* Seek out reality, leave things that seem.
> *The Heart.* What, be a singer born and lack a theme?
> *The Soul.* Isaiah's coal, what more can man desire?
> *The Heart.* Struck dumb in the simplicity of fire!
> *The Soul.* Look on that fire, salvation walks within.
> *The Heart.* What theme had Homer but original sin?

W. B. Yeats, *The Winding Stair and Other Poems* (New York: Macmillan, 1933), 47–53; here: 47 and 51–52. Roth praised Yeats among the Irish writers in whom he saw gentleness.

57　Compare Eda Lou Walton's discussion of e. e. cummings' sonnet "Unrealities IV" from *Tulips and Chimneys* (1923): The poet "is like a watcher near the shore who with passion and awe watches the melting together of the sea and sky." "Intolerable Towers," 278. See also Walt Whitman's "Crossing Brooklyn Ferry."

58　Although this scene may be a retelling of the Excalibur motif, it is also full of verbal echoes of the father as volcano, and continues the sword and light imagery that was initiated in the description of the Statue of Liberty. That "whiteness" is also racially coded becomes apparent in the gentile boys' taunts, "C'mon. He ain' w'ite"

175

(337) or "Dey ain' w'ite" (358) and in other references to black and white in America: Thus David wonders why a Negro can "breathe white when he is black" (273–274), and in the electrocution scene a voice says, "I bet he vuz mit a niggerteh last night!" (562). See also "Bronzeville" (12) and Luter's question about David's "white German skin" (48). The manuscript includes further references, including a startling one to the boxer Jack Johnson (Notes Additions IV, item 30).

59 Nahirny and Fishman 319, drawing on a 1961 *Commentary* symposium and on Daniel Bell; the second generation may also see in the struggle for universal justice and human brotherhood – rather than in observing rituals and identifying with Judaism – the "essence" of Jewishness, or proclaim "estrangement from ancestral roots" as a virtue that fosters the "detached" critical sense which makes the modern truth-teller assume "the role of the prophet." Roth redefined Judaism in a similar way: "Being Jewish does give one a different outlook, especially in two areas. One is justice, which was deeply ingrained. I didn't get it directly from Jewish studies, but it certainly was deeply ingrained in me from my mother. Justice took precedence over almost everything else tied in with the second area, the idea of compassion" (Lyons 1979, 54). The trolley-track experiment may also symbolize a *continuation* of the world of the father. David uses a milk dipper, emblematic of his father's new job that engendered the family's move to East 9th Street; and in the manuscript, David's father considers the job of street car conductor (2?H). In *Mercy of a Rude Stream* 111–115, Ira's father works as a conductor on the Fourth and Madison Avenue trolley line.

60 Roth said: "This scene is set here in order to do two things. First – to break that continual inner life, which is being presented, of the child. Had I continued, I felt, this inner life all the way to the end, that would introduce a certain overstrain or if you wish – that would introduce a certain sense of monotony. I would like to point out, too, that the rabbi's inner life has no particular message." (Manskleid-Makowsky 119–120).

61 The term "American" is often used to mark the "foreign," for example, when Genya speaks of "American" cake (139). Kazin 17 is among the critics who find this chapter "Dickensian," whereas Liptzin 112 believes that the Rabbi's traits conform to a stereotype in literature.

62 Compare Max Ernst's famous "The Virgin Corrects the Child Jesus

Before Three Witnesses," reproduced in *transition* in 1927 (McMillan 87).

63 See Ferraro 113–118 for an illuminating analysis of Roth's crosscutting technique. The manuscript suggests that Roth wrote sequential prose sections that he then cut up and inserted into each other according to a sixteen-point outline and a carefully devised system of Greek letters (booklet 59); his method thus resembled that of film editing.

64 See cummings' "Chansons Innocentes I" in Walton's *City Day* (69) for a similarly unusual word division. The word "cross-ing" calls attention to the Christian symbolism in such words as "crosstown." The "red cock" – an allusion to Peter's triple denial of Christ in Luke 22: 54–62 – may also allude to such folk beliefs as the Galician representation of the corn-spirit as a cock. It is brought down to the vulgar level immediately, however, as it is made to refer, perhaps, to a circumcised penis, and hence evokes David's fear of urinating with gentile boys (338). "Didja hear 'im, Mack? De goggle-eyed yid an' his red cock?" (567). See Fiedler 279; Redding 189–190, citing Frazer. Redding also reports from Frazer the sacrifice of the red cock as a protection against lightning, and cites Horatio's pertinent lines in *Hamlet* I.i; Wirth-Nesher, "Between" 310, refers to Emma Lazarus's poem "The Crowing of the Red Cock."

65 The allusion to the "face to face" of 1 Corinthians 13:12 is as unmistakable here as in Albert's earlier complaint about Luter: "Avoiding me as if the sight of my face were a stab! Looking past me darkly!" (160). Roth is also particularly attentive to a child's language acquisition, making his use of Paul's letter to the Corinthians somewhat ambivalent. Thus 1 Corinthians 11–12 begins with the words: "When I was a child, I spake as a child, I understood as a child, I thought as a child: but when I became a man, I put away childish things." What follows is the familiar verse to which the novel alludes: "For now we see through a glass darkly; but then face to face: now I know in part; but then shall I know even as also I am known."

66 This is a response to Luter's earlier suggestion of too much closeness between mother and son (44). Altenbernd 684 stresses that Albert hesitates when stating David's age.

67 The title of the novel may also allude to one of the most famous sentences near the beginning of Joyce's *Ulysses:* "History, Stephen said, is a nightmare from which I am trying to awake."

68 "Hamlet and His Problems," *The Sacred Wood: Essays on Poetry and Criticism* (1920, reprinted London: Methuen, 1964), 100. Eda Lou Walton, *This Generation* 289, defined Eliot's "objective correlative" as a "symbol that expresses very briefly a whole group of associated ideas. But, unlike the symbols of the symbolists which expressed highly personal reactions, the objective correlative is a social symbol." And in *City Day* 11 she called *The Sacred Wood* "one of the most important collections of modern criticism." Cleanth Brooks, however, criticized Walton as a representative "left-wing" critic who misrepresented early Eliot, viewing him as desperate and disillusioned. See "The Waste Land: An Analysis," in *T. S. Eliot: A Study of His Writings by Several Hands,* ed. B. Rajan (New York: Russell and Russell, 1966), 31. In 1977 Roth said about his own new turn toward Judaism and Israel: "My conversion reminds me of Eliot's conversion. *The Waste Land* verges on the unintelligible. The only way he reclaimed coherence was by conversion. It gave him a center."

69 Frazer 99; Bertha comments on the "spectacle of a stone wolf suckling two infants": "Woe is me! [. . .] Who would believe it – a dog with babies! No! It could not have been!" (195). See also the haunting exclamation in a children's game, "Wolf are yuh ready!" that is repeated seven times (551–554). Frazer 581 also makes an analogy between the primitive conception of "sacred or tabooed persons" and an electric charge; this analogy is more fully developed in the unabridged text of *The Golden Bough:*

the sacred man is charged just as a Leyden jar [an early device used for storing and discharging static electricity] is charged with electricity; and exactly as the electricity in the jar can be discharged by contact with a good conductor, so the holiness or magical virtue in the man can be discharged and drained away by contact with the earth, which on this theory serves as an excellent conductor for the magical fluid. Hence in order to preserve the charge from running to waste, the sacred or tabooed personage must be carefully prevented from touching the ground; in electrical language he must be insulated, if he is not to be emptied of the precious substance or fluid with which he, as a vial, is filled to the brim. And in many cases apparently the insulation of the tabooed person is recommended as a precaution not merely for his own sake but for the sake of others; for since the virtue of holiness or taboo is, so to say, a powerful explosive which the smallest touch may detonate, it is necessary in the interest of the general safety to keep it within narrow bounds, lest breaking out of it should blast, blight and destroy whatever it comes into contact with. (Vol. VII: Baldur the Beautiful; chapter i: Between Heaven and Earth; § 1; Not to touch the Earth; pp. 6–7)

70 Manskleid-Makowsky 114.

71 Manskleid-Makowsky 114. *Mercy of a Rude Stream* marks a new beginning with this project, though it does not yet reach the Village years.

72 Walton (19 January 1894–8 February 1961) was born in Deming, New Mexico, to a family of Quaker roots; her father was a member of the first New Mexico State Senate. She was trained in English and anthropology at Berkeley under Benjamin Putnam Kurtz and Alfred Kroeber, and defended her dissertation on "Navajo Traditional Poetry: Its Content and Form" in 1920. She also participated successfully in Witter Bynner's verse-writing class and soon published her own poems in journals and anthologies, and translations of Indian verse in *Dawn Boy* (1926). After teaching at Fresno State she accepted a position teaching modern literature at New York University in 1924, offering such courses as "English Poetry of the Nineteenth Century," "Modern English and American Poetry," and "The Writing of Original Verse." She was active in the field, published over three hundred book reviews, voluminous poetry, numerous scholarly articles, and edited impressively well selected literary anthologies. She associated with modern writers like Louise Bogan and Hart Crane as well as anthropologists like Ruth Benedict and Margaret Mead. By his own account Roth lived with her from 1928 to 1938. Rosen writes that "no understanding of Roth's creativity, or of his later inability to create, is possible without placing at the center Roth's relationship to the powerful woman who alternates as muse and demon in the saga of his life."

73 In interviews Roth also called Winter "one of the handsomest young Hungarian Jews that you ever laid eyes on," "polished, worldly, well-groomed" (Lyons 1976, 160), and "also much more assimilated than myself and knew about modern literature" (Manskleid-Makowsky 111) though he "had a lyric gift of a conventional sort" (Lyons 1979, 52). In Lyons 1979, 53, Roth dates this episode in 1925 (though Walton's trip to Europe in 1926 makes that year more likely); in Manskleid-Makowsky 112, he remembers other details and surmises that there was "a psychological competition" between the two young men.

74 It is interesting that Roth invokes the addictive experience of doubling. Abraham Cahan may also have based "Yekl" on the Yiddish spelling of Robert Louis Stevenson's famous Jekyll, using the figure of the double for thematizing ethnic assimilation.

75 See: "[I]n the death of art there is a beginning of the acceptance of
the necessity to live in a normal fashion, subject to all the demands
and all the exigencies and vicissitudes that life will bring. When I
say normal, I mean that now he's willing to accept marriage, he's
willing now to accept the getting of a livelihood" (*Shifting Landscape*
105). Or: "I was a dependent person; it was a real continuation of
infancy to be supported by a woman so long. More and more I felt
that I was collapsing inside myself. I probably would have gone on
indefinitely, except that in the summer of 1938 I went to Yaddo,
where I met Muriel [Parker, who became Roth's wife in 1939],
who had been invited as a composer. It was hardly a romantic love
affair. I feel that Muriel just retrieved me in time. I don't think I
would have lived very long; I just didn't feel like it" (Lyons 1976,
162).

76 Manskleid-Makowsky 114. The extant parts of the manuscript are
written on blue and pink examination booklets of New York University.

77 "I was admitted to a much older generation – well, not so much
older, but even five years of difference when you are only twenty-
two or twenty-three is a hell of a difference. You meet a guy who
already has his doctorate and so forth, and he may be teaching, and
you are still an undergraduate. And most of Walton's contemporaries were academics and teachers – a number of them with very well
established reputations: the Van Dorens, for example; Constance
Rourke. Then there were the poets, like Hart Crane, Léonie Adams,
Horace Gregory" (*Shifting Landscape* 20).

78 Bronsen 268. See also Manskleid-Makowsky 110, Lyons 1976, 159,
and Berman 12–18.

79 In this respect, Roth as a writer reenacts David's family romance to
a certain extent.

80 Manskleid-Makowsky 110.

81 The filial possessiveness and jealousy triggered in David by Luter,
for example, may thus be inspired and fed, not only by the writer's
memory of childhood examined through a Freudian lens, but also
by his experience of a sexual relationship symbolized as maternal –
and with an older "new woman" of the 1920s whose sexual conduct would give the writer sufficient cause to experience jealousy.
See Roth's statement about Walton: "She was both a mistress and
a mother. It was good, and it was bad" (*Shifting Landscape* 295).
According to Klein 193, Roth said that he had exchanged "a Jewish
Mama for a native American Mama," in describing biographically

the move from Leah Roth to Eda Lou Walton. In Walton's long poem "Jane Matthew" (1931) that opens a collection of the same title dedicated to "H.R." the relationship between Jane and Dale is rendered in a complementary fashion:

And Dale leaned
Quietly to her bosom and her side
As to his mother's, seeing nothing else
Except her gentleness. (74)

Or:

She told him awestruck how he was all three,
Boy, and sensualist, and tender lover (38)

In a letter of 25 June 1935 Walton said in praise of Roth's novel that he was "so far ahead" of her "generation that there is no comparison." Perhaps verbal parallels could support this approach. Genya calling David "little goose" (81) is similar to the line Roth ascribes to Walton, "Don't be a goose. Get under the covers!" (*Shifting Landscape* 295); and Walton's tone also resembles that of Genya's invitation to David, "Let's go to bed then, it grows late" (54). There may also be an allusion in the story of Ludwig the organist to Walton's poems evoking the organ mountains of New Mexico. See "Jane Matthew," "The Blue Room" (*Jane Matthew* 26, 106) and Greenhood, "Eda." Perhaps Leo Dugovka whose name falls short, by a few letters, of being an anagram for Eda Lou Walton, was also partly shaped in her image. One could think of "Eda Lou" and "Leo Du–." Since the age difference of twelve years is always emphasized, perhaps it is significant that Leo is "goin' on twelve" (416), and that he and David look at the cross on 12th Street and Avenue C (412), supposedly marking a (nonexistent) St. James Parochial School. The triangle of David, Leo, and Esther (478–479) is evocative of that of R, Eda Lou, and Lester in "Itinerant Ithacan" (*Shifting Landscape* 197–199), with the rosary in the novel taking the place of Eliot and Joyce in "Itinerant Ithacan."

82 In the manuscript, the radical political orator of Chapter XXI of "The Rail" was placed at Third Avenue beside Cooper Union, connected with David's epiphany by the same trolley tracks.

83 Georg Lukács, *The Historical Novel* (1937), trans. Hannah and Stanley Mitchell (Boston: Beacon Press, 1963).

84 Bronsen 267–268. Roth in Lyons 1976, 160, also criticized himself for representing himself in David as "a much finer sensibility than what was around me." Roth's suggestion to consider the historical context at the time he was writing the novel corresponds with

Nathan Glazer's attempt at historicizing discussions about immigrant generations (Kivisto 104–112). Roth spoke of a superimposition of the "hostile environment" of Harlem onto the protective East Side and supposed that the terror he felt inside when writing the book may have been prophetic of the Holocaust.

85 Lyons 1976, 56; see Buelens 6. The fact that Roth's and Walton's was a union between a Jewish man and a non-Jewish woman also mattered (*Shifting Landscape* 209, 212).

86 "It often seems to me, as I think of it, that the final image of the novel was in a way prophetic. . . . The short-circuit that occurs there seems to be the short-circuit that hit us all. I was short-circuited and I wasn't the only one. We were all somehow cut short" (Freedman 154). See also Freud, 1920, 39, for a use of the word "short-circuit."

BIBLIOGRAPHY

PRIMARY

Roth, Henry. *Call It Sleep.* New York: Robert O. Ballou, 1934; second printing, January 1935 (edition cited here).

Call It Sleep. New York: Avon Books, 1964. With an afterword by Walter Allen (cited in a few instances as "A"). Reprinted New York: Noonday Press/Farrar, Straus and Giroux, 1991, with some corrections, an introduction by Alfred Kazin, and an afterword by Hana Wirth-Nesher.

Shifting Landscape: A Composite, 1925–1987, ed. and introduction, Mario Materassi. Philadelphia: Jewish Publication Society, 1987.

Mercy of a Rude Stream. Vol. 1: A Star Shines Over Mt. Morris Park. New York: St. Martin's Press, 1994.

SECONDARY

Adams, Stephen J. "The Noisiest Novel Ever Written: The Soundscape of Henry Roth's *Call It Sleep." Twentieth Century Literature* (Spring 1989): 43–64.

Altenbernd, Lynn. "An American Messiah: Myth in Henry Roth's *Call It Sleep." Modern Fiction Studies* 35.4 (Winter 1989): 673–687.

Alter, Robert. *After the Tradition: Essays on Modern Jewish Writing.* New York: Dutton, 1969.

"Awakenings." *New Republic* (25 January 1988): 33–37.

[Anon.] "Brief Review." *New Masses* (12 February 1935): 27.

Baumgarten, Murray. *City Scriptures: Modern Jewish Writing.* Cambridge: Harvard University Press, 1982.

Berman, James. "Landscape, Silence, and Revelation: Modes of Symbolic Acculturation in Henry Roth's *Call It Sleep.*" Senior Thesis, English Department, Harvard University, 1990.

Bowman, James. "American Notes." *Times Literary Supplement* 4740 (4 February 1994): 14.

Bronsen, David. "A Conversation with Henry Roth." *Partisan Review* 36 (1969): 265–280.

Buelens, Gert. "The Multi-Voiced Basis of Henry Roth's Literary Success in *Call It Sleep.*" Ms. of lecture delivered at German Society for American Studies in Berlin, June 1992.

Burke, Kenneth. "More about Roth's *Call It Sleep.*" *New Masses* (26 February 1935): 21.

Chametzky, Jules. "Memories and Silences in the Work of Tillie Olsen and Henry Roth." Ms.1993; publication forthcoming in a collection edited by Amritjit Singh and Joseph Skerrett.

Diamant, Naomi. "Linguistic Universes in Henry Roth's *Call It Sleep.*" *Contemporary Literature* 27.3 (1986): 336–355.

Dickstein, Morris. "Call It an Awakening." *New York Times Book Review* (29 November 1987): 1, 33–36.

Dickstein, Morris. "The Tenement and the World: Visions of Immigrant Life." In William Boelhower, ed., *The Future of American Modernism: Ethnic Writing Between the Wars.* Amsterdam: VU University Press, 1990, 62–93 (European Contributions to American Studies XVII).

Epstein, Gary. "Auto-Obituary: The Death of the Artist in Henry Roth's *Call It Sleep.*" *Studies in American Jewish Literature* 5.1 (Spring 1979): 37–45.

Farr, Cecilia K. "Roth's *Call It Sleep.*" *Explicator* 46.2 (1988): 49–51.

Fein, Richard J. "Fear, Fatherhood, and Desire in *Call It Sleep.*" *Yiddish* 5.4 (1984): 49–54.

Ferraro, Thomas J. *Ethnic Passages: Literary Immigrants in Twentieth-Century America.* Chicago: University of Chicago Press, 1993.

Fiedler, Leslie. *The Collected Essays of Leslie Fiedler.* Vol. 2 (New York: Stein and Day, 1971).

Field, Leslie. "Henry Roth's Use of Torah and Haftorah in *Call It Sleep.*" *Studies in American Jewish Literature* 5.1 (Spring 1979): 22–27.

Forgue, Guy. "Un long sommeil." *La Quinzaine littéraire* 50 (May 1–15, 1968): 7.

Freedman, William. "A Conversation with Henry Roth." *Literary Review* 19 (Winter 1975): 149–157.

Geismar, Maxwell. "A Critical Introduction." *Call It Sleep.* New York: Cooper Square Publishers, 1960.

Girgus, Sam. *The New Covenant: Jewish Writers and the American Idea.* Chapel Hill: University of North Carolina Press, 1984.

Gollomb, Joseph. "Life in the Ghetto." *Saturday Review of Literature* 11.35 (16 March 1935): 552.

Greenhood, David. "Another View of 'Call it Sleep.' " *New Masses* (19 February 1935): 26.

Gregory, Horace. "East Side World." *Nation* 140 (27 February 1935): 255.

Guttmann, Allen. *The Jewish Writer in America: Assimilation and the Crisis of Identity.* New York: Oxford University Press, 1971.

Harris, Lis. "In the Shadow of the Golden Mountains." *New Yorker* (27 June 1988): 84–92.

Howard, Jane. "The Belated Success of Henry Roth." *Life* 53 (8 January 1965): 75–76.

Howe, Irving. *World of Our Fathers: The Journey of the East European Jews to America and the Life They Found and Made.* New York: Harcourt Brace Jovanovitch, 1976.

Immel, Horst. *Literarische Gestaltungsvarianten des Einwanderungsromans in der amerikanischen und anglokanadischen Literatur: Grove, Cahan, Rölvaag, Henry Roth.* Frankfurt: Peter Lang, 1987 (Mainzer Studien zur Amerikanistik 21).

Inge, M. Thomas. "The Ethnic Experience and Aesthetics in Literature: Malamud's *The Assistant* and Henry Roth's *Call It Sleep.*" *Journal of Ethnic Studies* 1.4 (1974): 45–50.

Kaganoff, Peggy. "Henry Roth." *Publishers Weekly* (27 November 1987): 67–68.

Kazin, Alfred. "The Art of 'Call It Sleep.' " *New York Review of Books* (10 October 1991): 15–18.

Kleederman, Frances Farber. "A Study of Language in Henry Roth's *Call It Sleep:* Bilingual Markers of a Culture in Transition." Dissertation, New York University, 1974.

    "The Interior Monologue in Henry Roth's *Call It Sleep.*" *Studies in American Jewish Literature* 5.1 (Spring 1979): 2–11.

Klein, Marcus. *Foreigners: The Making of American Literature, 1900–1940.* Chicago: University of Chicago Press, 1981.

Knowles, Jr., A. Sidney. "The Fiction of Henry Roth." *Modern Fiction Studies* 11.4 (1965–1966): 393–404.

Ledbetter, Kenneth. "Henry Roth's *Call It Sleep:* The Revival of a Proletarian Novel." *Twentieth Century Literature* 12.3 (October 1966): 123–130.

Lesser, Wayne. "A Narrative's Revolutionary Energy: The Example of Henry Roth's *Call It Sleep.*" *Criticism* 23.2 (1981): 155–176.

Liptzin, Sol. *The Jew in American Literature.* New York: Bloch, 1966.

Lyons, Bonnie. "The Symbolic Structure of Henry Roth's *Call It Sleep.*" *Contemporary Literature* 13.2 (1972): 186–203.

  Henry Roth: The Man and His Work. New York: Cooper Square Publishers, 1976 (with an excellent bibliography).

Maffi, Mario. *Nel mosaico della città: Differenze etniche e nuove culture in un quartiere di New York.* Milan: Feltrinelli, 1992.

Manskleid-Makowsky, Irit. "The 'Jewishness' of Jewish American Literature: The Examples of Ludwig Lewisohn and Henry Roth." M.A. thesis, John F. Kennedy-Institut, Freie Universität Berlin, 1978.

Materassi, Mario, ed. *Rothiana: Henry Roth nella critica italiana.* Firenze: Giuntina, 1985 (with excellent bibliography).

Michaels, Leonard. "The Long Comeback of Henry Roth: Call It Miraculous." *New York Times Book Review* (15 August 1993): 3.

Mooney, Theresa R. "The Explicable 'It' of Henry Roth's *Call It Sleep.*" *Studies in American Jewish Literature* 5.1 (Spring 1979): 11–18.

Mortara di Veroli, Elèna. "Da Babele al silenzio: Il romanzo sinfonico di Henry Roth." *Letterature d'America* 5 (1984): 135–151.

Nelson, Kenneth M. "A Religious Metaphor." *Reconstructionist* 31.5 (1965): 7–16.

Pinsker, Sanford. "The Re-Awakening of Henry Roth's *Call It Sleep.*" *Jewish Social Studies* 28.3 (July 1966): 148–158.

Portelli, Alessandro. *Il testo e la voce: Oralità, letteratura e democrazia in America.* Rome: Manofestolibri, 1992.

Redding, Mary Edrich. "Call It Myth: Henry Roth and *The Golden Bough.*" *The Centennial Review* 18.2 (Spring 1974): 180–195.

Rideout, Walter B. *The Radical Novel in the United States: Some Interrelations of Literature and Society, 1900–1954.* 1956; reprinted New York: Columbia University Press, 1992.

Roth, Fred A. "Henry Roth's *Call It Sleep.*" *Explicator* 48 (Spring 1990): 218–220.

Ruland, Richard, and Malcolm Bradbury. *From Puritanism to Postmodernism: A History of American Literature.* New York: Viking, 1991.

Samet, Tom. "Henry Roth's Bull Story: Guilt and Betrayal in *Call It Sleep.*" *Studies in the Novel* 7.4 (Winter 1975): 569–583.

Saperstein, Jeffrey. "Roth's *Call It Sleep.*" *Explicator* 46.1 (1987): 47–48.

Seaver, Edwin. "Caesar or Nothing." *New Masses* (5 March 1935): 21.

Sheres, Ita. "Exile and Redemption in Henry Roth's *Call It Sleep.*" *Markham Review* 6 (1977): 72–77.

Sherman, Bernard. *The Invention of the Jew: Jewish-American Education Novels (1916–1964).* New York: Yoseloff, 1969.

Sokoloff, Naomi. "Discoveries of Reading: Stories of Childhood by Bialik, Shahar, and Roth." *Hebrew Annual Review* 9 (1985): 321–341.

Walden, Daniel. "Henry Roth's *Call It Sleep:* Ethnicity, 'The Sign,' and the Power." *Modern Fiction Studies* 25.2 (Summer 1979): 268–272.

Wirth-Nesher, Hana. "Between Mother Tongue and Native Language: Multilingualism in Henry Roth's *Call It Sleep.*" *Prooftexts* 10 (1990): 297–312.

City Codes: Reading the Modern Urban Novel. Cambridge University Press, 1995.

Young, Debra B. "Henry Roth: A Bibliographic Survey." *Studies in American Jewish Literature* 5.1 (Spring 1979): 62–70.

RELATED WORKS

Brooks, Cleanth. "The Waste Land: An Analysis." In B. Rajan, ed., *T. S. Eliot: A Study of His Writings by Several Hands.* New York: Russell and Russell, 1966.

Cohn, Dorrit. *Transparent Minds: Narrative Modes for Presenting Consciousness in Fiction.* 1978; reprinted Princeton: Princeton University Press, 1983.

Crane, Hart. *The Selected Poems.* Ed. Marc Simon. New York: Liveright, 1986.

Eliot, T. S. *The Sacred Wood: Essays on Poetry and Criticism* (1920). Reprinted London: Methuen, 1964.

Erikson, Erik H. *Childhood and Society.* Second ed. New York: W. W. Norton, 1963.

Frazer, Sir James George. *The Golden Bough* (1890). Reprinted abridged edition, New York: Criterion Books, 1959.

Freud, Sigmund. "Family Romances" [orig. "Der Familienroman der Neurotiker" 1908]. *Standard Edition of the Complete Psychological Works,* trans. James Strachey, vol. 9 (1906–1908). London: Hogarth, 1959, 236–241.

"Beyond the Pleasure Principle" [orig. "Jenseits des Lustprinzips"

186

1920]. *Standard Edition of the Complete Psychological Works of Sigmund Freud*, trans. James Strachey, vol. 18 (1920–1922). London: Hogarth, 1955, 7–64.

Greenhood, David. "Eda Lou Walton's Use of Her Native Scene." *New Mexico Quarterly* 33 (1963): 253–265 (with bibliography and photograph).

Hamburger, Käte. *The Logic of Literature*, trans. Marilynn J. Rose, second ed. Bloomington: Indiana University Press, 1993.

Holt, Hamilton. *The Life Stories of Undistinguished Americans As Told by Themselves* (1908), reprinted New York: Routledge, 1990.

Howard, Helen Addison. "Literary Tran[s]lators and Interpreters of Indian Songs." *Journal of the West* (1973): 224–226.

James, William. *Talks to Teachers on Psychology: and to Students on Some of Life's Ideals*. New York: Holt, 1900.

Kivisto, Peter and Dag Blanck, eds. *American Immigrants and Their Generations: Studies and Commentaries on the Hansen Thesis after Fifty Years*. Urbana: University of Illinois Press, 1990.

McMillan, Dougald. *transition: The History of a Literary Era, 1927–1938*. New York: Braziller, 1976.

Mead, Margaret. *And Keep Your Powder Dry: An Anthropologist Looks at America* (1942). Expanded edition, New York: Morrow, 1965.

Nahirny, Vladimir C., and Joshua A. Fishman. "American Immigrant Groups: Ethnic Identification and the Problem of Generations." *American Sociological Review* 13.3 n.s. (November 1965): 311–326.

Perkins, David. *A History of Modern Poetry: From the 1890s to the High Modernist Mode*. Cambridge: Harvard University Press, 1976.

Poirier, Richard. *A World Elsewhere: The Place of Style in American Literature*. New York: Oxford University Press, 1966.

Rodriguez, Richard. "An American Writer" (1988). In Werner Sollors, ed., *The Invention of Ethnicity*. New York: Oxford University Press, 1988.

Selzer, Michael, ed. *"Kike!" A Documentary History of Anti-Semitism in America*. New York: World Publishing, 1972.

Steiner, Edward A. *On the Trail of the Immigrant*. New York: Fleming H. Revell, 1906.

Walton, Eda Lou, ed. *The City Day: An Anthology of Recent American Poetry*. New York: Ronald Press, 1929.

"Intolerable Towers." *The English Journal* 19.4 (April 1930): 267–281 (similar to introduction to *City Day*).

Jane Matthew and Other Poems. New York: Brewer, Warren & Putnam, 1931.

"The Scene in Books Today." *Signatures: Work in Progress* 1.1 (1936): n.p.

Walton, Eda Lou, and George K. Anderson, eds. *This Generation: A Selection of British and American Literature from 1914 to the Present with Historical and Critical Essays.* Chicago: Scott, Foresman, and Co., 1939.

Notes on Contributors

Leslie Fiedler is Samuel Clemens Professor of English Literature at the State University of New York at Buffalo. Among his numerous books and articles are *Love and Death in the American Novel, The Last Jew in America, Freaks, What Was Literature?, Fiedler on the Roof,* and *The Collected Essays of Leslie Fiedler.*

Karen R. Lawrence, Professor of English at the University of Utah, is the author of *The Odyssey of Style in Ulysses* and *Penelope Voyages: Women and Travel in the British Literary Tradition,* and the editor of *Decolonizing Tradition: New Views of Twentieth-Century "British" Literary Canons.*

Mario Materassi, who translated *Call It Sleep* into Italian, is Professor of American Literature at the University of Florence. He edited Henry Roth's *Shifting Landscape* and *Rothiana,* a volume of essays on Roth by Italian scholars, and has written critical books and essays in Italian on nineteenth- and twentieth-century American fiction.

Brian McHale is Eberly Family Distinguished Professor of American Literature at West Virginia University and co-editor of *Poetics Today.* He is the author of *Postmodernist Fiction* and *Constructing Postmodernism.*

Werner Sollors is Cabot Professor of English Literature and Professor of Afro-American Literature at Harvard University and the author of *Amiri Baraka/Leroi Jones: The Quest for a Populist Modernism, Beyond Ethnicity: Consent and Descent in American Culture,* and

Neither Black Nor White and Yet Both: Thematic Explorations of Inter-racial Literature, and the editor of *The Invention of Ethnicity* and *The Return of Thematic Criticism.*

Hana Wirth-Nesher, Associate Professor of English Literature at Tel Aviv University and Department Head, has written numerous articles on American, English, and Jewish literature. She is the author of *City Codes: Reading the Modern Urban Novel* and the editor of *What Is Jewish Literature?* and *The Sheila Carmel Lectures in English Literature.*

Ruth Wisse is Professor of Yiddish Literature at Harvard University and Director of the Center of Jewish Studies. Among her many publications on Jewish literature are *The Shlemiel as Modern Hero, I. L. Peretz and the Making of Modern Yiddish Culture, A Little Love in Manhattan: Two Yiddish Poets,* and *If I Am Not for Myself: The Liberal Betrayal of the Jews.* She is also the editor (with Irving Howe) of *The Best of Sholom Aleichem* and (with Irving Howe and Khone Shmeruk) *The Penguin Book of Modern Yiddish Verse.*

Selected Bibliography

Adams, Stephen J. "The Noisiest Novel Ever Written: The Soundscape of Henry Roth's *Call It Sleep.*" *Twentieth Century Literature* (Spring 1989): 43–64.

Altenbernd, Lynn. "An American Messiah: Myth in Henry Roth's *Call It Sleep.*" *Modern Fiction Studies* 35.4 (Winter 1989): 673–687.

Alter, Robert. *After the Tradition: Essays on Modern Jewish Writing.* New York: Dutton, 1969.

Baumgarten, Murray. *City Scriptures: Modern Jewish Writing.* Cambridge: Harvard University Press, 1982.

Diamant, Naomi. "Linguistic Universes in Henry Roth's *Call It Sleep.*" *Contemporary Literature* 27.3 (1986): 336–355.

Epstein, Gary. "Auto-Obituary: The Death of the Artist in Henry Roth's *Call It Sleep.*" *Studies in American Jewish Literature* 5.1 (1979): 37–45.

Fiedler, Leslie. "The Jew in the American Novel." *To The Gentiles.* New York: Stein and Day, 1971.

Ferraro, Thomas J. *Ethnic Passages: Literary Immigrants in Twentieth-Century America.* University of Chicago Press, 1993.

Freedman, William. "Mystical Initiation and Experience in *Call It Sleep.*" *Studies in American Jewish Literature* 5.1 (1979): 27–37.

Girgus, Sam. *The New Covenant: Jewish Writers and the American Idea.* Chapel Hill: University of North Carolina Press, 1984.

Guttman, Allen. *The Jewish Writer in America: Assimilation and the Crisis of Identity.* New York: Oxford University Press, 1971.

Howe, Irving. *World of Our Fathers: The Journey of the East European Jews to America and the Life They Found and Made.* New York: Harcourt Brace Jovanovich, 1976.

Kazin, Alfred. "The Art of 'Call It Sleep.' " *The New York Review of Books* (10 October 1991): 15–18.

Ledbetter, Kenneth. "Henry Roth's *Call It Sleep:* The Revival of a Proletarian Novel." *Twentieth Century Literature* 12 (October 1966): 123–130.

Lesser, Wayne. "A Narrative's Evolutionary Energy: The Example of Henry Roth's *Call It Sleep*." *Criticism* 23.3 (1981): 155–176.

Lyons, Bonnie. *Henry Roth: The Man and His Work.* New York: Cooper Square Publishers, Inc., 1976.

Pinsker, Sanford. "The Re-Awakening of Henry Roth's *Call It Sleep*." *ewish Social Studies* 28.3 (July 1966): 148–158.

Rideout, Walter. *The Radical Novel in the United States: 1900–1954.* Cambridge, Mass: Harvard University Press, 1956.

Robbins, Bruce. "Modernism in History, Modernism in Power," in Robert Kiely, ed., *Modernism Reconsidered.* Cambridge, Mass: Harvard University Press, 1983.

Samet, Tom. "Henry Roth's Bull Story: Guilt and Betrayal in *Call It Sleep*." *Studies in the Novel* 7.4 (Winter 1975): 569–583.

Walden, Daniel. "Henry Roth's *Call It Sleep:* Ethnicity, 'The Sign' and the Power." *Modern Fiction Studies* 25.2 (Summer 1979): 268–272.

Wirth-Nesher, Hana. "Between Mother Tongue and Native Language: Multilingualism in Henry Roth's *Call It Sleep*." *Prooftexts: A Journal of Jewish Literary History* 10 (1990): 297–312. Reprinted as the Afterword to the Farrar, Straus & Giroux edition of *Call It Sleep,* 1991.

Wirth-Nesher, Hana. "The Modern Jewish Novel and the City: Kafka, Roth, and Oz." *Modern Fiction Studies* 24 (Spring 1978): 91–111.

For EU product safety concerns, contact us at Calle de José Abascal, 56–1°, 28003 Madrid, Spain or eugpsr@cambridge.org.

www.ingramcontent.com/pod-product-compliance
Ingram Content Group UK Ltd.
Pitfield, Milton Keynes, MK11 3LW, UK
UKHW012346130625
459647UK00009B/561